7/24

ENGLISH FOR CONTRACT AND COMPANY LAW

ENGLISH FOR CONTRACT AND COMAPANY LAW

BY

Marcella Chartrand

Catherine Millar

Edward Wiltshire

SWEET & MAXWELL

Published in 2003 by Thomson Reuters (Legal) Limited
(Registered in England & Wales, Company No 1679046. registered Office and address for service: 100 Avenue Road, Swiss Cottage, London, NW3 3PF) trading as Sweet & Maxwell

For further information on our products and services, visit
www.sweetandmaxwell.co.uk

First edition published in 1997
Reprinted 2000 and 2002
Second Edition 2003
Reprinted 2007, 2008

Phototypeset by MFK Mendip, Frome, Somerset
Printed and bound in Great Britain by
Peartree Press, Stevenage.

No natural forests were destroyed to make this product:
only farmed timber was used and replanted

A C.I.P. Catalogue record for this book is available from the British Library
ISBN 978-0-421-79870-0

ACKNOWLEDGMENTS

The publishers and authors would like to thank the following for permission to reproduce material from publications in which they have copyright.

Extracts from various law reports reproduced with kind permission of the *Incorporated Council of Law Reporting for England and Wales*.

McGraw-Hill Higher Education for extracts from *Contemporary Business Law* by Hoeber, Reitzel, Lyden, Roberts and Severance, 1980.

Sweet & Maxwell Ltd for extracts from *Learning the Law* by Glanville Williams, 11th ed., 1982.

West Publishing Ltd for extracts from *Black's Law Dictionary*, 5th ed., 1979.

PUBLISHER'S NOTE

PREFACE

This book was born as an attempt to provide suitable material for University law under-graduates in a non-English speaking context. It is aimed at giving them the necessary background in specific legal English for their professional development.

In addition to law students and lawyers throughout the world who need to learn English for professional purposes, this book is also suitable for non-native speakers who wish to pursue their legal studies in English-speaking countries.

Ideally this book is for students having an upper-intermediate to advanced level of English.

The book is divided into two sections, English for Contract Law and English for Company Law. Each section is designed to provide material for approximately 50 hours of class contact.

The whole course is geared towards improving general language skills, achieved through an interactive methodology. However, the course provides a wide variety of exercises, thus allowing emphasis to be placed on any or all of the four skills (reading, writing, speaking and listening).

An exceedingly important legal content has been added to the extensive reading component. The texts are written in a formal register aimed at exposing students to a register with which they are not usually familiar, but with which they need to familiarise themselves in order to survive both academically and professionally.

One of the attractions of this book is its dual use in classroom teaching and self-study. To this end an answer key, a glossary of legal terms and a summary of cases have been included.

It is hoped that this unique book will fill the gap between English language and legal studies.

The authors would like to thank the publishers for their patience and help in producing this second edition. The assistance of various members of the staff of ICADE in Madrid is very much appreciated, and in particular, that of Mr Walter Cedar, Mr Antonio Castán and Dr Maria Luisa Aparicio.

Finally, on a personal note, the authors would like to thank their friends and families for all their support and in particular, Diana Millar, John Ross, Margaret Barry, Manolo Elisa and Daniel Espinosa, Ana Vázquez, Elizabeth and Peter Wiltshire, and Castropol.

CONTENTS

INTRODUCTION

READING

Justice is the basic value which a system of law in any country seeks to attain. The word justice comes from the Latin *jus*, which means a right deriving from a rule of law. Justice protects persons' rights and punishes their wrongs. If something is right, we say it is just, and if something is wrong we say it is unjust. Laws themselves may be just or unjust depending upon how you look at them, but they can be said to be just when they create the conditions leading to peace, happiness and prosperity for all persons.

Laws change from time to time in order to keep up with changes in a society's values and with developments in technology, but it is important that at any given moment these rules are both definite and known to the public.

On December 14, 1994 there was a debate in the House of Lords on the report of a commission concerning the legislative process. In that debate, Lord Lester of Herne Hill gave a good summary of the guiding principles to be observed in the legislative process.

"The five central principles which have guided and formed the Rippon Commission's recommendations need to be engraved in bold letters on the pillars of the Palace of Westminster and on the doors of every government department. They also need to be fully heeded by ministers, civil servants, and ourselves as parliamentarians. Perhaps I may remind your Lordships of those five principles.

First, laws are made for the benefit of the citizens of the state. All citizens directly affected should be involved as fully and openly as possible in the processes by which statute law is prepared. Secondly, statute law should be as certain as possible for the benefit of the citizens to whom it applies. Thirdly, statute law must be rooted in the authority of parliament and thoroughly exposed to open democratic scrutiny by the representatives of the people in parliament. Fourthly, ignorance of the law is no excuse. Therefore the current statute law must be as accessible as possible to all who need to know it. Fifthly, the Government need to be able to secure the passage of their legislation, but to get the law right and intelligible for the benefit of citizens is as important as to get it passed quickly. (...)

Year after year the volume of legislation continues to increase at a chokingly high rate, as does its quite bewildering complexity. This makes it essential for the legislative process to conform to democratic ideals, producing well-conceived, well-drafted and accurate legislation, with as much consultation of affected parties and relevant experts as is reasonably practicable. As the Rippon Report clearly demonstrates, successive governments of whatever colour and successive parliaments have paid lip service to these ideals without adopting effective measures to implement them."

VOCABULARY COMPREHENSION

Look back at the speech made by Lord Lester of Herne Hill in the House of Lords and find the word or words he used to express the following:

Paragraph One	cut/carved
	clear
	paid careful attention to
	member of, debater in parliament
Paragraph Two	fixed/established
	completely/deeply
	able to be reached
	passing
Paragraph Three	in such a way that stops you breathing
	very confusing
	written clearly
	praised but not adopted

READING

A distinction is made in most legal systems between criminal and civil law, but between each system there are slight differences as to what acts constitute public or criminal wrongs, and what acts constitute private or civil wrongs. It is difficult to arrive at an exact definition of criminal law: it could be said to govern the relationship of individual behaviour with the power of the State. It thus falls within the area of public law, the aim of a criminal charge being to convict and punish the offender. Civil law, on the other hand, concerns the individual's relations with his fellow human beings, and in the Anglo-American legal systems these relations are divided into two major branches: contract law, which covers all agreements made between two or more people with the intention of creating legal relations, and tort, which covers all civil wrongs other than a wrong which is a breach of contract, such as negligence, trespass or defamation. The word *tort* comes from the Latin word *tortus*, which means twisted or crooked, and from the French word meaning harm or wrong. Now, just as all cats are animals but not all animals are cats, all torts can be said to be wrongs, but not all wrongs are torts. Hence the importance of the distinction between civil and criminal wrongs.

Take for example the following case. A man was driving too fast along a road in a city suburb and as a result he knocked down and badly injured a pedestrian. In this one act he committed a criminal wrong (at the very least, careless driving) and a civil wrong (negligence). The legal consequences of his one act under criminal and civil law are different. He may be prosecuted by the police in the criminal courts for reckless driving (but may only be convicted for careless driving) and sued by the victim for negligence in the civil courts.

The language used for describing the criminal proceedings arising from his act is different from that used for describing the civil proceedings. You can learn some of the distinctions by reading this extract from *Learning the Law* by Glanville Williams (1982, pp.2–4):

"In fact the law is divided into two great branches, the criminal and the civil, and of these much the greater is the civil. Since the nature of the division must be grasped at the outset, I shall try to give a simple explanation of it.

The distinction between a crime and a civil wrong, though capable of giving rise to some difficult legal problems, is in essence quite simple. The first thing to understand is that the distinction does *not* reside in the nature of the wrongful act itself. This can be proved quite simply by pointing out that the same act may be both a crime and a civil wrong. Occasionally at a bus station there is someone who makes a living by looking after people's impedimenta while they are shopping. If I entrust my bag to such a person, and he runs off with it, he commits the crime of theft and also two civil wrongs – the tort of conversion and a breach of contract with me to keep the bag safe. The result is that two sorts of legal proceedings can be taken against him; a prosecution for the crime, and a civil action for the tort and for the breach of contract. (Of course the plaintiff in the latter action will not get damages twice over merely because he has two causes of action; he will get only one set of damages.) (...)

These examples show that the distinction between a crime and civil wrong cannot be stated as depending upon *what is done*, because what is done (or not done) may be the same in each case. The true distinction resides, therefore, not in the nature of the wrongful act but in *the legal consequences that may follow it*. If the wrongful act (or omission) is capable of being followed by what are called criminal proceedings, that means that it is regarded as a crime (otherwise called an offence). If it is capable of being followed by civil proceedings, that means that it is regarded as a civil wrong. If it is capable of being followed by both, it is both a crime and a civil wrong. Criminal and civil proceedings are (in the normal case) easily distinguishable: the procedure is different, the outcome is different, and the terminology is different.

In criminal proceedings the terminology is as follows. You have *a prosecutor prosecuting a defendant*, and the result of the prosecution if successful is a *conviction*, and the defendant may be *punished* by one of a variety of punishments ranging from life imprisonment to a fine, or else may be released on probation or discharged without punishment or dealt with in various other ways.

Turning to civil proceedings, the terminology generally is that *a plaintiff sues* (*e.g.* brings an *action* against) *a defendant*. The proceedings if successful result in *judgment for the plaintiff* and the judgment may order the defendant to pay the plaintiff money, or to transfer property to him, or to do or not to do something (injunction) or to perform a contract (specific performance). In applications for a writ of habeas corpus or for judicial review by means of an order of mandamus, prohibition or certiorari, or otherwise, the parties are called applicant and respondent respectively. In matrimonial cases in the Family Division the parties are called petitioner and respondent, and the relief sought concerns dissolution of the marriage, consequential financial arrangements, and the custody of children. (There are also other kinds of civil relief, but they need not concern us here.)

It is hardly necessary to point out that the terminology of the one type of proceedings should never be transferred to the other. "Criminal action" for example, is a misnomer; so is "civil offence" (the proper expression is "civil wrong"). One does not speak of a plaintiff prosecuting or of the criminal accused being sued. The common announcement "Trespassers will be prosecuted" has been called a "wooden lie", for trespass has traditionally been a civil wrong, not (generally) a crime. (There are some statutory offences of trespass, such as trespass on a railway line; and a "squatter" or other trespasser in a house that is occupied or required for occupation generally commits an offence if he fails to leave upon request.)

Again, the word "guilty" is used primarily of criminals. The corresponding word in civil cases is "liable"; but this word is also used in criminal contexts.

Civil and criminal courts are partly but not entirely distinct. The *Crown Court* has almost exclusively criminal jurisdiction. Magistrates are chiefly concerned with criminal cases, but they have important civil jurisdiction over licensing and family matters. On the other hand, the county court is only civil, and so is the *High Court* apart from appeals."

EXERCISES

1. Put the following words in the correct column:

sue, proceedings, plaintiff, punish, defendant, conviction, judgment, bring an action, guilty, jurisdiction, county court, magistrates' courts, imprisonment, prosecution, liable, offence, fine, civil wrong, Crown Court, appeal, injunction, trespass, release, discharge.

CIVIL	CRIMINAL	BOTH

2. How are the underlined words expressed in a more formal way?

   (a) The distinction between a crime and a civil wrong can <u>cause</u> some difficult legal problems.

   (b) This distinction <u>is not found</u> in the nature of the wrongful act.

   (c) ... but, rather, it can <u>be said to</u> depend on its legal consequences.

   (d) A trespasser commits an offence if <u>he doesn't leave an unoccupied house when asked</u>.

   (e) The language used to describe criminal proceedings is <u>different</u> from that used to describe civil proceedings.

   (f) Trespass is <u>principally</u> used in a civil context.

ENGLISH FOR CONTRACTS

INTRODUCTION

READING

Contract law is a branch of civil law which indicates to us when a promise is legally binding. There are many ways to define the meaning of a contract. Put quite simply, a contract is an agreement which the courts will enforce. However, there are certain agreements which the courts will not enforce for reasons we shall explain a little later on.

A contract may be oral, or in writing, and in every contract the parties to it have rights and obligations which arise from their agreement and which are personal to them. We call this special relationship between the parties privity of contract.

Case Law:

Panatown Ltd v Alfred MacAlpine Construction Ltd [2000] 4 All E.R. 97

Business and commerce rely on contract law to regulate their dealings, and the very basis of every business relationship is reflected in a contract which is a summary of the parties' agreement to comply with its terms.

The fundamental element of any contract may be expressed in Latin as *consensus ad idem* (consent to the same thing). This means that the parties must assent to all the terms of the agreement.

Every day of our lives we all make contracts, although we may not realise it. After all, agreements are usually in writing, or so it seems, but the majority of daily business transactions take the form of an oral, that is to say, a verbal contract. Buying a newspaper, paying for a coffee, purchasing a bus ticket or buying a packet of cigarettes are all examples of verbal contracts. It can therefore be said that contracts are the life-blood of business and as such, have to be carefully regulated to ensure that each and every contract is satisfactorily performed in so far as this is possible.

Case Law:

G. Percy Trentham Ltd v Archital Luxfer Ltd [1993] 1 Lloyd's Rep. (CA) 25

It is for this reason that both in the USA and in the UK there is so much emphasis on both legislation and jurisprudence for the guidance and protection of the consumer. As Denning J. said in the English case *John Lee & Son (Grantham) Ltd and Others v Railway Executive* [1949] 2 All E.R. 581, "... there is the vigilance of the common law which, while allowing freedom of contract, watches to see that it is not abused."

The importance and meaning of contract is brought out by this quotation from Hoeber, R., Reitzel, J., Lyden, D., Roberts, N. and Severance, G. *Contemporary Business Law* (1980):

"Contract law is worth attention not only because it governs contractual arrangements but also because it is basic to other areas of law. Much of the law governing sales of goods, commercial paper ("negotiable instruments"), agency, partnerships, corporations, and landlord and tenant is but the application to specialized situations of general contract principles. An understanding of the concepts, principles, and technical vocabulary presented in the chapters on contracts will be helpful in understanding other areas of business law."

Promises are basic to contracts and so we include a second quotation from The American Law Institute, *Restatement (Second) of the Law of Contracts* (1979), section 2(1).

"a manifestation of intention to act or to refrain from acting in a specified way, so made as to justify a promisee in understanding that a commitment has been made."

The party making the promise is called the "promisor". The person to whom the promise is made is called the "promisee". The *Restatement* definition lays special emphasis on both the promisee's expectations and the need for stability. When a promisor manifests (shows) an intention to act in a certain way, the promisee expects performance and may expend time or money in reliance on that expectation. A promise must satisfy certain requirements before it becomes binding. In Chapter One we shall consider these requirements, which are the essential ingredients of any contract.

EXERCISES

1. Having carefully read and thought about this introduction to contracts, discuss the following questions with your partner.

    (a)   When might individuals, businesses and governments **enter into** a contract?
    (b)   How would you define the role of both the courts and legislators with respect to contracts?
    (c)   What is the relevance of contract to business law?

2. Look back at the introduction and find words which mean:

    (a)   creating a legal obligation
    (b)   written
    (c)   agree with
    (d)   carried out
    (e)   cheques, bills of exchange, etc.

3. Fill in the spaces with words you found in the introduction:

    (a)   Contract law is a body of rules which regulate the formation of contracts so that contracts properly formed will be _____ on the parties involved, and the courts will be able to _____ them.
    (b)   Many court cases _____ from contracts which have been poorly **drawn up**.
    (c)   If a party enters _____ a binding contract, that party is legally obliged to _____ with the terms of that contract. Lack of _____ can result in litigation.

(d) A promisor leads the promisee to expect certain actions to be performed and frequently the promisee acts _____ reliance _____ those _____.

4. "an agreement which the courts will **enforce**." Many important verbs in English begin with "en-" or "em-". Complete the following sentences with a suitable verb of this kind.

(a) Parliament is _____ to make legislation.
(b) A warrant _____ the police to make an arrest.
(c) He _____ the education of his children to a private boarding school.
(d) All persons over the age of eighteen are _____ to vote.
(e) The system of legal aid was created to _____ that justice is equally available to all.
(f) The spirit of the French Revolution is _____ in the American Constitution.
(g) As a result of his accident, he became _____ in a complicated lawsuit.
(h) I wish to _____ the court as to the facts of the case.
(i) Parliaments exist all over the world to _____ legislation.

POINTS TO REMEMBER

1. *"to refrain/abstain from acting in a specific way"*
This verb has a reflexive meaning, and is the same as saying *"to stop oneself from acting"*. Compare with *"prevent someone from acting in a specific way"*. The verb *prevent* is used transitively.

2. *Lack of compliance with the terms of a contract can result in litigation.*
This can be expressed in another way: *Failure to comply with the terms of a contract can result in litigation.*

3. A *commitment* is made when you take it upon yourself to do something. It is an undertaking, a sort of promise. Look at the following examples:

Noun:–

(a) *An offer must contain language of* **commitment**.
(b) *His lifelong* **commitment** *to the company earned him the respect of his fellow-employees.*

Verb:– to commit yourself to doing something

(a) *She has* **committed herself to bringing** *the two sides together.*
(b) *Many developed countries* **commit** *0.7 per cent of their G.D.P.* **to helping** *developing countries.*

CHAPTER ONE

THE BIRTH OF A CONTRACT

A. *Classification of Contracts*

READ AND MATCH

A list of some common contract definitions is set out below. This is by no means intended to be either a definitive or exhaustive list of the various kinds of contracts that you may come across in daily business transactions. It is just a sample for you.

However, the list does not match the definitions. You and your partner have to match each type of contract with its definition. Partner A looks at the list of contracts on this page, and then the definitions which follow it. Partner B looks at the next page, and reads the definitions to A, who must find which kind of contract B is talking about. Then A reads his/her definitions, and B finds the type of contract from his/her list.

1. Contract of hire
2. Divisible contract
3. Contract of employment
4. Contract under seal
5. Open contract
6. Unilateral contract

   (a) A contract which is inferred from the conduct of the parties or from their relationship.
   (b) This is also called an indivisible contract. It is a contract in which there is an express or implied agreement, under which neither party may demand performance until it is ready to perform, or has performed its promise.
   (c) This is a contract between an employer and an independent contractor. This independence distinguishes such a contract from one of employment.
   (d) This is another name for a simple contract, and is one in which the parties must exchange reciprocal promises.
   (e) These comprise oral or written contracts which are not under seal, and which therefore require consideration.
   (f) Such a contract is an exception to the general rule that contracts may be oral or in writing. This kind of contract must be in writing.

Partner B looks first at the definitions of contracts which follow this list, and reads them aloud to A, who must match the definitions on his/her list. Then A will read his/her definitions.

1. Contract for the sale of land
2. Entire contract
4. Contract for services
5. Bilateral contract

3. Simple contract   6. Implied contract

    (a)   A contract set out in a document to which the parties' seals are affixed and which is delivered as "their deed". This is also known as a deed, and does not require consideration.

    (b)   This is a term which is used in the case of a contract for the sale of land which only contains very fundamental details, such as the names of the parties, price and description of the property. In this case, certain conditions are implied by law.
          Case Law: *Bigg and Another v Boyd Gibbins Ltd* [1971] 1 W.L.R. 913

    (c)   A contract arising where an offer is made in the form of a promise to pay a sum of money in return for the performance of an act. In such a case the performance of the act is taken to imply assent.
          Case Law: *Carlill v Carbolic Smoke Ball Co* [1893] 1 Q.B. 256

    (d)   This is a contract in which the parties express an intention that their mutual promises are to be independent of each other.
          Case Law: *Taylor v Webb* [1937] 2 K.B. 283

    (e)   A contract of service or apprenticeship where a relationship arises of employer and employee. Like most contracts, such a contract may be oral or written.

    (f)   This is a contract where payment is made for the temporary use of something. The object of such an agreement may be goods or a person's services.

READ AND DISCUSS

Three concepts which are often confused with contracts are:

    (a)   letters of intent
    (b)   heads of agreement
    (c)   quasi-contract.

(a) Letters of Intent

At times, it is quite usual to come across a letter written during negotiations by one party to another stating that it is their intention to enter into a contract at some future date. There are no established rules as to the legal effect of such letters which we call letters of intent.

Each case must be considered on its facts, but where the words and facts show an intention to contract, then the letter of intent can be construed as an acceptance.

Case Law: *British Steel Corp v Cleveland Bridge and Engineering Co Ltd* [1984] 1 All E.R. 504

(b) Heads of Agreement

Another term for "heads of agreement", which is quite often used, is "memorandum of understanding". Such a document records the intention of the parties prior to entering into a firm contract. It is very akin to a letter of intention, but is a more formal document, which contains a preamble with the proposed intentions for the object of the future contract and its proposed terms and conditions.

Such documents are normally used by future contracting parties to demonstrate that they are in earnest and wish to proceed to stabilise their relationship through a definitive contract.

(c) Quasi-contract
This is not strictly a contract as its name implies. However, in such a case, an obligation arises, as if it were an obligation of a contract. The law imposes this obligation upon a person, usually in cases of unjust enrichment. This means the unjust obtaining of money benefits at the expense of another person. Another example of a quasi-contractual obligation is the case of an executor or administrator of an estate who is bound to satisfy the liabilities of a deceased person to the extent of the assets, as if he had contracted to do so.

Case Law: *Craven-Ellis v Canons Ltd* [1936] 2 K.B. 403
What is the equivalent concept for these three figures under your country's law?

SENTENCE WRITING

Rewrite the following sentences in a more formal style, using the word given in brackets after the original sentence:
1. The court ordered the parties to perform the contract. (enforced)

2. The court ordered them to stop distributing the product in California. (refrain)

3. You've got to do what the contract says because you've signed it. (committed)

4. Many EU directives lead to new enactments. (arise)

B. *The Elements of a Contract*

READ AND DISCUSS

What does the word **agreement** mean?
What other related words can you think of?
How would you define **bargain**?

An insight into the concept of **bargain** is thus essential to an understanding of the Anglo-American idea of contracts. Examples of bargain are to be found in the following sentences:

(1) They were fully aware of the fact that the new regulations would not be popular among the students, but they had not **bargained** for such opposition.

(2) The typical modern contract is the bargain struck by the exchange of promises (Cheshire, Fifoot Furmston, *Cheshire and Fifoot's Law of Contract* (12th ed., 1991) p.73).

(3) Although it is argued that **plea bargaining** may result in a mutually beneficial compromise for the guilty defendant and the prosecution, there is a widespread concern about the legitimacy of such a practice.

(4) Why not agree ... to put the whole Maastricht timetable back a little? Spain can be a hard **bargainer**, and on this issue can count on allies ... (*The Economist*, March 4, 1995).

(5) In due course, ... investors will decide that the dollar is cheap enough ... to be a **bargain** (*The Economist*, March 11, 1995).

(6) The National Labour Relations Act provides for **collective bargaining** in labour disputes.

Discuss with a partner what you think **bargain** means in each sentence.

POINTS TO REMEMBER

1. *Undertake* is a formal word used in two slightly different ways.

(a) *to undertake a task, job, mission, post, etc.* means to accept the responsibility of it.

I am not in a position to undertake such an extensive research project at the moment.
A more informal way to express the same meaning is *to take on*.

(b) When you *undertake to do something*, you commit yourself to doing it.

The supplier undertakes to deliver the products within a 90 day lead time.
A more informal way to express the same meaning is *to promise or agree to do something*.

2. *Detrimental* in everyday language means *harmful*.
Smoking is detrimental to your health.
A *legal detriment*, however, is not necessarily harmful.
A promisee incurs legal detriment when he/she gives up a legal right or undertakes a legal burden.
When Anne agrees to buy Bob's video recorder for $40.00, she has incurred *legal detriment*. It consists of giving up her right to use those $40.00 in any other manner, such as purchasing something else or investing the money.

3. *Forbearance* in legal terms means refraining from doing something one has a legal right to do, *e.g.* deliberately choosing not to claim for a debt.
An example of forbearance is the following:
Paul gives up smoking for one year in order to get the car his father promised him in return for not smoking. Paul's refraining from smoking constitutes forbearance.

READING

It can be said that the essential ingredients of any agreement to constitute a contract are the following:

— an **offer**,
— which is **accepted**,
— both parties **intending** to enter legal relations.
— both parties having **capacity** to contract.
— there being no **mistake, misrepresentation** or **undue influence**.
— the object being **lawful**.

Now, before the law will enforce such an agreement, there must be something promised or actually done by one party in return for the promise of the other party. This something is called **consideration**. Without consideration, if the something is missing, the agreement will not be legally enforceable, unless it is in the form of a deed under seal, which is an exception to the rule.

1. Consideration

What is consideration? It is a term used for the price. It need not be money; it may be an exchange of goods, but a basic principle is that an agreement must amount to a **bargain**, each of the parties paying a price for what he receives from the other. See *Currie and Others v Misa* [1875] L.R. 10 E.x. 153 which contains a classic definition of consideration. It was held that a valuable consideration "may consist either in some right, interest, profit, or benefit accruing to the one party, or some forbearance, detriment, loss, or responsibility given, suffered, or undertaken by the other". So, if a party to an agreement gives a right or benefit he gives consideration. Equally, if a party incurs or undertakes responsibility, he gives consideration. So, consideration is something which is actually given or accepted in return for a promise.

Consideration must be valuable and it is often referred to as valuable consideration. This means that it must be something which is of some value in the eyes of the law. It does not matter how small the value is so long as it is worth something.

Case Law: *Thomas v Thomas* [1842] 2 Q.B. 851

There are some important rules governing consideration which need to be considered in a little more detail. You have seen that a contract must be supported by valuable consideration. Consequently, it cannot be sufficiently emphasised that a contract, to be valid and enforceable, needs consideration.

Consideration has been defined in the following way:

> The inducement to a contract. The cause, motive, price or impelling influence which induces a contracting party to enter into a contract. The reason or material cause of a contract. Some right, interest, profit, or benefit accruing to one party, or some forbearance, detriment, loss or responsibility, given, suffered or undertaken by the other (*Black's Law Dictionary*).

DISCUSSION

Here are four hypothetical situations which will illustrate the idea of consideration. Decide with a partner whether or not consideration is present in each case.

1. When Mr Smith learns that his nephew is thinking of dropping out of university, he promises to give him a car if he completes his university studies and obtains his degree. The nephew does this. Was consideration involved?

2. As a graduation present, Mary Brooks promises to take her granddaughter on a trip to China. When she graduates, can Mary's granddaughter legally hold her grandmother to this promise?

3. John's uncle promises to pay John £5,000 if he refrains from drinking, smoking and swearing until he is 21. John agrees and keeps his part of the promise. On John's 21st birthday is the uncle legally bound to keep his promise?

4. X and Y enter into a contract whereby X promises Y that he will sail around the world in a canoe departing from Manila and visiting all the islands that he comes across during a period of 365 days. X also undertakes that he will furnish palpable evidence of the islands visited.

5. And, to end with, a leading case:
Bainbridge v Firmstone [1838] 8 Ad. & E. 743. The plaintiff, at the request of the defendant, consented to allow the defendant to weigh two boilers. The defendant promised to return the boilers in perfect and complete condition. The defendant dismantled the boilers and then refused to put them back together again. The plaintiff sued for damages and the defendant argued that the plaintiff had given no consideration to support the promise to return the boilers in complete condition.

The following rules govern consideration:
1. Consideration must be sufficient, but need not be adequate.
2. Consideration need not move to the promisor.
3. Consideration must move from the promisee.
4. Past consideration is no consideration.
5. Consideration must not be illegal.
6. Consideration must be real.
7. Consideration must be possible of performance.

DISCUSSION

1. In the following cases the courts held that there was no consideration. Read the cases and decide with a partner which of the above rules were broken in each case.

(i) *Parkinson v College of Ambulance Ltd & Harrison* [1925] 2 K.B. 1

Mr Harrison, the second defendant, was the secretary of the defendant company, which was a charity. He fraudulently represented to the plaintiff that he was in a position to nominate persons to be given titles. He told the plaintiff that he or the charity could arrange for him to be given a knighthood if the plaintiff would make an adequate donation to the charity. The plaintiff paid £3,000 to the charity but did not receive a knighthood in return for this donation. The plaintiff brought an action to recover the £3,000.

(ii) *In Re McArdle* [1951] Ch. 669

Mr McArdle and his wife lived in a house which formed part of the estate of his father in which he and his brother and a sister had a beneficial interest, expectant on the death of their mother, who was the tenant for life. In the years 1943 and 1944 his wife paid the sum of £488 for improvements and decorations to the property. In 1945, after the work had been completed, the beneficiaries, including Mr McArdle, signed a document addressed to his wife which stated: "In consideration of your carrying out certain alterations and improvements to the property, we the beneficiaries under the will (of their father) hereby agree that the executors … shall repay to you from the said estate, when so distributed, the sum of £488 in settlement of the amount spent on the improvements."

   Later, in 1945, the tenant-for-life died and the daughter-in-law claimed payment of the sum of £488.

(iii) *John Price v Easton* [1833] 4 B. & Ad. 433

The defendant agreed with William Price that if the latter carried out certain work for the defendant, the defendant would pay £13 to the plaintiff, John Price, who was owed this amount by William Price. William Price carried out the work but the defendant did not pay the money to the plaintiff. The plaintiff sued for the money.

EXERCISE

---

1. Complete the sentences with the correct preposition.

  (a) A contract for the sale of land must be _____ writing.
  (b) Many claims arise _____ breach of contract.
  (c) This contract has been made _____ seal.
  (d) The parties _____ a contract may be referred to as the contracting parties.
  (e) When you enter _____ a contract you are bound _____ the terms of that contract and could become involved in litigation if you do not comply _____ those terms.
  (f) In the USA much emphasis is placed _____ consumer protection.
  (g) We have been ordered to refrain _____ using that symbol in our advertising campaign.
  (h) The plaintiff has acted _____ reliance _____ the commitment made by the defendant.

2. Offer

READ AND MATCH

In order for a contract to be **binding**, there must be a valid **offer** and **acceptance**.

What constitutes a valid offer? There are four basic requirements:
1. The offer must be communicated from the **offeror** to the **offeree**.
2. The offer must contain language of **commitment**.
3. The offer must be made with serious intention by the offeror.
4. The offer must be reasonably definite, usually containing the names of the **parties** involved, the **subject-matter**, the **consideration** (price) and the time and place for **performance**.

In daily business you will come upon many statements which look like offers, but which do not amount to offers. For example, you might hear or read the following:

1. A quotation for 50 laser printers CIF Hong Kong.
2. The price tag on any item of clothing.
3. (In a shop window) "The cheapest prices in town"
4. When John's car breaks down for the fourth time in a month, he says," If anyone offers me £500 for this load of scrap metal, I'll sell my car to them".

Match each example with one of the following concepts:

(a) Trade Puffs

This is not an offer but merely a statement boasting about a situation which may or may not be correct.

(b) Declaration of intention

It is intended to be an exclusively unilateral statement merely indicating a purpose or intention.

(c) Invitation to treat

A price ticket in a shop, goods advertised for auction, and requests for tenders, although they might appear to be offers, are merely requests for offers.
Case Law: *Pharmaceutical Society of Great Britain v Boots Cash Chemists (Southern) Ltd* [1952] 2 Q.B. 795; [1953] 1 Q.B. 401

(d) Requests for information, or the response to such requests

Frequently in preliminary negotiations to a contract, there is an exchange of information which lacks some of the elements of a valid offer.

POINTS TO REMEMBER
1. Tender
    (a) a formal offer to furnish goods or perform a service, together with the price of these goods or services. *We have submitted a tender for the construction of the new bridge.*
    (b) formally to offer something: a proposal, money, performance or resignation. *That firm tendered for the construction of the new bridge.* (In the U.S., the word "bid" is often used for "tender".)
2. Bring an action against somebody
Sue somebody for damages/for breach of contract
File suit for damages
3. (a) The court held that
            ruled that ⎰ the defendant had been negligent.
            found that
   (b) The court found ⎱ for the claimant.
            ruled
delivered judgment for/in favour of plaintiff/claimant.

WRITING

In well-written sentences explain the difference between the following concepts:

1. unilateral contract/bilateral contract.

2. valid offer/invitation to treat.

3. detrimental/legal detriment.

3. Acceptance
    1. Acceptance is a voluntary act by the offeree who shows **assent** to the terms specified by the offeror.
    2. It can be manifested by the **performance** of an act or by a **return promise**.
    3. Normally acceptance must be **communicated** to the offeror.
    4. Sometimes the offeror may **waive** the necessity of communication of acceptance.

Case Law: *Entores Ltd v Miles Far East Corp* [1955] 2 Q.B. 327

POINTS TO REMEMBER
1. In a shop, you can often hear *"All those items amount to £78."* That is, they add up to £78. An extended meaning of this is found in these two examples:

    (a) *"many statements ... do not amount to offers."*
    (b) *"An agreement must amount to a bargain ..."*

2. Waive –

    (a) give up, relinquish a right: *On settling the matter privately he waived his right to take an action against the XYZ company.*
    (b) not enforce a requirement: *Given the tenant's precarious financial situation, the landlord waived the requirement of timely payment.*

3. *Assent to* and *consent to* are used as synonyms in legal English.

---

4. Intention

READING

Intention to enter legal relations is a vital element of an enforceable contract. A leading case is *Rose and Frank Co v J.R. Crompton and Brothers Ltd* [1925] A.C. 445.

In this case, a commercial agreement stated: "This arrangement is not entered into as a formal or legal agreement, and shall not be subject to legal jurisdiction in the law Courts". Scrutton L.J. in the Court of Appeal said:

> "It is quite possible for parties to come to an agreement by accepting a proposal with the result that the agreement does not give rise to legal relations. The reason of this is that the parties do not intend that their agreement shall give rise to legal relations. This intention may be implied from the subject matter of the agreement, but it may also be expressed by the parties. In social and family relations such an intention is readily implied, while in business matters, the opposite result would ordinarily follow."

This case clearly defines a line to be drawn between social or family matters on the one hand and business matters on the other. Where agreements are of a social or family nature, there is a presumption that the parties do not intend to create legal relations. This, in effect, means that in such cases the burden is on the plaintiff to rebut the presumption that there is not the necessary intention to contract. A leading case is *Balfour v Balfour* [1919] 2 K.B. 571. The facts are as follows: the defendant and his wife returned to England on leave. The wife, on her doctor's advice, remained in England and the defendant returned alone to Ceylon. The defendant promised to pay his wife £30 per month as maintenance. He failed to keep up the payments and his wife sued him. The court held that there was no intention to create legal relations and the wife's claim could not succeed.

Unlike a family agreement, in the case of a commercial agreement there is a presumption that the parties intended to create legal relations. This means that the plaintiff does not have to prove such an intention to succeed with his claim, as the court will presume its existence. However, this presumption can be rebutted if a contrary intention is expressed and this is clearly illustrated in the case of *Rose and Frank Co v J.R. Crompton and Brothers Ltd*. But this was an express rebuttal and in other cases it is normally more difficult to establish that the burden of proof has been rebutted, and is a question of fact.

POINTS TO REMEMBER

There are many different ways to express **contrast**. Here are four different examples which may be useful for you.

1. Linking word – **Whereas/While** *other countries were inspired by the Enlightenment to codify laws and draft constitutions, Britain clung to a common law tradition.*
2. Verb – *Most countries* **differ from/are different from** *England* **in that** *they have a written constitution.*
3. Adverb – *The English judge takes no part in deciding guilt or innocence. The French judge,* **in/by contrast**, *reaches a verdict together with the jury.*
4. Preposition – *The American legal system,* **as distinct from** *the British one, allows lawyers to charge contingency fees.*

WRITING

Having read the above paragraph on intention, write a short formal paragraph explaining the differences between commercial and family agreements. The following words may be useful:

give rise to	presume/presumption	implied
expressed	rebut/rebuttal	intend/intention

EXERCISES

1. Learners of English often encounter difficulty with the formation of verbs from the following nouns. As you can see from these examples, there is no general rule to follow.

NOUN	VERB
litigation	litigate
specification	specify

Now form verbs from the following abstract nouns:

NOUN	VERB
notification	
invitation	
termination	
manifestation	
regulation	
communication	
obligation	
diversification	
expectation	
certification	
contemplation	
consideration	
implication	
repudiation	
revocation	
allegation	
examination	
quotation	
determination	
application	
simplification	
interpretation	
annotation	
implementation	
resignation	
qualification	

2. LIKE   LIKELY   UNLIKE   UNLIKELY   DISLIKE   ALIKE
Use one of the above words to complete the following sentences:

(a) _____ though it is, I think judgment will be for the defence.
(b) The law books used this semester are _____ the ones used last semester.
(c) _____ counsel for the plaintiff, counsel for the defence did not base his arguments on precedents.
(d) The judge is _____ to dismiss the case.
(e) The two subjects you have chosen for your course are _____ .
(f) The new statute was _____ the one it replaced in any way.
(g) They say that the jury will convict because they _____ counsel for the defence's style.
(h) Any further examination conducted in a _____ manner will be rejected.
(i) It was unfortunate that both lawyers _____ found the case so difficult.

19

5. Capacity

READ AND REPORT

Persons may be **natural** or **artificial**. Natural persons are, of course, human beings. Artificial persons are corporations.

In the case of natural persons, the general rule is that all natural persons have full **contractual capacity**, with some exceptions which we will refer to below.

In the case of corporations, their contractual capacity depends upon how the corporation was created.

Below you will find three instances where capacity to contract may be limited. Working in groups of three, each of you will read one section (a, b or c) and then describe what you have read to your group. Finally, discuss contractual capacity under your country's law.

(a) Minors

The Family Law Reform Act, 1969, defines a **minor** as a person under the age of 18. A minor **attains his or her majority** at the first moment of time on the 18th anniversary of his or her birth.

English law aims to protect minors but not to prevent them from entering into contracts. A fundamental rule of common law is that contracts are enforceable by minors, but not against them.

Contracts involving minors may be divided into two classes: (i) binding; (ii) voidable.

   (i)   **Binding contracts** — There are two kinds: contracts for necessaries and beneficial contracts of service.

       In the former case, "necessaries" means goods and services necessary to maintain the minor in the style to which he is accustomed, having regard to his social position and suitable to his actual requirements at the time of their delivery. The second kind of contract is one which is for the minor's benefit. These include contracts of apprenticeship, or for education or training.

  (ii) **Voidable contracts** — The general rule is that all other contracts entered into by a minor exist unless or until he **avoids** them during infancy or within a reasonable time after attaining his majority. In this context, the word "avoid" means to repudiate. Let us take the case of a minor who enters into a contract and then avoids it a few months later. From that moment of repudiation he will have no further liabilities thereunder. However, he will be liable to meet any obligations which may have arisen up to the date of its repudiation.

(b) Mentally disordered persons and drunken persons

These two incapacities come under the same heading, and they are treated in a very similar way.

A person who is certified as being mentally unsound, under the Mental Health Act 1983, is incapable of entering into contracts. Other cases of mental disorder are regarded as conditions of temporary insanity, akin to the condition of drunkenness. In these cases, any contract is **voidable** at the option of the incapacitated party if they can prove that they were so insane or so drunk that they did not know what they were doing and the other party was aware of their condition. There is one exception to this general rule. As in the case of minors, a drunken person or a temporarily insane person is bound by contracts for necessaries and cannot **avoid** them on regaining sobriety or sanity.

(c) Aliens

Generally they enjoy full contractual capacity. However, they may not directly own, or hold shares in a British ship or aircraft, but they are permitted to be shareholders of a British company owning a British ship or aircraft.

When the United Kingdom is in a state of war, alien enemies cannot contract and any existing contracts are automatically suspended. Furthermore, alien enemies cannot sue in the British Courts but they may be sued, in which case they may defend the **action**, **counter-claim** and **appeal**. A leading case is *Arab Bank Ltd v Barclays Bank (Dominion, Colonial and Overseas)* [1954] A.C. 495, in which Lord Reid, in the House of Lords, said:

> "... with certain exceptions, the outbreak of war prevents the further performance of contracts between persons in this country and persons in enemy territory."

EXERCISES

1. Finish these sentences in an appropriate way:

    (a) On his/her 18th birthday, a minor ...
    (b) Regarding contractual capacity, a mentally unsound person is incapable ...
    (c) On signing the contract, you have committed ...
                    you have undertaken ...
    (d) If there is no consideration, an agreement will not be binding unless ...
    (e) We have submitted a tender ...
    (f) I'm afraid our action for breach of contract has not been successful; the court has delivered judgment ...
    (g) That advertisement is merely an invitation to treat; it does not amount ...
    (h) Family arrangements do not always result ...
    (i) The court has held that our product is infringing Kraft's patent and has issued an injunction ordering us to refrain ...
    (j) English law does not prevent minors ...

2. Finish each sentence with a word made from the word in brackets.

    (a) A contract needs consideration to be valid and _____ (force)
    (b) A promisee expects the promisor to fulfil certain obligations and may act on these _____ (expect)
    (c) _____ instruments are used to transfer good title to a transferee, and include bills of exchange, letters of credit and cheques. (negotiate)
    (d) Your lack of _____ with the terms of the agreement can be considered a breach of contract. (comply)
    (e) Consideration may be defined as the _____ to a contract. (induce)
    (f) The _____ parties have agreed to submit this contract to the jurisdiction of the Irish courts. (contract)

(g) _____ capacity is limited in three instances. (contract)

(h) When an agreement is of a family nature, courts operate under the _____ that the parties do not intend to create legal relations. (presume)

(i) _____ of contract only operates as anticipatory breach of contract if the promisee decides to treat it as such and brings an action for damages. (repudiate)

(j) The defence's _____ of the plaintiff's arguments was a brilliant piece of oratory. (rebut)

6. No mistake, misrepresentation or undue influence

These elements are often referred to as **vitiating factors** when they arise in a contract. The word "vitiate" means invalidate. There is an additional factor to which we shall refer, known as **duress**.

WRITING

Before reading about the effects of these vitiating factors under Anglo/American law, write a definition of each and then discuss their effects under your country's law.

1. _____
_____
_____

2. _____
_____
_____

3. _____
_____
_____

4. _____
_____
_____

READ AND ANSWER

Working in pairs, **Partner A** must carefully read *Mistake* and *Misrepresentation* and be prepared to clarify some points for your partner without looking back at the reading passage. Then find out the following information from your partner.

1. When might a court rule that a contract was formed under undue influence?
2. How would the case be dealt with and what sort of remedy be applied?

3. How does undue influence differ from duress?
4. Are cases of duress and undue influence dealt with in the same way in the courts?

Partner B must carefully read *Undue Influence* and *Duress* and be prepared to clarify some points for your partner without looking back at the reading passage. Then find out the following information from your partner.

1. Will a mistake always render a contract void?
2. What is meant by an operative mistake?
3. How does misrepresentation differ from mistake?
4. Must misrepresentation always be intentional?

1. *Mistake*: The general rule is that mistake does not affect the validity of a contract. However, this depends upon the seriousness of the mistake, and it may lead to rendering a contract void. This only arises where there is a mistake of fact, never in the case of a mistake of law. Hence the addage, "ignorance of the law is no defence" (*Ignorantia juris non excusat*).

Serious mistakes which affect the validity of a contract are known as operative mistakes, because they operate so as to avoid the contract. Such mistakes can arise in the cases of documents, identity of the other party and the identity and existence of the subject matter of the contract.

Operative mistakes can be common, mutual or unilateral. A Court will declare a contract to be void where there is a mistake of fact which effectively prevents the formation of a contract.

Case Law: *Great Peace Shipping Ltd v Tsavliris Salvage (International) Ltd* [2002] Lloyd's Rep. 653, CA; *Clarion v National Provident Institution* [2000] 2 All E.R. 265

2. *Misrepresentation*: This arises where a false statement of a material fact is made by one party to the other party prior to the making of the contract, with a view to inducing the other party to act on it. It is important to note that such a statement must have been intended to be acted on and it must in fact have induced the other party to make the contract. The misrepresentation, as in the case of mistake, must be one of fact, and statements of law are therefore excluded. There are four categories of misrepresentation:

(a) fraudulent;
(b) negligent;
(c) those made under s.2(1) of the Misrepresentation Act 1967;
(d) innocent.

In the leading case of *Curtis v Chemical Cleaning and Dyeing Co* [1951] 1 K.B. 805 Denning L.J. offered a very succinct definition of misrepresentation:

"In my opinion any behaviour, by words or conduct, is sufficient to be a misrepresentation if it is such as to mislead the other party about the existence or extent of the exemption ... If it conveys a false impression, that is enough. If the false impression is created knowingly, it is a fraudulent misrepresentation; if it is created unwittingly, it is an innocent misrepresentation; but either is sufficient to disentitle the creator of it to the benefit of the exemption."

Case Law: *Spice Girls Ltd v Aprilia World Service BV The Times*, April 5, 2000

3. *Undue influence*: This is what we call an equitable doctrine, and arises in cases where confidential or personal relationships exist.

A transaction can be **set aside** in equity in certain cases where undue influence is presumed on account of the special relationship between the parties. In these special cases, the presumption may be rebutted, and the onus is on the party receiving the benefit to establish that he did not obtain it by undue influence.

The following relationships are ones where undue influence is presumed:

    (a)   parent and child;
    (b)   guardian and ward;
    (c)   solicitor and client;
    (d)   doctor and patient;
    (e)   trustee and beneficiary;
    (f)   religious adviser and disciple.

You should note that this presumption does not arise in the case of a husband and wife. However, it may arise in the case of engaged couples although the position has not been clearly defined.
Case Law: *Allcard v Skinner* [1887] 36 Ch. D. 145

4. *Duress* was well defined by Lord Scarman in the House of Lords case, *Pao On and Others v Lau Yiu Long and Others* [1980] A.C. 614: "Duress, whatever form it takes, is a coercion of will so as to vitiate consent".

Consequently, where a person has been coerced into a contract whereby he did not contract of his own free will, that person may apply to the court for **relief**. What form will the relief take? The contract may be **avoided or set aside**. The remedy will be either a **common law** one or an **equitable** one, and this will depend upon whether the coercion was in fact duress or undue influence.

If it is patently clear that a particular act of coercion amounts to duress, then the common law remedy is available, and the contract may be avoided. If, however, the act of coercion amounts to undue influence then the equitable remedy will be available, and the contract may be set aside, at the discretion of the court. In practice, if there is doubt as to whether the act of coercion amounts to duress or undue influence, an action may be brought before the court applying to have the contract avoided for duress, and pleading in the alternative that the contract be set aside on the grounds of undue influence. If the court is satisfied that duress existed, then the court will order the contract to be avoided and that will be the end of the matter. But if the plaintiff fails to establish the existence of duress, the court will go on to consider whether undue influence existed. If the court finds that there was undue influence, then it will exercise its equitable jurisdiction and order the contract to be set aside.

POINTS TO REMEMBER

1. *To set aside* means to annul, cancel or make void. It is usually used in the context of a motion to the Court of Appeal to set aside a High Court judgment on the grounds that the judgment was wrong.

To avoid means to set aside or make null or void. It is used, *e.g.* when a case is brought to enforce a contract and the defendant alleges that it contains some defect which prevents it from being enforceable.

2. *These elements are often referred to as vitiating elements.*

Notice the passive construction. *Refer to* is a transitive verb. For example:

The word "construction" refers to a way of interpreting a written document.

He referred to the political situation in his speech.

In business English, we often begin letters with the words *With reference to ...*

3. *due/undue/duly*

Due and *undue* are two adjectives frequently used in legal English. Examples are:

due diligence, in due time, at the due date, in due course, undue influence.

Duly is the adverb of *due.*

He duly paid on the specified date.

She duly used the medicine three times daily.

4. *It may lead to rendering a contract void.*

Render is a more formal way of saying *make or cause to be.*

A second useful meaning is *give:*

You have just rendered me a great service.

5. *They operate so as to avoid the contract.*

So as to is a formal way of saying *in such a way that.* It is commonly used in legal English.

EXERCISES

1. Look back at the passages on mistake, misrepresentation, undue influence and duress and find a more formal way of expressing the following:

mistake: make + something + adjective
       come up
       in such a way that
misrepresentation: in order to induce
             to do something because of something else
             get across, pass
undue influence: proved that what was said is not true.
          burden
          person with legal title to assets in trust for another
duress: a legal solution
      does not/is not able to
      make use of

2. Put one of the following prefixes in front of each of the words in the list: UN-, IN-, MIS-, IL-, IM-, DIS-.

enforceable	stability	lead
enacted	divisible	aware
legal	legitimate	representation
take	capacity	adequate
valid	qualify	natural
existence	reasonable	agreement

7. The object being lawful

READING

The word lawful means something that is authorised by law, or something that is not contrary to or forbidden by law. If the object of a contract is unlawful, we refer to the contract as being illegal. There are several situations which render the object of a contract unlawful. These include the following examples:

1. Contracts expressly prohibited by statute law.
2. Contracts in restraint of trade.
3. Contracts to defraud the Inland Revenue.
4. Contracts involving corruption in public life.
5. Contracts to commit a crime.
6. Contracts contrary to public policy.
7. Contracts to commit a civil wrong.
8. Contracts which would be unlawful in the jurisdiction of a foreign state.

In *Archbolds (Freightage) Ltd v S. Spanglett Ltd* [1961] 1 Q.B. 374, Devlin L.J. said:

"The effect of illegality on a contract may be threefold. If at the time of making the contract there is an intention to perform it in an unlawful way, the contract, although it remains alive, is unenforceable at the suit of the party having that intent; if the intent is held in common, it is not enforceable at all. Another effect of illegality is to prevent a plaintiff from recovering under a contract if in order to prove his rights under it, he has to rely on his own illegal act; he may not do that even though he can show that at the time of making the contract he had no intent to break the law and that at the time of performance he did not know that what he was doing was illegal. The third effect of illegality is to avoid the contract ab initio, and that arises if the making of the contract is expressly or impliedly prohibited by statute or is otherwise contrary to public policy."

POINTS TO REMEMBER:

1. *. . . in restraint of.*

This is a compound preposition which means *limiting*. The verb is *to restrain – hold back, keep down.* For example:

I had to restrain myself from laughing.

2. *threefold = treble*

The suffix *-fold* may follow any number to indicate magnitude *e.g.*:

The cost of living has increased twenty-fold over the last forty years.

3. On p.18, you saw some ways of expressing contrast.

Here are some more, together with some examples of making comparisons.

1. Linking word – **As** *in the rest of the world, English law can be divided into public and private.*
2. Preposition – **Like** *the American constitution, many constitutions protect freedom of speech.*
3. Linking word/general lexis – **Although** *there* **is** *much* **in common between** *the French and Italian systems,* **the following contrast may be mentioned.**
4. Noun – **This is the key difference between** *the American version of the law of tort and that of the British system.*
5. Preposition – *Civil law judges,* **as opposed to** *their British counterparts, reach their positions through a series of professional examinations.*
6. Verb – *Inquiry conducted by an examining judge* **distinguishes** *inquisitorial criminal procedure in civil law countries* **from** *that in England, which is accusatorial.*
7. Verb – *This characteristic of the common law* **contrasts** *with the European civil law.*
8. Preposition – *Louisiana,* **unlike** *the rest of the US, follows the civil law tradition.*

WRITING

Now that you have seen the essential elements of a contract in the common law system, name the essential elements in a contract under your legal system and discuss the differences between the two systems. Try to incorporate the ways of expressing contrast found on p.18, as well as the preceding constructions.

C. *Leading Cases*

READING

In order to obtain a better understanding of the elements of a contract, we are going to read and discuss two leading cases. This short extract from a well-known book on contract law lays down guidelines as to the interpretation of the language of offers.

> "... The first and strongest guide is that the particular expression is to be judged on the basis of what a reasonable man in the position of the offeree has been led to believe. This requires an analysis of what the offeree should have understood under all of the surrounding circumstances, with all of his opportunities for comprehending the intention of the offeror, rather than what the offeror, in fact, intended. ... The most important of the remaining guides is the language used. If there are no words of promise, undertaking or commitment, the tendency is to construe the expression to be an invitation for an offer or mere preliminary negotiations in the absence of strong, countervailing circumstances." *Murray on Contracts* (1977) pp.37–40, Section 24.

READ AND REPORT

Case One: *Harvey v Facey* [1893] A.C. 552

There was a dispute between the Mayor of Kingston, Jamaica, Dr James Ogilvy, and Mr Larchin Facey over the sale of the latter's property. The plaintiffs, the Mayor and his Town Council, sued Mr Facey for breach of contract when the property in question was not transferred.

You and your partner should each read one of the following conversations, one between the Mayor and his solicitor, and the other between Mr Facey and his solicitor. Then tell each other your side of the story and work out what the judgment was in the ensuing court case.

Conversation A

Mayor: I've never been so insulted in my whole entire life! We were on the point of closing the deal when he walked off.

Solicitor: Wait a minute! Calm down! What deal are you talking about!

Mayor: Bumper Hall Pen. The Council was interested in buying it from that Facey chap. But they hadn't taken a vote yet. An urgent call from my wife made me put off all my arrangements for the rest of that day and then Facey disappeared.

Solicitor: Well, had you informed him about the postponement?

Mayor: Of course I had! He was quite understanding. He told me he was in no hurry. But lo and behold, the next day, when we had definitely voted to buy the property, I couldn't get hold of him. After asking around I found out he had gone to Porus on the train, so I telegraphed the fellow.

Solicitor: What exactly did the telegraph say?

Mayor: "Will you sell us Bumper Hall Pen? Telegraph lowest cash price. Answer paid." And he said OK, £900.

Solicitor: But what exactly did his telegraph say?

Mayor: "Lowest price for Bumper Hall Pen £900."

Solicitor: How did you word your acceptance?

Mayor: "We agree to buy Bumper Hall Pen for the £900 asked by you. Please send us your title deed in order that we may get early possession." And we haven't heard a thing from him since.

Conversation B

Mr Facey is speaking to his solicitor.

Facey: I've just received a letter from the Kingston Town Council's solicitor informing me that they are bringing a case against me. You see, I'd been negotiating the sale of my property in Porus, Bumper Hall Pen, with them, and as they'd taken such a long time in answering me and at the end of that the only answer I got was that they had deferred their decision to a later date, I got fed up and went off to Porus the next day. To my surprise, I received a telegram on the train from the Mayor and Council asking me for a price. The telegram actually said "Will you sell us Bumper Hall Pen? Telegraph lowest cash price. Answer paid". As the answer had been paid, I thought I might as well reply, so I sent them the following telegram "Lowest price for Bumper Hall Pen £900", although I had no serious intention of continuing negotiations with that inconsiderate lot. It was obvious from the Mayor's immediate reply that he had misinterpreted my telegram because he was already asking for the title deed as if he was the owner. He seemed to think that we had closed the deal. That was not my view of the situation, so I took no notice of his last telegram. What did the telegram say? It went like this: "We agree to buy Bumper Hall Pen for the £900 asked by you. Please send us your title deed in order that we may get early possession."

Now answer these questions on the case.

1. Would **a reasonable person** in the position of Mayor Ogilvy have believed that Facey was making him an offer to sell the property?
2. Did Facey do or say anything **to lead him to believe** so?
3. Can we **construe** Facey's telegraph to be an offer?
4. Has the offer been **revoked**? or **rejected**?
5. Does the exchange of telegrams **constitute a binding** contract?

EXERCISES

1. Complete the following table:

ADJECTIVE	NOUN	VERB
valid		
	acceptance	
	definition	
		try
		comprehend
		revoke
	judgment	
	existence	
		intend
		rely

2. The following words are often confused. Insert the correct word from the list in each sentence.

COUNSEL   TO COUNSEL   COUNCIL   COUNCILLOR   COUNSELLOR

(a) The judge asked _____ for the defence to explain his point.
(b) He has been elected to the district _____ .
(c) She's an excellent _____ . I'd listen to her if I were you.
(d) The _____ in charge of roads objected to the plan.
(e) After the terrible floods, the local farmers took _____ together to work out a plan of action.
(f) Priests _____ people who have serious problems.

WRITING

1. Below are statements made orally by Facey to his lawyer. Using the words given in brackets, show how his lawyer would have expressed the same ideas in a written brief.

(a) I didn't get a reply from the Mayor and Council, so I started talking to a new buyer. (in the absence of ... negotiations)

_____

(b) The Council took so long to reply that day in Kingston that I thought that they didn't want the property. (led. .... believe)

_____

(c)   The Mayor thinks that just because I didn't send the title deed I breached the contract. (failure ... breach of contract)

_____

(d)   I never said I'd sell him the property. (committed)

_____

_____

READ AND DISCUSS

Case Two: *Carlill v Carbolic Smoke Ball Co* [1893] 1 Q.B. 256

It is also important to remember the *Carbolic Smoke Ball* case, which is a good illustration of an offer which is made to the world at large, where a valid acquiescent non-communicated acceptance may be made by a person with notice of the offer. What do you know about offers?

_____

What do you know about unilateral offers?

_____

_____

BLANK-FILLING

Read the following passage on **communication of acceptance** and fill in the blank spaces with an appropriate word.

Acceptance takes different forms. It may, *e.g.* be _____ writing or orally, or made at an _____ at the fall of a hammer, but it must normally be _____. This communication has to be made by somebody with the authority to do so. Silence cannot amount _____ acceptance unless there is a _____ consent of the offeree. This is implied in circumstances such _____ those in the *Carlill* case. In some cases the offeror is regarded as having waived communication of acceptance. This arises in the case of unilateral contracts such_____ promises to pay a sum of money in _____ for some act to be _____ out by the offeree. _____ of the act constitutes acceptance, and communication is not necessary.

Carlill v Carbolic Smoke Ball Co deals with this concept as well as offers to **the world at large** and the **intention to create legal relations**.

READING

The following advertisement was placed in the *Pall Mall Gazette* of November 13, 1891, by the Carbolic Smoke Ball Co.

> "£100 reward will be paid by the Carbolic Smoke Ball Company to any person who contracts the increasing epidemic of influenza, colds, or any diseases caused by taking cold, after having used the carbolic smoke ball three times daily for two weeks according to the printed directions supplied with each ball. £1000 is deposited with the Alliance Bank, Regent Street, showing our sincerity in the matter. During the last epidemic of influenza many thousand carbolic smoke balls were sold as preventives against this disease, and in no ascertained case was the disease contracted by those using the carbolic smoke ball. One carbolic smoke ball will last a family several months, making it the cheapest remedy in the world at the price, 10s. post free. The ball can be refilled when empty at a cost of 5s. Address, Carbolic Smoke Ball Company 27, Princess Street, Hanover Square, London."

Mrs Carlill read the advertisement, and on the strength of it bought the balls, and used them according to the instructions. Unfortunately, they did not afford her much protection, for in January 1892 she contracted influenza. She immediately claimed the reward, but the Carbolic Smoke Ball Co refused to give it to her. She did not hesitate in bringing an action against the company for breach of contract, and the court of first instance ruled for her. The Carbolic Smoke Ball Co appealed.

When one of the parties is not satisfied with the judgment delivered, they can **appeal** to a court with **appellate** jurisdiction. The party appealing is referred to as the **appellant** and the opposite party as the **respondent**. The appeal judges can **uphold/affirm** the original judgment, or **reverse** it or **set** it **aside**. When the original judgment is upheld, the appeal is **dismissed**.

Lindley L.J. delivered judgment dismissing the appeal Bowen L.J. concurred in the following terms:

> "I am of the same opinion. We were asked to say that this document was a contract too vague to be enforced. The first observation which arises is that the document itself is not a contract at all, it is only an offer made to the public. The defendants contend next, that it is an offer the terms of which are too vague to be treated as a definite offer, inasmuch as there is no time limit fixed for the catching of the influenza, and it cannot be supposed that the advertisers seriously meant to promise to pay money to every person who catches the influenza at any time after the inhaling of the smoke ball. It was urged also, that if you look at this document you will find much vagueness as to the persons with whom the contract was intended to be made – that, in the first place, its terms are wide enough to include persons who may have used the smoke ball before the advertisement was issued; at all events, that it is an offer to the world in general, and, also, that it is unreasonable to suppose it to be a definite offer, because nobody in their senses would contract themselves out of the opportunity of checking the experiment which was going to be made at their own expense. It was also contended that the advertisement is rather in the nature of a puff or a proclamation than a promise or offer intended to mature into a contract when accepted. But the main point seems to be that the vagueness of the document shows that no contract whatever was intended."

NOTE-TAKING

1. List the main points made for the defence.

_____

_____

_____

_____

_____

2. How are these arguments introduced? Find two different introductory phrases. Can you think of any other phrases which are not in the text?

_____

_____

_____

_____

_____

_____

WRITING

1. Now write a short paragraph summarising the arguments for the defence.

_____

_____

_____

_____

_____

_____

EXERCISES

1. Without looking back at the text, see if you can remember the formal expressions used instead of the underlined items:

    (a)   The first observation that *comes up* is ...
    (b)   The terms are very vague *because* there is no fixed time limit.
    (c)   You will find much vagueness *about* the terms of the contract.
    (d)   It is unreasonable to *think it is* a definite offer.
    (e)   ... and that, *anyway*, it is a contract with the world in general.

2. Rewrite the following sentences using the word(s) in brackets.

    (a)   When accepted, does this offer form the basis of a binding contract? (acceptance)
    (b)   Have they followed the instructions in the contract? (conditions, laid)
    (c)   Let us consider the contract we are talking about. (question)
    (d)   I thought you would give me a discount for such a large order. That was the impression you gave me. (led)
    (e)   We are not obliged to fulfil the promise. (obligation)

READ AND TAKE NOTES

In the preceding paragraph Bowen L.J. was summarising the defence's arguments. Now he goes on to comment on various points and deliver his judgment. While reading the judgment (pp.34–36), make notes on what he says about the following points:

1. the intention of the advertisement

_____

_____

_____

_____

2. the time limits of the advertisement

_____

_____

_____

_____

3. when the contract is formed

_____

_____

_____

_____

4. the notification of acceptance

_____

_____

_____

_____

5. consideration

_____

_____

_____

_____

"It seems to me that in order to arrive at a right conclusion we must read this advertisement in its plain meaning, as the public would understand it. It was intended to be issued to the public and to be read by the public. How would an ordinary person reading this document construe it?

It was intended unquestionably to have some effect, and I think the effect which it was intended to have, was to make people use the smoke ball, because the suggestions and allegations which it contains are directed immediately to the use of the smoke ball as distinct from the purchase of it. It did not follow that the smoke ball was to be purchased from the defendants directly, or even from agents of theirs directly. The intention was that the circulation of the smoke ball should be promoted, and that the use of it should be increased.

The advertisement begins by saying that a reward will be paid by the Carbolic Smoke Ball Company to any person who contracts the increasing epidemic after using the ball. It has been said that the words do not apply only to persons who contract the epidemic after the publication of the advertisement but include persons who had previously contracted the influenza. I cannot so read the advertisement. It is written in colloquial and popular language, and I think that it is equivalent to this: "£100 will be paid to any person who shall contract the increasing epidemic after having used the carbolic smoke ball three times daily for two weeks." And it seems to me that the way in which the public would read it would be this, that if anybody, after the advertisement was published, used three times daily for two weeks the carbolic smoke ball, and then caught cold, he would be entitled to the reward.

Then again it was said: "How long is the protection to endure? Is it to go on for ever, or for what limit of time?" I think that there are two constructions of this document, each of which is good sense and each of which seems to me to satisfy the exigencies of the present action. It may mean that the protection is warranted to last during the epidemic, and it was during the epidemic that the plaintiff contracted the disease. I think, more probably, it means that the smoke ball will be a protection while it is in use. That seems to me the way in which an ordinary person would understand an advertisement about medicine, and about a specific against influenza. It could not be supposed that after you have left off using it you are still to be protected for ever, as if there was to be a stamp set upon your forehead that you were never to catch influenza, because you had once used the carbolic smoke ball. I think the immunity is to last during the use of the ball. That is the way in which I should naturally read it, and it seems to me that the subsequent language of the advertisement supports that construction. (...)

Was it intended that the £100 should, if the conditions were fulfilled, be paid? The advertisement says that £1,000 is lodged at the bank for the purpose. Therefore, it cannot be said that the statement that £100 would be paid was intended to be a mere puff. I think it was intended to be understood by the public as an offer which was to be acted upon. But it was said there was no check on the part of the persons who issued the advertisement, and that it would be an insensate thing to promise £100 to a person who used the smoke ball unless you could check or superintend his manner of using it. The answer to that argument seems to me to be that if a person chooses to make extravagant promises of this kind he probably does so because it pays him to make them, and, if he has made them, the extravagance of the promises is no reason in law why he should not be bound by them.

It was also said that the contract is made with all the world – that is, with everybody; and that you cannot contract with everybody. It is not a contract made with all the world. There is the fallacy of the argument. It is an offer made to all the world: and why should not an offer be made to all the world which is to ripen into a contract with anybody who comes forward and performs the conditions? It is an offer to become liable to anyone who, before it is retracted, performs the conditions, and, although the offer is made to the world, the contract is made with that limited portion of the public who come forward and perform the condition on the faith of the advertisement. It is not like cases in which you offer to negotiate, or you issue advertisements that you have got a stock of books to sell or houses to let, in which case there is no offer to be bound by any contract. Such advertisements are offers to negotiate – offers to receive offer – offers to chaffer, as, I think, some learned judge in one of the cases has said. If this is an offer to be bound, then it is a contract the moment the person fulfils the condition. That seems to me to be sense, and it is also the ground on which all these advertisement cases have been decided during the century. (...)

Then it was said that there was no notification of the acceptance of the contract. One cannot doubt that, as an ordinary rule of law, an acceptance of an offer made ought to be notified to the person who makes the offer, in order that the two minds may come together. Unless this is done, the two minds may be apart, and there is not that consensus which is necessary according to the English law – I say nothing about the laws of other countries – to make a contract. But there is a clear gloss to be made upon that doctrine, that as notification of acceptance is required for the benefit of the person who makes the offer, the person who makes the offer may dispense with notice to himself if he thinks it desirable to do so, and I suppose there can be no doubt that where a person in an offer made by him to another person expressly or impliedly intimates a particular mode of acceptance as sufficient to make the bargain binding, it is only necessary for the other person to whom such offer is made to follow the indicated method of acceptance; and if the person making the offer, expressly or impliedly intimates in his offer that it will be sufficient to act on the proposal without communicating acceptance of it to himself, performance of the condition is a sufficient acceptance without notification. That seems to me to be the principle which lies at the bottom of the acceptance cases, of which two instances are the well-known judgment of Mellish L.J. in *Harris v Nickerson* [1873] L.R. 8 Q.B. 286 and the very instructive judgment of Lord Blackburn in *Alexander Brogden and Others v The Directors of the Metropolitan Railway Company* [1877] 2 H.L. 666, in which he appears to me to take exactly the line I have indicated.

Now, if that is the law, how are we to find out whether the person who makes the offer does intimate that notification of acceptance will not be necessary in order to constitute a binding bargain? In many cases you look to the offer itself. In many cases you extract the answer from the character of the transaction that notification is not required and in the advertisement cases it seems to me to follow as an inference to be drawn from the transaction itself that a person is not to notify his acceptance of the offer before he performs the conditions, but that, if he performs the condition, notification is dispensed with. It seems to me that from the point of view of common sense no other idea could be entertained. If I advertise to the world that my dog is lost and that anybody who brings the dog to a particular place will be paid some money, are all the police or other persons whose business it is to find lost dogs to be expected to sit down and write me a note saying that they have accepted my proposal? Why, of course they at once look after the dog, and as soon as they find the dog, they have performed the condition. The essence of the transaction is that the dog should be found, and it is not necessary under such circumstances, as it seems to me, that in order to make the contract binding, there should be any notification of acceptance. It follows from the nature of the thing that the performance of the condition is sufficient acceptance without the notification of it, and a person who makes an offer in an advertisement of that kind makes an offer which must be read by the light of that common sense reflection. He does, therefore, in his offer impliedly indicate that he does not require notification of the acceptance of the offer. (...)

Then as to the alleged want of consideration. The definition of "consideration" given in Selwyn's *Nisi Prius*, 8th edn., p. 47, is this:

'Any act of the plaintiff from which the defendant derives a benefit or advantage, or any labour, detriment, or inconvenience sustained by the plaintiff, provided such act is performed or such inconvenience suffered by the plaintiff with the consent, either express or implied, of the defendant.'

Can it be said here that if the person who reads this advertisement applies thrice daily, for such time as may seem to him tolerable, the carbolic smoke ball to his nostrils for a whole fortnight, he is doing nothing at all – that it is a mere act which is not to count towards consideration to support a promise (for the law does not require us to measure the adequacy of the consideration)? Inconvenience sustained by one party at the request of the other is enough to create a consideration. I think, therefore, that it is consideration enough that the plaintiff took the trouble of using the smoke ball. But I think also that the defendants received a benefit from this user, for the use of the smoke ball was contemplated by the defendants as being indirectly a benefit to them, because the use of the smoke balls would promote their sale. (...)"

SMITH, L.J., delivered judgment to the same effect.

WRITING

Now write a paragraph summarising his decision.

POINTS TO REMEMBER:
1. As we have already seen, the following phrases are used to introduce different points contained in a judgment:
The Court held that ... The Court found that ... The Court decided that ...
It is also possible to use an impersonal construction to express judgments:
It was held that ... It was found that ... It was decided that ...
Other impersonal constructions are also used by Bowen L.J. to express his opinions, and are commonly used in formal English.
It was also said that ... Was it intended that ...? It could not be supposed that ...
2. *The advertisement began by saying*
We begin /start/ continue/ finish up /end our speech **by** saying/ pointing out/ remarking that. ...
3. The construction with *seem* ... can be made personal in English. Look at the example taken from the text:
It seems to me that that is exactly the line which he takes.
Performance as acceptance seems to me to be the principle which lies at the bottom of the acceptance cases.
In the first example the construction is impersonal and is followed by a *that* – clause. In the second the subject is specified (it is a noun) and because it has a direct reference, it can be followed by the infinitive.
4. ... *Then as to the alleged want of consideration*
as to is another way of drawing attention to a subject that you want to speak about. We can also say
As regards the alleged want ... Regarding the alleged want ...
and, more informally,
As far as the alleged want of consideration is concerned, ...

EXERCISES

---

1. Rewrite the following sentences beginning in the way indicated so that the new sentence means the same as the previous one.

   (a) A person is immune as long as he uses the ball.
     Immunity is _____

   (b) Was it their intention that the £100 reward should be paid?
     Was the £100 reward _____

   (c) For the past century, all cases involving advertisements have been decided on those grounds.
     Those are the grounds _____

    (d)   The offeree never notified the offeror that he was accepting the offer.
        There was no _____

_____

2. Join these groups of sentences to form one longer one in each case.

    (a)   A reward will be paid by the Carbolic Smoke Ball Company to a person.
    (b)   This person uses the smoke ball.
    (c)   After this he contracts the increasing epidemic.

_____

_____

_____

_____

    (a)   It would be an insensate thing to promise £100 to a person.
    (b)   This person used the smoke ball.
    (c)   In this case you could not check or superintend his manner of using it.

_____

_____

_____

_____

3. Complete this table:

VERB	NOUN	ADJECTIVE
contend		
	advertisement	
	document	
	definition	
mature		
	intention	
		alleged
promote		
imply		
endure		
	argument	
ripen		
apply		
receive		

CROSSWORD ONE

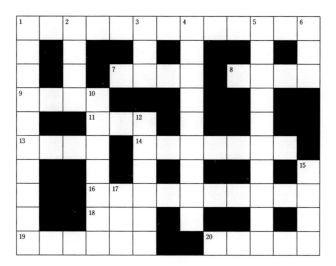

Across
1. Without this, a contract is not binding.
7. The hammer _____ and closed the deal at yesterday's auction.
8. I would like to call _____ Mr Smith to make a speech.
9. = sole.
11. At present.
13. A civil wrong.
14. He brought an action _____ that company.
16. When the offeror takes the offer back.
18. See 17 down.
19. They are going to make a _____ to supply hospital equipment.
20. This contract _____ both parties.

Down
1. It's not a serious offer: there's no language of _____.
2. In the _____ future.
3. The contract is _____ to expire on July 1st.
4. The state of being applicable to a subject, pertaining to.
5. The witness had a negative _____ on the jury.
6. Switzerland is a _____-EU country.
10. This contract is _____ into the sixth day of June, 1995.
12. The relinquishment of a right, giving up a claim.
15. A burden, a heavy duty.
17. What you see with.

CHAPTER TWO

THE LIFE OF A CONTRACT

A. *The Terms of a Contract*

1. Implied and express terms

BLANK FILLING

Read the explanation of implied and express terms and fill in the blank spaces with words we saw in Chapter One. Some terms will be repeated several times.

The contents of a contract are known as its terms, and the terms reflect the agreement _____ (1) between the _____ (2) to the contract. There are two kinds of contractual terms: express and implied. Express terms are express statements made by the _____ (3) with the _____ (4) of being _____ (5) by them. Where terms have not been included specifically in the contract, in certain circumstances the missing terms are inferred by _____ (6). The general rule is that a term may be implied in a contract either by statute or to give effect to the presumed _____ (7) of the parties. The _____ (8) case of *Shirlaw v Southern Foundries (1926) Ltd* [1940] A.C. 701 _____ (9) what has come to be known as the "officious bystander" test. It was _____ (10) by the court:

> "Prima facie that which in any contract is left to be implied and need not be expressed is something so obvious that it goes without saying; so that, if while one of the _____ (11) were making their _____ (12), an officious bystander were to suggest some express **provision** for it in their agreement, they would testily suppress him with a common, 'Oh, of course' ".

An implied term is one which will be implied, either from statute or custom and where it is necessary to carry out the presumed _____ (13) of the _____ (14) An implied term will not **override** an express term.

   A good example of the regulation of implied terms can be found in the Sale of Goods Act 1979. Section 2 of this Act lays down implied terms as to the title to goods when these are being sold. Under s.3 of the same Act the goods must correspond to their description. Section 4 is designed to protect quality. It **provides that** an implied condition on the sale of goods is that the goods are of merchantable quality, **provided (providing)** the seller sells the goods during the course of business.

POINTS TO REMEMBER
1. ... *if an officious bystander were to suggest some provision* ...
This is another way of expressing the second conditional which indicates difficulty of performance or facts contrary to reality. It is the same as saying
... *if an officious bystander suggested some provision* ...
2. *It provides that an implied condition on the sale of goods is that the goods are of merchantable quality, provided/providing the seller sells the goods during the course of business.*
Provided can be used both as a verb and a subordinating conjunction. It is important to distinguish between these two uses.

EXERCISE

Rewrite the following sentences, using a form of "provide".
1. The contract should establish both terms and method of payment.

2. Our clients will only enter into the contract if you include a clause limiting their liability as to defective products.

3. The contract established that all promotional material be approved by the Company.

4. The distributor will give us all the advertising material.

2. Conditions and warranties

NOTE-TAKING

Read the passage and take notes on the following points:

	CONDITIONS	WARRANTIES
nature		
remedy for breach		

The terms of a contract reflect the rights and obligations of the parties expressed as a consequence of their free negotiation and subsequent agreement. The more important terms of a contract are called **conditions**, and the less important terms **warranties**. It is therefore important to remember that every term of a contract is either a condition or a warranty. This difference is important when it comes to a **breach of contract**. In this context, the difference can be explained like this: if a party to a contract breaches a condition in any respect and however slight, the other party has the right to elect to treat itself as effectively **discharged** from any further obligations or **liability** under the contract, and to claim for damages. Now, if the **aggrieved party** does not exercise its right to terminate the contract, then it can choose to treat the breach of condition as a mere breach of warranty. What does this mean? It means that the contract will continue as a perfectly valid one, and the wronged party can **claim for damages** in respect of the other party's breach of warranty.

But, if a party to a contract breaks a warranty, the remedy available to the other party is a claim for damages for the breach. In such a case there is no right to treat the contract as terminated.

As the distinction between conditions and warranties is important, we shall refer to the *obiter* in a leading case.

In *Hong Kong Fir Shipping Co Ltd v Kawasaki Kisen Kaisha Ltd* [1962] 2 Q.B. 26, Upjohn L.J. said:

> "The question to be answered is, does the breach of the stipulation go so much to the root of the contract that it makes further commercial performance impossible, or, in other words, is the whole contract frustrated? If yea, the innocent party may treat the contract as at an end. If nay, his claim sounds in damages only."

Case Law: *Cehave NV v Bremer Handelsgesellschaft mbH The Hansa Nord* [1976] Q.B. 44

EXERCISES

1. The passage you have just read contains several basic concepts related to contract law. Try to extract their meaning from the context, and then match them with the correct definition.

1. breach of contract	(a)	the victim of a breach of contract, also known as the non-breaching party
2. to discharge	(b)	to bring civil proceedings against
3. to sue	(c)	legal responsibility
4. aggrieved/wronged party	(d)	non-performance of contractual obligations
5. damages	(e)	to free someone from something
6. liability	(f)	financial compensation awarded in civil cases

2. Read each of the following cases and write down whether there was a breach of condition or a breach of warranty and what the aggrieved party was **entitled** to do.

(a) Poussard v Spiers and Pond [1876] 1 Q.B.D. 410

An actress was contracted to play the leading part in a French operetta as from the beginning of its London run. The actress fell ill and was unable to appear until a week after the show had opened. The producers had to contract a substitute actress.

(b) Bettini v Gye [1876] 1 Q.B.D. 183

A singer was under a contractual obligation to sing in a series of concerts and to participate in six days of rehearsals before the first performance. He arrived three days late, and in consequence, was only able to participate in three days of rehearsals.

POINTS TO REMEMBER

1. *yea* and *nay*. These are old-fashioned ways of saying yes and no.

2. Use of **as**.

The contents of a contract are known **as** its terms, …

As the distinction … is important, …

… **as** a consequence of their free negotiation …

… to treat himself **as** effectively discharged …

… the contract will continue **as** a perfectly valid one …

The word **as** is very common in legal English. Study the examples given, and try to find the text from which they were taken. Here are some more uses of **as**, also common in legal English:

to construe something as …, to define something as …, to refer to something as …

3. *The wronged party can sue for damages in respect of the other party's breach of warranty.*

Compound prepositions are used extensively in legal English, and can sometimes substitute simple prepositions (here "for").

Other examples are *by reason of, in consequence of.*

EXERCISES

---

1. Complete these unlikely situations by applying one of the legal principles we have seen in this course. Be careful to use the correct terminology.

   (a) Andros Ltd has been your company's reliable supplier for 15 years. If Andros **were suddenly to breach** a warranty established in your distribution agreement, …

   (b) If, in a moment of weakness, your sister **were to promise** to do all the cooking and cleaning in the apartment you share with her for the entire exam period, …

   (c) If, at the age of 17, Peter **were to enter** into a contract under which he committed himself to buying the full 75 volume set of books on contemporary music, …

   (d) A Canadian company has a licensing agreement with a British one. If a war **were to break out** between England and Canada, …

   (e) If you **were to leave** your notice of acceptance on a broken answering machine, …

2. Test your knowledge of English and Law by completing the following items with **as**:

    (a)   The person who makes a promise is known ...

    (b)   Regarding contractual capacity, drunken persons are treated much the same ...

    (c)   A serious mistake is frequently called an operative mistake because it operates so ...

    (d)   Consideration may be defined ...

    (e)   In the case of a unilateral offer performance acts ...

    (f)   The courts construed the Carbolic Smoke Ball advertisement ...

    (g)   The price tag in a shop is regarded ...

    (h)   Mistake, misrepresentation and undue influence are referred to ...

    (i)   If the aggrieved party does not wish to terminate his contract he can choose to treat the breach of condition ...

3. Substitute the underlined items for a word or expression that would be more suitable in a formal legal context.

    (a)   A request for a tender <u>is not</u> an offer; it is <u>only</u> an invitation to treat.

    (b)   This is an <u>example</u> of what I had <u>in</u> mind in citing that case.

    (c)   The new non-smoking regulations will be effective <u>as long as</u> the authorities <u>make people obey</u> them.

    (d)   A price quotation is not <u>thought to be</u> an acceptance.

    (e)   The defendant has clearly <u>shown</u> his intention to create legal relations.

    (f)   We are not in a position to <u>take on</u> such a costly reorganization.

    (g)   You must be fully aware that if you reach an out-of-court settlement with your supplier, you will <u>give up</u> any right to take further legal action.

    (h)   He will be held <u>responsible</u> for any obligations which may have <u>come up</u> before the repudiation of the contract.

    (i)   As there has been a breach, the plaintiff <u>has a right</u> to damages.

    (j)   He has <u>withdrawn</u> his offer.

B. *The Clauses in a Contract*

1. Exclusion clauses

READING AND DISCUSSION

1. Discuss with a partner how the law regulates exclusion clauses in your country.
2. Read the following paragraphs, and compare the law in England with that of your country regarding exclusion clauses.

Quite often a contract contains an exclusion clause. This is a term of the contract which purports to limit or exclude obligations which would otherwise attach to one of the parties to the contract. This in effect means that a party to a contract who introduces an exclusion clause is usually trying to limit his liability for breach of contract or in tort for negligence. However, such a clause is construed by the courts *contra preferentem*, which means, against the interests of the person seeking to rely on the clause.

The Unfair Contract Terms Act, 1977, serves to impose limits on the extent to which liability for breach of contract or for negligence can be avoided by means of contract terms. The Act provides that certain kinds of exclusion clauses are to have no effect at all, and certain other kinds are to be effective only in so far as they satisfy the requirements of reasonableness.

An example of the first kind of exclusion clauses are clauses excluding or restricting liability for death or personal injury resulting from negligence. An example of the latter kind are clauses excluding or limiting liability for negligence other than liability for death or personal injury.

Case Law: *Mitchell (George) (Chesterhall) Ltd v Finney Lock Seeds Ltd* [1983] 1 All E.R. 108; *Photo Production Ltd v Securicor Transport Ltd* [1980] A.C. 827

READING COMPREHENSION

In the leading case of *Thornton v Shoe Lane Parking Ltd* [1971] 2 Q.B. 163, Lord Denning gave a characteristically brilliant explanation of the principle of the exclusion clause, which has come to be known as the "Red-Hand Rule".
Read the case and choose the correct statement.
1.   (a)   The conditions were written on the back of the ticket.
     (b)   The conditions were on a notice near the entrance.
     (c)   The conditions exempted the defendants from liability.

2. One of the conditions provided for
     (a)   the car owner's exemption in case of injury.
     (b)   damages for all car-park owners on the premises.
     (c)   exemption of the defendants from liability in case of injury.

3.   (a)   The court of first instance held that the plaintiff was not bound by the condition.
     (b)   The Court of Appeal held that the plaintiff was bound by the condition.
     (c)   The Court of Appeal held that the defendant was liable for injury.

4. Lord Denning felt that
     (a)   this case could be construed in the same light as cases involving actual clerks instead of machines.
     (b)   the court was not bound to follow the principles laid down in cases involving clerks.
     (c)   a new precedent had to be established in this case.

5. Lord Denning ruled in favour of the plaintiff because
     (a)   the plaintiff had proved he was not aware of the exemption condition.
     (b)   the defendant had not properly informed the plaintiff of the exemption condition.
     (c)   the exemption of liability claimed by the defendant was totally unreasonable.

The facts of the case are as follows:

The plaintiff drove his car into a multi-storey automatic car-park. At the entrance to the car park there was a notice headed "Shoe Lane Parking" and details of the parking charges and other information concerning the use of the car park. At the end of the notice were the following words: "ALL CARS PARKED AT OWNERS' RISK". When the plaintiff reached the entrance to the car park, there was no sign of any employee on the control gate. There was an automatic traffic light which turned from red to green and a ticket automatically emerged from the machine. The plaintiff took the ticket and parked his car in the car park. Later, when the plaintiff returned to his car, he was badly injured while loading the car. In the trial, the plaintiff and the defendants were each held to be 50 per cent to blame for the accident. The defendants claimed exemption from any liability by reason of certain conditions which had become part of the contract. The defendants argued that the ticket was a contractual document which incorporated a condition exempting them from liability. The ticket contained the following words: "This ticket is issued subject to the conditions of issue as displayed on the premises." The plaintiff had looked at the ticket to see the time printed on it, but he had not read the print on the ticket. The plaintiff did not see the conditions displayed on a pillar opposite the ticket machine. One of these conditions provided that the defendants would not be responsible or liable for injury to a customer when the customer's motor vehicle was in the car park. The defendants relied on the condition to exclude them from liability. It was held by the Court of Appeal that the exempting condition did not bind the plaintiff because he did not know of it, and the defendants did not do what was reasonably sufficient to give him notice of it.

Lord Denning M.R. said:

"Assuming, however, that an automatic machine is a booking clerk in disguise, so that the old fashioned ticket cases still apply to it. We then have to go back to the three questions put by Mellish L.J. in *Parker v South Eastern Railway Company* 2 C.P.D. 416, 423, subject to this qualification: Mellish L.J. used the word 'conditions' in the plural, whereas it would be more apt to use the word 'condition' in the singular, as indeed the Lord Justice himself did on the next page. After all, the only condition that matters for this purpose is the exempting condition. It is no use telling the customer that the ticket is issued subject to some 'conditions' or other, without more: for he may reasonably regard 'conditions' in general as merely regulatory, and not as taking away his rights, unless the exempting condition is drawn specifically to his attention. (Alternatively, if the plural 'conditions' is used, it would be better prefaced with the word 'exempting' because the exempting conditions are the only conditions that matter for this purpose.) Telescoping the three questions, they come to this: the customer is bound by the exempting condition if he knows that the ticket is issued subject to it; or, if the company did what was reasonably sufficient to give him notice of it.... Counsel for the defendants admitted here that the company did not do what was reasonably sufficient to give Mr Thornton notice of the exempting condition. That admission was properly made. I do not pause to inquire whether the exempting condition is void for unreasonableness. All I say is that it is so wide and so destructive of rights that the court should not hold any man bound by it unless it is drawn to his attention in the most explicit way. It is an instance of what I had in mind in *J. Spurling Ltd v Bradshaw* [1956] 1 W.L.R. 461, 466. In order to give sufficient notice, it would need to be printed in red ink with a red hand pointing to it – or something equally startling.... But, although reasonable notice of it was not given, counsel for the defendants said that this case came within the second question propounded by Mellish L.J., namely that Mr. Thornton 'knew or believed that the writing contained conditions'. There was no finding to that effect. The burden was on the company to prove it and they did not do so. Certainly there was no evidence that Mr. Thornton knew of this exempting condition. He is not, therefore, bound by it."

POINTS TO REMEMBER
1. *This term purports to limit or exclude obligations . . .* (p.44)
to purport is a formal regular verb which means *to have the purpose of, to have the intention of*
2. *An example of the latter kind are clauses . . .* (p.45)
Do not forget the use of *the former* and *the latter* to refer back to the first of two items previously mentioned (*the former*) and the second of two (*the latter*). They are very common – and useful – in formal written English.
3. *They were each 50 per cent to blame for the accident.* (p.46)
Blame can be used as a verb (*to blame somebody for something*), a noun, and in the expression *to be to blame*.

EXERCISES

1. Fill in the grid with the correct form of each word.

NOUN	VERB
implication	
	presume
provision	
negotiation	
	sue
	entitle
exclusion	
negligence	
compensation	
	rely

2. Rewrite the following sentences using forms of *blame* as appropriate.

    (a) People say that in marriage break-ups the responsibility is never wholly on one side.

_____

    (b) In a case of negligence it is the court's task to decide who is responsible.

_____

    (c) Our clients feel it is totally your fault that they were unable to open their hotel in time for the tourist season.

_____

    (d) The police said the rise in traffic accidents was the fault of the poor city lighting.

_____

MULTIPLE CHOICE

Choose the alternative that is most suitable in the context to complete the following passage:

Exclusion clauses are regulated by the policy of the European Union concerning unfair contract terms.

On April 5, 1993 the Council of Ministers of the European Community adopted Directive 93/13/EEC _____ (1) unfair terms in consumer contracts. This is the first time that the European Union has entered into the _____ (2) of general contract law in relation to its programme of the _____ (3) of laws. The _____ (4) of this Directive is to regulate a class of terms in consumer contracts defined _____ (5) unfair. Article 3 of the Directive defines "unfair terms".

    (1) A contractual term which has not been individually negotiated _____ (6) be regarded as unfair if, contrary to the requirement of good _____ (7), it causes a significant imbalance in the parties' rights and obligations _____ (8) under the contract, to the _____ (9) of the consumer.

    (2) A term shall always be regarded as not individually negotiated where it has been drafted in advance and the consumer has _____ (10) not been able to influence the substance of the term particularly in the context of a pre-formulated standard contract.

        The fact that certain aspects of a term or one specific term has been individually negotiated shall not _____ (11) the application of this Article to the rest of a contract if an overall assessment of the contract indicates that it is _____ (12) a pre-formulated standard contract.

        Where any seller or supplier _____ (13) that a standard term has been individually negotiated, the burden of _____ (14) in this respect shall be incumbent _____ (15) him.

(3)   The annex shall contain an indicative and non-exhaustive list of the terms which may be regarded as unfair.

The Annex to the Directive contains a list of seventeen sub-paragraphs of terms, the object or effect of _____ (16) are to be regarded as unfair. As you may expect, exclusion clauses feature in this list. So, this Directive effectively establishes a control structure for all contract terms _____ (17) unfair, _____ (18) of their particular function in the contract in _____ (19); the terms which are subject _____ (20) control are all those which are not individually negotiated.

1 (a) relating	(b) concerning	(c) about	(d) relative
2 (a) circle	(b) subject	(c) ambience	(d) sphere
3 (a) harmonization	(b) harmony	(c) regulation	(d) regulate
4 (a) purport	(b) proposition	(c) target	(d) purpose
5 (a) like	(b) how	(c) as	(d) being
6 (a) must	(b) will	(c) shall	(d) ought to
7 (a) consideration	(b) faith	(c) intention	(d) will
8 (a) arising	(b) raising	(c) coming up	(d) rising
9 (a) injury	(b) damage	(c) detriment	(d) loss
10 (a) so	(b) however	(c) then	(d) therefore
11 (a) do away with	(b) exclude	(c) exempt	(d) refrain
12 (a) nevertheless	(b) despite	(c) although	(d) so
13 (a) claims	(b) demands	(c) denies	(d) admits
14 (a) prove	(b) approval	(c) right	(d) proof
15 (a) in	(b) on	(c) in	(d) over
16 (a) whose	(b) that	(c) what	(d) which
17 (a) called	(b) deemed	(c) sentenced	(d) said
18 (a) notwithstanding	(b) no matter	(c) regardless	(d) despite
19 (a) discussion	(b) vain	(c) light	(d) question
20 (a) of	(b) under	(c) to	(d) in

2. *Force Majeure* clauses

DISCUSSION

1. Make a list of the events which could be considered *force majeure*.

2. What constitutes an Act of God?

A *force majeure* clause is always necessary in any contract. The object of these clauses is to release both parties from any liability under the contract in the event of any failure to perform obligations as a result of circumstances beyond their reasonable control.

In 1970 The European Court of Justice defined the concept of *force majeure* in Case 11/70 *Internationale Handelsgesellschaft mbH v Einfuhr und Vorratsstelle Für Gertreide und Futtermittel* [1972] C.M.L.R. Pact. 56 255. The court stated:

   "The notion of *force majeure* is not limited to absolute impossibility but should be extended to cover abnormal circumstances, outside the control of the importer or exporter, and the consequences of which could not have been avoided except at the price of excessive sacrifice, in spite of using all diligence."

This definition has been consistently applied in subsequent cases before the court involving *force majeure*.

Case Law: *Taylor v Caldwell* [1863] 122 E.R. 309

C. *Types of Agreement and European Law*

Having looked at some of the different clauses to be found in an agreement, we are now going to learn about some kinds of agreements.

READING AND REPORTING

These definitions will help you do the exercise.

Hire: Hire can be defined as the payment for the temporary use of something, for example, the hire of goods or the hire of services. Hire purchase is a form of paying for goods in instalments.

Bailment: Bailment occurs when a person takes possession of goods belonging to another party with the consent of that party.

Now, in groups of five, A should read about option agreements, B should read about hire purchase agreements, C about conditional sales agreements, D about leasing contracts and E about consumer hire agreements. Be able to tell the rest of the class about the differences between the five.

(a) *Option agreements*: An option is a right which may be acquired by contract to accept or reject a present offer within a given period of time. An option agreement, like any other agreement, will set out the terms and conditions agreed between the parties. There is usually an option price which is the consideration to be paid upon the signing of the agreement, although it is possible to grant a gratuitous option.

(b) *Hire Purchase Agreements*: These are defined as agreements for the bailment of goods under which the hirer gives possession of the goods to the debtor/bailee in return for periodical payments. Upon complete payment of the instalments, the debtor/bailee may exercise an option to purchase, and the ownership will pass to the debtor. You should distinguish this kind of option from an option agreement.

(c) *Conditional Sales Agreements*: These are agreements for the sale of goods or land under which the whole or part of the purchase price is payable in instalments, and while the buyer is in possession of the goods or land, the property in these remains in the seller until the conditions of the agreement are fulfilled.

(d) *Leasing agreements*: If you wish to purchase the use of a motor vehicle without incurring the capital cost involved in owning it, you would enter into such a contract with a finance house which would purchase the motor vehicle from the seller and lease it to you under the contract for a specific period of time. You would then have the use of the motor vehicle. The fundamental difference from a hire purchase agreement is that the user does not, as a result of the lease, become the owner of the item, even when the lease expires. However, these contracts can lead to sales agreements.

(e) *Consumer Hire Agreements*: These are similar to leasing agreements but have a payment limit of £15,000. The Consumer Credit Act of 1974 introduced certain protection to the consumer in respect of such an agreement, such as the right to cancel.

POINTS TO REMEMBER

1. *These are defined as agreements for the bailment of goods under which the hirer gives possession . . .* (p.50)

Notice the use of preposition + which/whom in formal English.

Here are two more examples from the text:

(a) *. . . a list of 17 sub-paragraphs of terms, the object or effect of which are to be regarded as unfair.* (p.49)

(b) *These are agreements under which the whole or part of the purchase price is payable in instalments.* (p.50)

2. *Property in the goods remains in the seller.* (p.50)

This is the same as saying *The seller remains the owner of the goods.*

3. *The object of these clauses is to release both parties from any liability* (p.50)

Release can be used in the following ways:

(a) *The prisoner was released on licence.*

(b) *The terrorists released their hostage.*

(c) *This clause will release you from any obligation/liability/further duties/undertakings.*

EXERCISE

Complete the following sentences by adding the correct preposition in each gap.

1. We have inserted a clause to provide _____ untimely delivery.
2. _____ the Sale of Goods Act, 1979, goods must be of merchantable quality.
3. His payment _____ the hire of the refrigerated truck was not made _____ the specified time limits.

4. Goods can be hired by the bailee ——————— return ———————
   regular payments.
5. We wish to enter ——————— a hire purchase agreement.
6. ——————— the contract, payment has to be made on the last day of every
   month.
7. Several contract cases have come ——————— the European Court of
   Justice.
8. Her title ——————— the house is not secure.

READ AND DISCUSS

The European Union affects contracts, especially as far as restrictive practices are
concerned. In pairs, A should read the paragraphs on Art.85 of the Treaty of Rome, and
be prepared to report its contents to B, and B should be prepared to do the same with
Art.86.

1. Article 85

Article 85 of the Treaty of Rome covers the Law of Competition. This is an extremely
important aspect of Community Law. In the preamble to the Treaty of Rome, the term
"Fair Competition" is recognised as one of the tenets of the European Union. Although
the Treaty purports to institute "a system ensuring that competition in the Common
Market is not distorted" (Art.3), competition, fair or otherwise, has not been defined
either by the Treaty or by the European Court of Justice. It seems to be a self-explanatory
term. The Treaty sets out to establish a system of sound competition based on three sets
of rules; rules applying to undertakings (the Treaty does not define the meaning of the
word, but it is clear that it would include companies or firms which are referred to in
Art.58). So, by analogy, we can say that "an undertaking" means a legal entity, whether a
physical person or a corporation or an association or legal entity engaged in a
profit-making activity, such as a partnership; secondly, there are rules against dumping,
and thirdly, rules governing State aids.

Article 85 prohibits as "incompatible with the Common Market all agreements
between undertakings, decisions by associations of undertakings, and concerted
practices which may affect trade between member states, and which have as their object
or effect, the prevention, restriction or distortion of competition within the common
market".

As this Article is intended to combat price fixing, the powers of the European
Commission are draconian – and they have to be – to be able to identify cartels.

2. Article 86

Article 86 of the Treaty is also important. This Article prohibits abuse of a dominant
position in the market. Now the classic definition of a monopoly is a market in which
there is only a single seller or producer. If there is a single seller and a single buyer, the
situation is called a bilateral monopoly. In 1972, in *Continental Can Co Inc, EC
Commission Decision, 72/21 [1972]*, the European Commission decided that a market
share in the range of 50 per cent to 55 per cent may constitute a dominant position, in

other words, a monopoly. You should note that the key word in the circumstances is abuse. The Treaty does not define "dominant position".

You should also note that in the case of Arts 85 and 86 the European Commission assumes for itself, on a unilateral basis, extraterritorial jurisdiction. In practice, the European Commission, upon hearing of an abuse which might affect the market, will notify the party or parties concerned and invite them to comply with the provisions of Arts 85 and 86. An example of this would be, and this happened recently, two United States companies merging in the United States and then seeking to trade actively within the European Union. The European Commission may exclude them until it is satisfied that the merged company is complying with Arts 85 and 86.

SENTENCE WRITING

The following statements were made by laymen. Rewrite them so as to sound like a lawyer in a professional setting.

1. It is the courts' job to make sure that the people who sign a contract do what they are supposed to do.

_____

2. Mr Brown hasn't promised anything. He has only shown that he wants to make a contract some day.

_____

3. We're talking about family relations, so we have to imagine that these people weren't thinking about any sort of legal relation.

_____

4. Unless you say you are not interested in continuing with this contract before you turn 18, you will be responsible for everything in it.

_____

5. The man that brought the action won the case.

_____

6. My client has gone without doing something he has got a right to do and that is consideration.

_____

7. The party that does not breach the contract can take the other party to court to try to get some financial compensation.

_____

8. He performed the contract in the established way.

_____

D. *Contracts – Examples*

1 The language of contracts

VOCABULARY

The following words and expressions are commonly found in contracts. In the short paragraphs below, which are taken from contracts, substitute the italicised words or expressions for suitable ones from the list.

grants	all due
pursuant to	timely pay
undertake	be deemed to terminate
assign	prior written consent of
furnished	the outstanding amount
arising	prior to
expiration	foreseeable
to fulfil	to hold harmless and indemnify
hereto	set forth
infringement	

1. Area services will not charge recipient under this agreement a service fee *as established in* a certain Research Management Agreement entered into on April 1.

2. Neither party may *transfer to a third party* its rights or obligations hereunder without *obtaining written permission first from* the other party.

3. The consultants *promise* for the duration of this agreement not to enter into any other oral or written arrangement with any other party.

4. Any dispute concerning the existence, validity, interpretation, performance or non-performance, whether *happening* before or after the *final date* of the agreement, will be settled by arbitration.

5. With respect to any patent included in the Industrial Property Rights, the licence granted hereunder shall *be considered ended* two weeks *before* the expiration date of the patent.

6. Both parties are obliged to perform the services stipulated in the present agreement and *to do* them with *the necessary* care and diligence.

7. In the event that either party does not *pay the other when they are supposed to* an invoice rendered to it as stipulated in the provisions of this agreement, interest shall accrue on *the money owed* at the official legal interest rate current at the time in the debtor's country.

8. If any of the obligations of the parties *to this contract* cannot be fulfilled by reason of Force Majeure in consequence of any of the following events and if the event and its consequences were neither avoidable nor *could have been seen beforehand* ...

9. Licensor hereby *gives* to Licensee the exclusive right to manufacture, produce, use, transfer and sell the Licensed Products using the Industrial Property Rights and Technical Information *supplied* by Licensor in the Contract Territory.

10. The Contributing Author agrees *to protect and to compensate* the Publisher against any claim, suit, action, proceeding, recovery or expense of any nature whatsoever arising from any claim of *violation* of copyright or proprietary right.

11. "Licensed Products" shall mean the products *presented* in Schedule A hereto.

> **POINT TO REMEMBER**
> Compound adverbs/prepositions.
> You have just seen how *hereto* can be used.
> *Here* is used in a legal document to refer to the document itself and is combined with different prepositions depending on the context, so that you will find the following combinations:
> *hereunder* – the rights and obligations established under the contract
> *hereof* – the date of a contract
> *hereinafter* – from that point throughout the rest of the document
> *hereafter* – from the moment established in the document onwards in time

2. Example of a contract

READING

DISTRIBUTION AGREEMENT

THIS AGREEMENT is made the 1st day of January 2099 BETWEEN Cinderella plc, having its registered office at 3 Ugly Sisters Street, Fairyland (hereinafter called "the Company" which expression shall where the context so admits or requires include its successors and assigns) of the one part and Prince Charming plc having its registered office at 1 Palace Road, Wonderland (hereinafter called "the Distributor" which expression shall where the context so admits or requires include its successors and assigns) of the other part.

WHEREAS:

1. The company is the owner of certain intellectual property in respect of the Products specified in Schedule 1 hereto ("the Products" which expression shall include all components, spares, drawings, designs, production details, updates and alterations thereto).

2. The Distributor is desirous of purchasing the Products pursuant to the terms of this Agreement for distribution and sale within the following territory/territories ("the Territory"):

WHEREBY IT IS AGREED AS FOLLOWS IN CONSIDERATION OF THE MUTUAL COVENANTS CONDITIONS AND PAYMENTS HEREINAFTER SET FORTH:

1.   (a) The Distributor shall purchase the Products for sale within the Territory pursuant to the terms and conditions hereinafter appearing.

      (b) It is intended between the Company and the Distributor that if new products are developed and manufactured by the Company during the continuance of this Agreement that the Distributor shall purchase such new products for sale within the Territory pursuant to the terms and conditions of this Agreement subject to agreement on price, minimum sales and minimum orders in respect thereof.

2. The Distributor is responsible for ensuring that all the Products comply with local legislation in the Territory as to safety and operation. The Company will use its reasonable endeavours to assist the Distributor in relation to its said responsibility.

3.   (a) The Company undertakes to supply the Products to the Distributor at the prices currently as per the Price List set out in Schedule 2 hereof PROVIDED ALWAYS that on giving to the Distributor not less than 3 months' notice by telex or telefax the Company shall be entitled to make any price adjustments which it considers necessary and prudent.

(b)   The price which the Distributor shall charge its customers for the Products shall be the price (converted into local currency) set out in Schedule 2 hereof which price shall only be varied to take account of (i) currency fluctuations between the Fairyland dollar and local currency and (ii) freight charges incurred by the Distributor in delivery to its customers.

(c)   Any other variation of the prices to be charged by the Distributor to its customers may only occur with the prior consent of the Company. The Company may, from time to time, agree variations in respect of local promotions and market conditions.

4. The Distributor shall pay the company for all Products by bank guaranteed Bills of Exchange payable thirty days from date of delivery of the Products by the company FOB Fairyland Port. Title to the Products shall only pass to the Distributor when payment has been received by the Company. The Distributor is responsible for all taxes (including value added tax) applicable to the Products.

5.   (a)   The Company undertakes to use its best endeavours to make all Products available with a delivery period not exceeding 8 weeks from date of receipt of order to FOB Fairyland Port. The Distributor is responsible for all costs of freight after delivery by the Company FOB Fairyland. The company and the Distributor will liaise as to the most appropriate manner of arranging for delivery of the Products by the Company FOB Fairyland.

(b)   Minimum orders for Product One shall be one unit thereof and minimum orders for Product Two shall be such number as may be conveniently transported, which is currently 6 such units. Minimum Orders for any other of the Products shall be agreed between the company and the Distributor from time to time.

6. The Distributor undertakes to purchase during the first period of 12 months following signature hereof the number of units of the Products as set out in Schedule 3 hereof. The minimum Orders for the Products during each quarter shall be in accordance with the details set out in Schedule 3 hereof. The Company and the Distributor will endeavour to agree minimum sales and minimum orders for the products for each succeeding period of 12 months and each succeeding quarter, respectively.

7. This Agreement shall be for a period of two years from the date hereof and shall thereafter be renewed for further successive periods of two years PROVIDED ALWAYS that the Distributor shall have achieved a level of sales to the satisfaction of the Company within such periods and also subject to the provisions for termination hereinafter appearing.

8. The Distributor agrees with the Company as follows:

(a)   To make every effort to maximise the sales of the Products in the Territory including the production of suitable technical literature, data, exhibitions/demonstrations, mail shots and the provision of adequate sales and technical personnel all at the expense of the Distributor.

(b)   Prior to each successive period of 12 months of this Agreement, to furnish to the Company in respect of the following period of 12 months (i) its projected sales for the Products and (ii) a marketing plan for sales of the Products detailing matters pertaining to the Products including, resources being used, demonstrations and promotions proposed, provision of back up services and such other details as the Company shall reasonably require so as to enable the Company to ascertain its role in assisting the Distributor in fulfilling its obligations hereunder.

9. The Distributor confirms that it will at its own cost and expense make available for the benefit of its customers all necessary after-sales repair and maintenance personnel, spare parts and facilities to ensure prompt and efficient servicing of the Products *provided however* that the Company warrants that the Products shall be, for a period of 12 months from the date of delivery thereof, to end customers free from defects due to faulty components or bad workmanship and if such defects occur within such period because of faulty components or bad workmanship the Company shall deliver to the Distributor replacement components at the cost of the Company.

10. Any enquiries received by the Company for the Products for sale within the Territory shall be referred by the Company to the Distributor. The Distributor shall refer to the Company any

enquiries received by the Distributor in respect of the Products originating from outside the Territory. The Distributor shall make no attempt whatsoever to supply any customer other than within the Territory whether directly or indirectly and in addition shall use its best endeavours to ensure that any customer of the Distributor shall take no steps whatsoever to export the Products without the due notice being given to the Company and the Distributor.

11. The Distributor hereby indemnifies and will keep indemnified the Company against all actions, costs, claims and demands arising from the sale or distribution of the Products by the Distributor wheresoever, whensoever and howsoever arising excluding matters of a product liability nature.

12. The Company agrees with the Distributor as follows:

    (a)   To furnish to the Distributor reasonable product support documentation, operation and maintenance manuals and technical information.

    (b)   To provide training for service and maintenance personnel of the Distributor. All costs of travel, accommodation and expenses of employees of the Company in this regard shall be paid by the Distributor but the Company shall be responsible for the wages of its own employees so engaged.

    (c)   To provide at the cost of the Company reasonable marketing support including making available existing marketing and promotional material, attending exhibitions, shows and seminars and assisting in sales demonstrations and new product launches.

    (d)   To control, insofar as the Company shall be able to do so, sales prices to customers of other distributors throughout Fantasia it being the desired object that the basic sale price of the Products throughout Fantasia shall be uniform.

13. Either party may terminate this agreement immediately by written notice if the other:

    (a)   breaks any material term or condition of this agreement or any order and fails to remedy the breach within 30 days' notice requiring it to be remedied.

    (b)   becomes insolvent, enters into an agreement with its creditors, has a receiver or trustee in bankruptcy appointed, is unable to pay its debts or goes into liquidation.

14. The Distributor hereby undertakes that it will not at any time after the signature of this Agreement disclose any information in relation to the Company's method of manufacture or design or the Distributor's method of distribution in relation to the Products and that it will not during this Agreement or for a period of two years after the termination of this Agreement for any reason whatsoever be associated whether as principal, partner, agent, contractor or employer in the manufacture, sale or distribution in the Territory of any Products of a like or similar kind to or designed to perform functions like or similar to the Products which the Distributor or any of its selling agents have distributed under this Agreement without the prior consent in writing of the Company or its successors in title first being obtained.

15. (a)   Upon termination of this Agreement from any cause whatsoever or at any time prior to such termination, at the request of the Company, the Distributor shall promptly return to the Company or otherwise dispose of as the Company may instruct all samples, patterns, instruction books, technical pamphlets, catalogues, advertising material and other material documents and papers whatsoever in the Distributor's possession relating to the Products and also deliver up to the Company a note of the names and addresses of all customers to whom the Products have been supplied during the currency of this Agreement together with a note of the specific terms referable to such supply in each individual case.

    (b)   In addition, upon termination of this Agreement for whatever reason, the Distributor shall forthwith re-deliver to the Company or otherwise dispose of to the Company's nominees as the Company directs the Products which the Distributor may have in its possession or under its control at the same price that the Distributor shall have paid to the Company therefor less any costs incurred by the Company in rendering the said Products into the same condition of such Products when they were delivered by the Company to the Distributor.

16. To ensure a correct interpretation and performance of the present agreement four copies thereof will be prepared two in English and two in Fairylandese and will be executed by each of the parties, each party keeping one copy of each version and each version having the same value and

effectiveness. In the case of any conflict with regard to the interpretation thereof, the version of the Fairyland language shall prevail.

17. Neither party shall be liable to the other for any failure to perform or delay in performance of its obligations hereunder, other than an obligation to pay monies, caused by any circumstances beyond its reasonable control, including but not limited to defaults of suppliers or sub-contractors for any reason whatsoever, and all types of industrial disputes, lockouts and strikes.

18. Neither party may assign its rights or obligations hereunder without the prior written consent of the other party, which consent may be withheld arbitrarily, nor may this agreement be assigned by operation of law. Any purported assignment in the absence of such written consent shall be null and void.

19. Any notice required or permitted to be served hereunder shall be in writing and may be served in any of the following ways:

  1. By prepaid registered post or delivery addressed or delivered to the addressee party at its address set out herein or such other address as the addressee party shall advise from time to time.

  2. By facsimile
      (a) in the case of the Company to Fax No.
      _____
      marked for the attention of
      Mr _____
      (b) in the case of the Distributor to Fax No.
      _____
      marked for the attention of
      Mr _____
      or in either (a) or (b) above to such other number marked for the attention of such other person as the addressee shall advise from time to time.

Notice shall be deemed served:
  (i)   if delivered, upon delivery;
  (ii) if posted as aforesaid, 72 hours after posting; or
  (iii) if sent by facsimile as aforesaid, upon correct transmission thereof to the addressee.

20. This agreement shall be binding upon and shall inure to the benefit of the parties hereto and their respective successors and permitted assigns.

21. Any dispute arising or which may arise at any time hereafter between the Company and the Distributor touching on the true construction of this Agreement shall be submitted to arbitration by reference to the President for the time being of the International Chamber of Commerce, Geneva, who shall appoint an Arbitrator to deal with such dispute or difference and the decision of such Arbitrator shall be final and binding on the parties hereto.

22. This agreement and all orders shall be governed by the laws of Fairyland and the parties hereby agree to submit to the jurisdiction of the Courts of Fairyland. This agreement is the entire agreement between the parties and supersedes all prior written and oral agreements, contracts, understandings and commitments between the parties.

SIGNED for and on behalf of   SIGNED for and on behalf of

_____   _____

Witnessed by   Witnessed by

_____   _____

READING COMPREHENSION

1. Contracts always begin in the same way. Read the introductory section and decide what information is found there.

This is usually followed by the "whereas clauses". These clauses are not an essential part of the operating portions of the contract. Read the clauses in the contract and decide if *whereas* stands for

It is agreed   Considering that   Notwithstanding

This is usually followed by the main body of the contract, containing the stipulations. The main body is preceded by the following introduction:

WHEREBY IT IS AGREED AS FOLLOWS IN CONSIDERATION OF THE MUTUAL COVENANTS CONDITIONS AND PAYMENTS HEREINAFTER SET FORTH

What does **whereby** refer to?

Look at the contract and find answers to the following questions (the numbers in brackets after the questions refer to the number of the relevant clause in the contract). Be prepared to explain this information in your own words, as you would if you were talking to a client.

1. Is a new contract needed in the event that the Company launches a new product? (1)
2. Under what conditions is the Company entitled to alter the prices? (3)
3. What modifications can the Distributor make to the selling price stipulated in the contract? (3)
4. What transport responsibilities will the Company bear? What transport responsibilities will the Distributor bear? (5)
5. Must the Distributor purchase a specified quantity of products? How is this established? (6)
6. How long is the contract valid? Under what conditions will the contract be renewed or terminated? (7)
7. Does the Distributor have any other obligations other than to pay for the products? (8)
8. Does the responsibility of the post-sales maintenance fall entirely on one party? Explain. (9)
9. Which party must bear the costs arising out of legal problems concerning the sale of the products? (11)
10. Does this contract bind the Distributor even after the termination of the agreement? In what way? (14)
11. What must the Distributor do on termination of the agreement? (15)

2. Read this short paragraph on Boiler-plate clauses.

Boiler-plate clauses are to be found in practically every commercial contract. As the name suggests, such clauses deal with the way in which the contract operates. These clauses protect the contract and the origin of the name comes from the plating of iron or steel covering the hulls of ships. The typical boiler-plate clauses include, *inter alia*,

THE LIFE OF A CONTRACT

confidentiality and **disclosure**, commencement and termination, standard warranties, guarantees and indemnities, the **service** of notices, exclusions of liability, whole agreement, disputes and conflict of laws, and *force majeure*.

Now go back to the contract on pp.55–58, and find as many as possible of the above clauses.

VOCABULARY

1 What verb tense/modal is frequently used to show legal obligation?
2. Put the correct compound adverb/preposition in the following sentences:

hereto	**whereby**	**hereof**	**hereafter**
hereinafter	**hereunder**	**hereby**	**herein**

(a) This agreement is made between James Wright (_____ called the tenant) and ...
(b) In consideration of all the agreements _____ the parties _____ agree as follows:
(c) Industrial Property Rights shall mean any and all rights under patents, trademarks and copyrights presently owned or _____ acquired by Licensor.
(d) "Contract Territory" shall mean the countries set forth in Appendix 2 _____.
(e) Licensor _____ grants to Licensee the exclusive rights to manufacture, produce, use, transfer and sell the Licensed Products.
(f) Neither party may assign its rights or obligations _____ without the prior written consent of the other party.
(g) Running royalty shall be computed and paid every six months, terminating the last day of each six-month period (the first period shall begin as of the date _____).
(h) Clause Two provides for a procedure _____ both parties _____ can modify the terms of credit.

COMPREHENSION PRACTICE

Find a partner. Partner A should follow the instructions on this page, and Partner B should go immediately to the next page and follow the instructions there.

Partner A

Read the following clauses from different contracts. Your partner will play the role of different clients who have questions about contracts you have drawn up for them. Find the clause which relates to his/her doubts and explain the answer to the question in your own words.

The failure of any party to enforce at any time any of the provisions of this agreement shall not be construed to be a waiver of any such provision or to affect the validity of this agreement or the right of any party to enforce each and every provision.

Licensee shall pay Licensor, as an advance on royalties to be earned by Licensor under the running royalty clause below an advance royalty of X pounds. Licensee shall make payment of running royalty to Licensor semi-anually within 60 days of each six-month period, to the extent not already deemed paid through the advance royalty referred to in clause (a) (1).

The quoted System prices in SCHEDULE III and Spare Part Prices in SCHEDULE IV may be changed subject to 3 (three) months' written notice. Only in the case where the Distributor informs ABC in writing that the Distributors are submitting tenders requesting longer validation, can the prices be fixed for a longer period.

Now play the role of the different clients and consult your partner, who is your lawyer, about the following:

1. Does the contract provide for assignment?
2. Does this agreement only cover the patents the Licensor holds at the time of signing the contract?
3. Our agreement expired three months ago but the supplier is still shipping us the minimum orders. We no longer wish to distribute their products. Where do we stand?

Partner B

Your partner is a lawyer who has drawn up contracts for several different clients. Play the role of three different clients and consult your partner about the following doubts.

1. Are the prices fixed for the duration of the contract? Can we rely on them when calculating firm bids?
2. The contract says that there will be a 10 per cent charge for late payment, but we've paid late at least two times and they've never asked us to pay the charge. Can they ask us to pay it now if we make a late payment?
3. After we calculate the royalty to be paid to the licensor in the first period, do we pay that full amount or do we deduct the amount we've already paid in advance?

Now read the following clauses from different contracts. Your partner will play the part of different clients who have questions about contracts you have drawn up for them. Find the clause which relates to his/her doubts and explain the answer to the question in your own words.

If not terminated in writing by either party two months prior to the date of expiration the agreement shall continue in force and either party shall be entitled to serve the other party a three month termination notice.

This agreement shall inure to the benefit of, and be binding upon, the parties thereto and their respective successors and assigns provided that any assignment of this agreement or of the rights hereunder by any party hereto without the written consent of the other parties shall be void.

"Industrial Property Rights" shall mean any and all rights under patents, design patents, trademarks and copyrights and applications thereof, presently owned or hereafter acquired by Licensor and which are applicable to or may be used in the manufacture or sale of the Licensed Products.

READ AND MATCH

Below are the name of five types of clauses typically found in a contract. Match them with the clauses that follow them.

1. An implied clause
2. An express clause
3. A waiver
4. A *force majeure* clause
5. An exclusion clause.

(a) No waiver or modification of this agreement, or of any condition herein contained, shall be valid unless in writing and duly executed by the parties hereto. Furthermore, no event of waiver or modification shall be offered or received as evidence in any proceeding, arbitration or litigation between the parties arising out of or affecting this agreement, or the rights or obligations of the parties hereunder, unless such waiver or modification is in writing, duly executed by such parties.

(b) A Limited shall not be liable to B Limited for any damages of any kind or nature whatsoever, including, but not limited to, loss of business or claims by B Limited's customers relating to consequential damage as a result of B Limited's use of the technology or the improvements. All such risk of loss, cost or damage shall be borne solely by B Limited.

(c) A Limited hereby agrees to grant exclusively unto the licensee from the date of this agreement for the life of the last to expire of the patents detailed in the first schedule or any patent granted in the territory to A Limited in respect of any improvement of the subject utilised by the licensee, the right as hereinafter provided to install linings of A Limited in the territory and for this purpose to use the inventions claimed in the patents.

(d) This agreement may be terminated by either party for cause. In this event, the party giving notice of termination shall be entitled to terminate this agreement forthwith and without delay upon delivery of such notice.

(e) Neither party shall be liable to the other for any failure to perform or for any delay in performance of its obligations hereunder, other than an obligation to pay monies, caused by any circumstances beyond its reasonable control, including but not limited to defaults of suppliers or sub-contractors for any reason whatsoever, and all types of industrial disputes, lock-outs and strikes.

Now look back at the contract on pp.55–58 and find the counterparts of the above five clauses.

EXERCISE

Rewrite the following sentences in a style more suitable to a lawyer by using the word given in brackets.

1. An express term is always more powerful than an implied term. (overrides)

2. The promisee expected a certain price and relied on it when he submitted his tender. (reliance)

3. A contract for the sale of land differs from other sale contracts in that it must be in writing. (distinct)

4. As your client has breached a condition, my client feels no longer bound by this contract. (discharged)

5. He has been served with a writ concerning his breach of contract. (respect)

CROSSWORD TWO

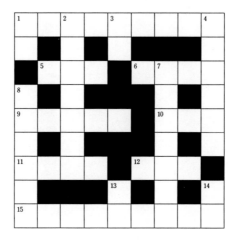

Across

1. A contract is an _____ between two parties.
5. A B.Sc. is to science as an _____ is to law.
6. To treat, to consider.
9. A contract for the renting of property.
10. This expression shall include _____ components, spares, drawings and designs.
11. This clause will protect us for _____.
12. You can _____ to buy the goods when you have paid all the instalments.
15. Assigns, makes over.

Down

1. _____ common law.
2 The court will _____ him from his contract.
3. *exempli gratia*.
4. The goods must be delivered _____ and not late.
7. This is a good _____ of an exemption clause.
8. That company is a _____ of the best law firm in town.
13. XYZ was treated _____ the aggrieved party.
14. Please advise _____ if you feel we should change any clauses.

CHAPTER THREE

THE DEATH OF A CONTRACT

A. *The Discharge of a Contract*

READING

In life, most things have to come to an end, and the contract is no exception. As you will have seen, every contractual obligation in a contract gives rise to a corresponding contractual right. Rights and obligations are complementary necessities in contracts. Consequently, when the obligation of a party is discharged, the corresponding right of the other party is said to be extinguished. So, when all the obligations contained in a contract are discharged, automatically all the corresponding rights are extinguished, and nothing is left. The contract is therefore said to be discharged.

There are basically five ways in which a contract may be discharged.

(1) By complete performance

For a contract to be discharged by performance, it is essential that there is a complete and definitive performance of the contract. You will recall that the parties to a contract are known as the promisor and the promisee. Now, the promisee is entitled to the benefit of the complete performance of the contract exactly in accordance with the promisor's obligation. If the promisor is unable or unwilling to offer more than a partial performance, then there can be no discharge. The performance must be total to be valid.

(2) By agreement

A contract may be discharged by agreement, and just as an agreement between the parties gives rise to the birth of a contract, so may the parties destroy what they created if they are in agreement to do so, in which event the contract dies.

The agreement may take various forms, such as a simple waiver of a breach promising not to sue to enforce the contract; voluntary rescission by both parties; novation, in the case of a new contract; or accord and satisfaction, where the performance obligations only are changed after the maturity or breach of the contract.

(3) By operation of law

A contract may be discharged by operation of law in various ways. An example is a contract for personal services which is automatically discharged by death. Another case would be a merger, where a contract is merged into a higher obligation. This would arise where a contract is merged into a deed on the same terms and between the same parties.

(4) By frustration

Where there is an event or change of circumstances so fundamental as to strike at the root of a contract as a whole, and beyond what was contemplated by the parties, then the contract is said to be frustrated.

This may occur when supervening events make the performance of the contract impossible, illegal or radically different from what the parties contemplated when they executed the contract.

Case Law: *Joseph Constantine Steamship Line Ltd v Imperial Smelting Corp Ltd* [1942] A.C. 154; *Krell v Henry* [1903] 2 K.B. 740; *Davis Contractors Ltd v Fareham Urban District Council* [1956] A.C. 696; *Taylor v Caldwell* [1863] 122 E.R. 309

(5) By acceptance of breach

Finally, a contract may be discharged by acceptance of a breach. The usual remedy for a breach of contract is an award of damages. However, in certain cases a party may treat the contract as repudiated by the breach, in which event the aggrieved party may consider himself discharged from any further liability and sue for damages.

If the breach occurs before the date fixed for performance of the contract, it is known as anticipatory breach.

DISCUSSION

You have just read how a contract may be discharged under Anglo/American law. Discuss the following points with a partner:

1. Can you think of any examples of discharge by frustration?
2. Why might a businessman waive a breach of contract rather than sue to enforce it?
3. Are contracts discharged in the same way in your country?
4. What legislation or jurisprudence governs this aspect of contract law in your country?

POINTS TO REMEMBER

1. *"Every contractual obligation in a contract gives rise to a corresponding contractual right."* This highly formal way of expressing cause and result is very frequent in legal English. However, you are probably aware of many other ways of indicating cause and result.

Frequently used expressions include:

thus, lead to, result in, as a consequence of, result from, is because, explains, hence

2. *"In certain cases the party may treat the contract as repudiated by the breach. In this event the aggrieved party ..."*

In the text these two sentences were joined in the following way:

"In certain cases the party may treat the contract as repudiated by the breach, in which event the aggrieved party ..."

In this context, an alternative would be: *in which case.*

Other expressions include:

on whose behalf, both of which, the rest of which, half of which.

EXERCISES

1. Join these sentences using a relative clause.

(a) Both parties may agree that circumstances have changed. In this case, their contract may be changed by novation.

(b) My client wishes to remain anonymous. I am appearing on his behalf.

(c) There were four parties to this contract. All of them will have to appear in court.

(d) Restrictions may be placed on the export of computer technology. In this event your contract will be deemed to be frustrated.

(e) The plaintiff will probably be awarded damages. He will have to pay a third of this to his lawyer.

2. Language of cause and result.
(a) Study the following expressions, and decide whether each introduces a cause or a result, *e.g.: result = bring about*

result		**cause**
_____	because	_____
_____	due to	_____
_____	lead to	_____
_____	result from	_____
_____	as a consequence	_____
_____	Hence,	_____
_____	result in	_____
_____	give rise to	_____
_____	arise from	_____

(b) Rewrite the following sentences using the words given in brackets.

(i) The fact that you have signed this document means that you have waived your right to sue. (resulted in)

(ii) Becno Inc. have withdrawn their take-over bid because of our financial problems. (led to)

_____

_____

(iii) Mr Smith's failure to give us 30 days' notice has given rise to a breach of contract. (Hence)

_____

_____

(iv) As a result of the faulty drafting of the contract, there were two important court cases. (gave rise to)

_____

_____

B. *Remedies for Breach of Contract*

BLANK-FILLING

Fill the blanks with one word from the following list. Some words are used more than once.

compliance	rise	discharge
which	of	denies
demand	against	injured
upon	constitutes	fails
raise	victim	to
when	arises	in
performance	perform	by
sue	towards	victimised
amounts	for	from

If one of the parties _____ (1) a contract _____ (2) to perform its terms, his conduct_____ (3) to a breach of contract. A breach of contract does not automatically serve to _____ (4) the contract. The situation will depend _____ (5) the nature of the breach, but a breach of contract does give the _____ (6) party a remedy. A remedy is the means provided _____ (7) the law to recover rights or to obtain redress or compensation for a wrong. A breach of contract generally gives _____ (8) to a loss, but this is not always the case. However, a breach gives the _____ (9) party a right of action _____ (10) the party breaking the contract.

A term _____ (11) you may encounter is "anticipatory breach", which _____ (12) where the breach occurs before the time established for the _____ (13) of the contract. In such a case, the _____ (14) party may _____ (15) for damages without having to wait until the date established for the _____ (16) of the contract.

There are several remedies available for breach of contract, and some of them are equitable as opposed to common law remedies.

READ AND DISCUSS

Read about the common law remedy for breach and with a partner discuss in what circumstances a different sort of remedy might be necessary.

1. The common law remedy of damages

It is important to remember that whenever damages are awarded, they are intended to compensate the injured party for any loss or damage arising from the breach, but they are not intended to punish the party committing the breach. The basic principle is that the injured party should be restored financially as nearly as possible to the position it would have been in had the contract been performed. It is also important to note that damages are assessed by the court on the actual loss to the injured party, and not on the basis of any gain made by the other party.

If an injured party, who will be the plaintiff in the action, sues to recover damages for breach of contract, it must set out in the **writ** and **statement of claim** the relief it is seeking. In the case of a claim for damages, this relief may take the form of a claim for liquidated or unliquidated damages.

Liquidated damages are usually based on a pre-estimate for an anticipated breach of contract which is specifically set out as a clause of the contract. An anticipated breach should be distinguished from an anticipatory breach.

The general rule is that a claimant may recover financial compensation for his actual loss, provided it is not too remote.

Case Law: *Hadley v Baxendale* [1854] 9 Exch. 341

2. Equitable remedies

READING FOR DEFINITIONS

Equity supplements common law remedies by providing remedies where the common law remedy of damages may be inadequate. Equitable relief is also available in cases of mistake, where the contract could be perfectly valid at common law. When granting equitable relief, the court may choose one of the following remedies.

The definitions have been mixed up. Match the definition to the type of remedy.

(1) Specific Performance

       (a) A remedy granted in the event of fraud or mistake which releases the innocent party from its obligations.

(2) Injunction	(b) An equitable remedy allowing the terms of a contract to be changed when these terms do not reflect either party's true intentions.
(3) Rescission	(c) A court order compelling a defendant to perform his part of the contract. The court will normally award this remedy where damages would be inadequate.
(4) Rectification	(d) A court order which is usually negative, or prohibitory, and which forbids a person to do something. In rare circumstances it can be mandatory and command a person to do something, and is consequently positive.

EXERCISES

1. Supply the negative form of the following words

valid	able	willing
earned	reasonable	performed
complete	necessary	legal
foreseen	effective	practical
available	adequate	due

2. Rewrite the following sentences using the word given in brackets.

(a) By giving up their rights to make a claim, both parties were discharged from their contract. (waived)

_____

(b) The plaintiff considered that she was entitled to receive money for the inconvenience she had suffered because of the airline's negligence. (recover)

_____

(c) A contract is discharged when both parties perform their obligations. (performance)

_____

(d) The court ordered the plaintiff to be paid damages of £50,000 (awarded))

_____

3. Find the words which express the opposite concept to the words in the following list:

(1) performance	(2) right
(3) promisor	(4) partial
(5) wholly	(6) signed
(7) frequent	(8) plaintiff
(9) trustee	(10) landlord

CROSSWORD THREE

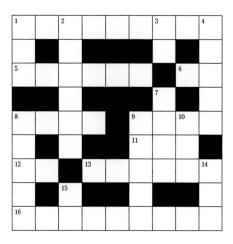

Across
1. The release from a contract.
5. He _____ a lot of money through that contract.
6. The injured party will _____ the plaintiff in the action.
8. _____ all your obligations are extinguished, you will be released from your contract.
9. The defence _____ doubt on the plaintiff's allegations.
11. There are several forms of breach: _____ of them is anticipated breach.
12. *id est.*
13. In a fiduciary relationship each party _____ the other.
16. The contract was _____ from the date it was signed.

Down
1. _____ to the strike, they were unable to meet the order.
2. Put in order.
3. In _____ McArdle [1951] Ch 669.
4. ... in which _____ the aggrieved party may ....
7. Forbids, does not allow to enter.
8. The aggrieved party may _____ his right to sue.
9. The _____ awarded damages.
10. The plaintiff must _____ out his claim in his writ.
14. They will _____ for breach.
15. _____ they lose the case, they will have to pay costs.

ENGLISH FOR COMPANY LAW

INTRODUCTION

The importance of the leading case of *Salomon v Salomon & Co Ltd* [1897] A.C. 22 is that the House of Lords held that a company duly registered under the Companies Acts is a separate legal entity, and a distinct person from the shareholders, even if it is what is commonly called "a one-man company".

READ AND ASK

Below there are two versions of the facts of the case. In pairs, A should read version A and prepare questions that will elicit answers to fill the gaps in the text, and B should do likewise, so that A can provide the information that B needs to complete the text.

Version A

Aaron Salomon had for many years carried on business as a leather merchant and wholesale boot manufacturer, and the business had been very successful. In 1892 he decided to form a limited company to (1) _____, which was duly registered in the name of Salomon and Co Ltd. Mr Salomon wished to retain control over the running of the business, and so his plan was that the shareholders should be restricted to himself and (2) _____. The memorandum of association was signed by Mr Salomon, his wife, a daughter and four sons, thus making seven members.

After the company was formed, it bought the business from Mr Salomon for (3) _____. In payment, Mr Salomon took 20,000 £1 shares in the company, and his wife and children (4) _____ each. He also received an issue of debentures (a secured form of loan) for £10,000 and (5) _____.

At the time of the transfer of the business to the company, the business was solvent but shortly afterwards the company went through a difficult time. In an effort to keep the business going, Mr Salomon arranged for (6) _____ to be made by an outsider to the business. The company failed to pay interest on the loan, and so in 1893 liquidation proceedings were started to enforce the (7) _____. The liquidation (sale of the company's assets) raised enough money to meet the company's debt on the loan but not the (8) _____, who, unlike Mr Salomon, had no secured interest. Mr Salomon claimed all the remaining assets in priority over the unsecured creditors, because of the first debentures which had been issued to him, but the liquidator contended that the company (and the unsecured creditors) were entitled to be repaid personally by Mr Salomon. The liquidator claimed that (9) _____, and that the company was merely a sham designed to limit Mr Salomon's liability for debts incurred while carrying it on. The liquidator argued that in these circumstances, Mr Salomon should be ordered to indemnify the company against its debts, and that payment of the debenture debt to him should be postponed until the (10) _____ were satisfied.

Version B

Aaron Salomon had for many years carried on business as a (a) _____, and the business had been very successful. In 1892 he decided to form a limited company to purchase the business, which was duly registered in the name of (b) _____.
Mr Salomon wished to retain control over the running of the business, and so his plan was that the shareholders should be restricted to himself and members of his family. The (c) _____ was signed by Mr Salomon, his wife, a daughter and four sons, thus making seven members.

After the company was formed, it bought the business from Mr Salomon for £39,000. In payment, Mr Salomon took (d) _____ in the company, and his wife and children one £1 share each. He also received an issue of (e) _____ for £10,000 and the balance in cash.

At the time of the transfer of the business to the company, the business was solvent but shortly afterwards the company (f) _____. In an effort to keep the business going, Mr Salomon arranged for another loan of £5,000 to be made by an outsider to the business. The company failed to pay interest on the loan, and so in 1893 (g) _____ were started to enforce the repayment of the loan. The liquidation (sale) of the company's assets raised enough money to meet (h) _____ but not the debts owed to the company's trade creditors, who, unlike Mr Salomon, had no secured interest. Mr Salomon claimed all the remaining assets in priority over the unsecured creditors, but the liquidator contended that the (i) _____ were entitled to be repaid personally by Mr Salomon. The liquidator claimed that the company's business was in reality still Mr Salomon's, and that the company was merely a sham designed to limit Mr Salomon's liability for debts incurred while carrying it on. The liquidator argued that in these circumstances, Mr Salomon should be ordered to (j) _____, and that payment of the debenture debt to him should be postponed until the company's other creditors were satisfied.

EXERCISES

---

1. Working with a partner, orally read and finish these sentences without looking back. Pay attention to the structure as well as to the content.

    (a)   Before forming Salomon and Company Ltd, Aaron Salomon had ...

    (b)   The membership of Salomon and Company Ltd. was limited ...

    (c)   Mr Salomon sold his company for £39,000. He and his family received 20,006 £1 shares and £10,000 in debentures, leaving a balance ...

    (d)   Shortly after the transfer of the business, the company ...

    (e)   Liquidation proceedings were started because ...

    (f)   The liquidation of the company's assets raised only enough money to ...

    (g)   Mr Salomon claimed he had a right to be paid before the unsecured creditors because ...

    (h)   The liquidators contended that ...

2. Below is a short summary of the facts of the case. Fill in each underlined blank with a preposition and each dotted blank with a verb in the correct form.

In 1892 Aaron Salomon decided to form a limited company to purchase his own business. Upon .... this limited company, Mr Salomon restricted the membership _____ family members so that he .... control _____ the running of the business. After the company .... , it .... Mr Salomon's business for £39,000. _____ payment, Mr Salomon and his family .... 20,006 £1 shares and £10,000 in debentures and the balance _____ cash.

   Not long afterwards, the company had financial problems. _____ an effort .... these problems, Mr Salomon arranged for a loan .... by an outsider. When the company failed .... interest _____ the loan, liquidation proceedings .... The sale of the company's assets .... enough money .... the debt on the loan, but not the debts .... to the company's creditors. Mr Salomon .... he had priority _____ the unsecured creditors, but the liquidator .... that the unsecured creditors were entitled .... by Mr Salomon personally. An action .... by Mr Salomon.

POINTS TO REMEMBER

1. *The company failed to pay the interest due on the debenture.*
The regular verb *fail* is used extensively in formal English and it simply means not to do something, generally a duty.
He failed to notice the red traffic light, and crashed into the police car.
The abstract noun derived from *fail* is *failure*, and can be found on public notices and in contracts.
Failure to comply with the terms of this contract may lead to court action being taken against you.
2. *Mr Salomon's liability for debts incurred.*
You *incur* losses/debts/someone's displeasure by the way you act. The verb *incur* is not followed by a preposition.
3. *Mr Salomon was under no liability to the company.*
A formal and stylish way to express the idea of being free from liability or obligation is to use the verb *to be* + *under no obligation/liability.*
I am under no obligation to disclose those facts.
4. *A sum sufficient to meet its liabilities in full.*
Meet (met, met) can be used in many expressions with the meaning of *to satisfy.*
You can meet needs/bills/standards/approval/demands, etc.
What other words can you find to follow *meet*?

READING

At the hearing of the case, *Salomon v Salomon & Co Ltd* [1897] A.C. 22, the trial judge, Vaughan Williams J. agreed with the liquidator. The judge held that the subscribers of the memorandum, other than Mr Salomon, held their shares as mere nominees for him, and that Mr Salomon's sole purpose in forming the company was to use it as an agent to run his business for him.

The Court of Appeal reached the same conclusion as the trial judge. It held that the Companies Acts were intended to confer the privilege of limited liability only on genuine, independent shareholders who had combined their capital to enable an enterprise to be started, and not upon a person who was really the sole owner of a business and who merely found six nominees to join him in going through the formalities of incorporating a company.

Lopes L.J. argued:

> "It never was intended that the company to be constituted should consist of one substantial person and six mere dummies, the nominees of that person, without any real interest in the company. The Act contemplated the incorporation of seven independent *bona fide* members, who had a mind and a will of their own, and were not the mere puppets of an individual who, adopting the machinery of the Act, carried on his old business in the same way as before, when he was a sole trader."

Lindley L.J. said:

> "I do not go so far as to say that the creditors of the company could sue Mr Salomon. In my opinion, they can only reach him through the company. Moreover, Mr Aaron Salomon's liability to indemnify the company in this case is, in my view, the legal consequence of the formation of the company in order to attain a result not permitted by law. The liability does not arise simply from the fact that he holds nearly all the shares in the company ... His liability rests on the purpose for which he formed the company, on the way he formed it, and the use which he made of it."

It was therefore the view of the court that Mr Salomon had incorporated the company for an unlawful purpose, and that relief should be given to the company's creditors by requiring Mr Salomon to indemnify the company against its liabilities and to contribute to the company's assets a sum sufficient to meet its liabilities in full.

On appeal to the House of Lords, the decision of the Court of Appeal was reversed, and it was held that the company was a distinct person from Mr Salomon and not his agent, that Mr Salomon was under no liability to the company or its creditors, and that his debenture was valid as against the company.

Lord Halsbury L.C. reasoned:

> "I must pause here to point out that the statute enacts nothing as to the extent or degree of interest which may be held by each of the seven subscribers of the memorandum, or as to the proportion of influence possessed by one or the majority of the shareholders over the others. One share is enough. Still less is it possible to contend that the motive of becoming shareholders or of making them shareholders is a field of enquiry which the statute itself recognises as legitimate. If they are shareholders, they are shareholders for all purposes ..."

In the course of his speech Lord MacNaghten said:

> "The company attains maturity on its birth. There is no period of minority – no interval of

incapacity. I cannot understand how a body corporate thus made 'capable' by statute can lose its individuality by issuing the bulk of its capital to one person, whether he be a subscriber to the memorandum or not. The company is at law a different person altogether from the subscribers to the memorandum; and, though it may be that after incorporation the business is precisely the same as it was before, and the same persons are managers, and the same hands receive the profits, the company is not in law the agent of the subscribers or trustee for them."

In his opinion, Lord Herschell said:

"In a popular sense, a company may in every case be said to carry on business for and on behalf of its shareholders; but this certainly does not in point of law constitute the relation of principal and agent between them or render the shareholders liable to indemnify the company against the debts which it incurs."

The House of Lords refused to accept that there was anything improper in the purpose for which the company was formed by Mr Salomon, or in the manner in which the company was formed. It also rejected the trial judge's view that the company must be treated as Mr Salomon's agent appointed to run his business for him. The most important principle established by the House of Lords was that a company has a separate legal personality, and is quite distinct from the individuals who are its members. This principle is of vital and fundamental importance and has been rigorously applied by the courts ever since the case of Mr Salomon.

NOTE-TAKING

1. What did the trial judge, Vaughan William J. hold about the principal and agent relationship?

2. What did the Appeal Court Judge, Lopes L.J., say about the division of shares in the company?

3. What opinion did Lindley L.J. have with regard to Mr Salomon's purpose in forming the company?

4. How did the three judges in the House of Lords reverse the decisions of the judges in the lower courts?
(a) Lord Herschell: _____

(b) Lord Halsbury: _____

(c) Lord MacNaghten: _____

SUMMARY-WRITING

Complete the following summary, basing your answers on the text and on the notes you have taken.

The court of first instance and the Court of Appeal held Mr Salomon _____, saying that all shareholders in a company should be _____ and that Mr Salomon had incorporated the company for _____. However, in the House of Lords the decision _____ and it _____ that a company is a separate _____ and as such it is _____ from the moment it is formed. It was also held that the statute made no provision for _____. Therefore, Mr Salomon was under no legal obligation to _____.

EXERCISE

Prepositions.

1. Mr Wright deposited £5,000 in your account _____ payment _____ your services.
2. We have restricted membership in the organisation _____ graduates _____ law.
3. You will be expected to refund the money _____ cash.
4. What rate of interest are you paying _____ that loan?
5. They are expected to lower their prices _____ an effort to compete with the larger retail outlets.
6. The Companies Act confers the privilege of limited liability _____ all shareholders.
7. _____ appeal to the Supreme Court, the judgment was reversed.
8. A limited company is a separate legal entity, distinct _____ its shareholders.

CHAPTER ONE

THE BIRTH OF A COMPANY

READING

The following are four kinds of businesses. Match each one to the four situations described below and give reasons for your choice.

       (a) sole trader   (b) public limited company
       (c) private limited company   (d) partnership

1. Henry Leverett wanted to *set up* an import-export business but had no capital, so he *looked round* for someone to finance him. Barry Goldfinger provided *financial backing* and now the two men are in business together. Henry is working very hard because he knows that if things go badly his house will be repossessed by the building society to which it is mortgaged.
2. Bill Cuthbert trained as a car mechanic. His dad left him £5,000 to set up his own workshop. He worked very hard at first until the business *got off the ground*. Now he employs two junior mechanics who get £150 *take-home pay* a week. He *takes in* an average of £5,000 a month, which leaves him about £1,700 after paying *the lads*, tax and overheads.
3. At the last annual general meeting Alison Reeves was pleased to hear that the managing director was being replaced, as Only Askus' profits had slumped and the share price had plummeted. She had already contacted her stockbroker about selling her stake in the company, but decided to keep the shares for another few months to see if the price *picked up* and a dividend was declared after two years of receiving nothing.
4. James Bell, Meriel Hutchinson and Anthony Little studied computer science together. They all obtained prizes for creativity when at university, and decided to work together to produce computer software. They each *put in* £10,000 to *get going*. Sensibly, they took legal advice, and set up a company. Things have not gone too well for them: debts are *mounting up* and they are thankful they will never lose more than the £10,000 they each originally invested.

EXERCISES

---

1. Find the formal equivalent for the words italicised in the text.
2. Rewrite the following sentences in a formal style, such as one lawyer would write to another.

(a) Each friend put in £10,000 to get the business going, but it never got off the ground.

(b) ABC's results have picked up and they've decided how much to give as a dividend.

_____

(c) His dad left him £5,000 to set up his own workshop.

_____

(d) He takes in about £1,700 after paying the lads, the rent and tax.

_____

_____

CLASSIFYING

The following is a list of characteristics of the four different kinds of businesses listed below. Discuss to which kind of business each characteristic would correspond. (Some characteristics are common to different kinds.)

> (a) sole trader   (c) private limited company
> (b) partnership   (d) public limited company

1. an artificial, not a natural person
2. dissolution upon death or retirement
3. minimum of one member and two directors + one secretary
4. perpetual succession regardless of changes in membership
5. minimum authorized share capital of £50,000
6. one quarter of share capital paid up
7. no minimum capital requirement
8. an entity separate from its members
9. only one director required + one member + secretary
10. no minimum share payment requirement
11. compliance with registration procedures under company legislation
12. no deed of incorporation required
13. unlimited number of members
14. limited to 20 members
15. members not entitled to take part in management unless they are directors
16. members are agents
17. public inspection of accounts and compulsory annual audit
18. limited liability
19. unlimited liability
20. managed by the owner(s)
21. finance obtainable by a charge attached to company's assets

QUESTIONS

1. Are there four types of businesses in your country that correspond to the four types listed above?

2. Which items in the above list fit the characteristics of the four kinds of businesses that you have named?

LETTER-WRITING

Rupert Blake, a junior partner in The Fried Partnership's London office, has to answer the following letter.

127 Sunset Boulevard

R. Blake, Esq.   *Los Angeles*
The Fried Partnership   *CA. 80332*
25 Charing Cross Road   *U.S.A.*
London
England   *February 28, 2003*

Dear Mr Blake,

As I was very pleased with the way in which you dealt with the conveyancing of my property in the Isle of Wight, I am writing to you to enquire whether your firm would be able to assist me with a business venture in Europe.

As you might know, I have recently moved into the restaurant business, and in the last year I have been expanding throughout the United States. The time is now ripe to move into Europe and I consider London, Paris and Marbella obvious launch-pads for the rest of the E.U. At present I would like to open one restaurant in each city with a view to possible expansion.

My knowledge of E.U. law is extremely limited, and so I would greatly appreciate it if you could clearly explain the differences between the kinds of businesses I could set up, and advise me as to the most suitable one for this type of venture.

I thank you in advance for your help.

Yours sincerely,

Bruce Wallis

If you are familiar with the legal framework of companies in your own country, write an appropriate reply to a potential English client.

POINTS TO REMEMBER
1. *thankful/grateful*
Although very similar, both words are not always interchangeable.
Grateful is used in professional correspondence to request something.
I would be grateful if you could send me the following information.
Thankful is more limited in that it expresses a general feeling of gratitude.
She came out of the accident unscathed and was thankful to be alive.
2. *"perpetual succession regardless of changes in membership."*
regardless of is a prepositional expression which means "even if there is"
He voiced his disapproval of the CEO's policy regardless of the consequences for his career.
3. *R. Blake, Esq.*
Esq. stands for *esquire*, a word which dates back to the Middle Ages, and was used to indicate the lowest rank of nobility. Nowadays it is a courtesy title for men, and is put on envelopes and in the addressee column of formal letters. It is used in the US to address lawyers, and is still used in the UK in formal letters.

EXERCISE

Rewrite the following sentences using the word in brackets so that the new sentence means the same as the original one.

1. When a partnership is dissolved, the first step is to pay any debts to outsiders. (upon)

2. He has more shares in that company than anybody else. (stake)

3. The two companies have come together to build a bridge across the Nile. (venture)

4. The company continued with its plan, without paying attention to the fact that the managing director was very doubtful. (regardless)

READING

Read the following newspaper article from *The Rag Trade Press*, June 14, 2004:

RECORD YEAR FOR PRETTYWOMAN

Prettywoman p.l.c. has recorded its highest ever profits. A delighted chairman, Arthur Young, said that this was due to increased store traffic, especially in France, and to downsizing at its production facilities outside Birmingham.

Not surprisingly, the Stock Market reacted favourably to this news, and Prettywoman's shares were up 7 points on yesterday's F.T. closing price.

Shareholders, who have already been enjoying a healthy return on their investment, can look forward to an even more sizeable dividend.

The company has come a long way since Arthur and his wife Jean acquired an off-the-shelf company for the price of £100 back in the 1980s.

BLANK-FILLING

Although Arthur and Jean Young could have set up a completely new company, they chose to buy an already-formed company, thereby avoiding a fairly costly and complicated procedure. The paragraph below describes the option that they chose.

Off-the Shelf Companies

Fill the blank spaces in the following passage by choosing one of the alternatives listed below.

A ready-made registered company may be acquired from company formation agencies specialising in the sale of what we call off-the-shelf companies. This is a company which has been incorporated in (1) _____ with the registration (2) _____ of the Companies Act, and has a minimal (3) _____ capital usually of two £1 shares. The advantage of purchasing such a company is that if you require one urgently and at a low cost, you can _____ (4) corporate status very rapidly, thus avoiding the time and expense of having to incorporate the new company yourself. Upon payment of a (5) _____ to the agency, the shares and the company's (6) _____ of members will be (7) _____ to the purchasers of the company. At the same time the (8) _____ directors and secretary of the company will resign and new ones will be (9) _____ in their place. (10) _____ of the change of the address of the company's registered office, its directors and secretary, will then be given to the Registrar of Companies. The new shareholders may also change the company's name, its objects, its articles and the contents of its memorandum.

1. (a) according
   (b) respect
   (c) agreement
   (d) accordance
4. (a) arrive
   (b) attain
   (c) reach
   (d) get
7. (a) conveyed
   (b) translated
   (c) transferred
   (d) relocated
10. (a) advice
    (b) news
    (c) notification
    (d) information

2. (a) laws
   (b) provisions
   (c) regulations
   (d) proceedings
5. (a) fee
   (b) sum
   (c) salary
   (d) tip
8. (a) existing
   (b) actual
   (c) real
   (d) functioning

3. (a) share
   (b) stock
   (c) bond
   (d) security
6. (a) logbook
   (b) manual
   (c) catalogue
   (d) register
9. (a) placed
   (b) recruited
   (c) approached
   (d) appointed

READING

Had Jean and Arthur not chosen to acquire an off-the-shelf company, they would have had to go to the Company Registry to file the following documents with the Registrar of Companies.

1. Memorandum of association ⎫ (in the US, the articles of incorporation)
2. Articles of association ⎭ (in the US, the bylaws)
3. A statutory declaration signed by the solicitor or director or secretary of the company to the effect that all the requirements of the Companies Act have been complied with.
4. The address of the registered office and the names of the first directors and secretary.

Before issuing a certificate of incorporation, the Registrar of Companies must be satisfied that the company has met all the statutory requirements. The Registrar may refuse to register a company whose objects are unlawful or whose name is offensive. However, the certificate of incorporation is not conclusive evidence of the lawfulness of the objects of the company. If a company with unlawful or immoral objects is registered, the courts may cancel the registration effected by the Registrar.

Can you think of any objects of a company which might be unlawful?

In *Attorney-General v Lindi St Claire (Personal Services) Ltd* [1981] 2 Co. Law 69, the High Court quashed a decision by the Registrar of Companies to register the business of a prostitute under the name Lindi St Claire (Personal Services) Ltd. This name had been registered in 1979 after the Registrar had refused to accept Miss St Claire's alternative names, Prostitutes Ltd, Hookers Ltd and Lindi St Claire French Lessons Ltd. Miss St Claire's accountants had advised her to register a company after they had received a letter from the Inland Revenue in which it was stated that prostitution was considered to be a trade. The Attorney-General objected arguing that the company should never have been formed in the first place as it had clearly been formed for sexually immoral purposes, and as such, was contrary to public policy and consequently illegal. The High Court accepted the Attorney-General's argument and the registration was quashed.

POINTS TO REMEMBER

1. *in the event of* + noun
This complex prepositional phrase is frequently found in legal English when referring to a possible future event and its consequences. *e.g.*:
In the event of his resignation, the committee will appoint a new chairman.
This is the same as saying:
If he resigns, the committee will appoint a new chairman.
2. *Before issuing a certificate of incorporation ...*
The word "*issue*" has many meanings. In the extract of the text quoted above it is

used to indicate an official body granting a document to another person. (*issue* a passport, licence, etc.)

Shares are *issued* (an extended use of the same meaning).

We also talk about a first day of *issue* of stamps, today's *issue* of the newspaper.

Finally, one of the most usual meanings is to indicate a *question, a controversial subject.*

None of the members present at the meeting dared raise the issue of possible redundancies.

3. *Register/Registry*

A *register* is a book in which important information is stored, and which is often available for public inspection.

A *registry* is the office in which registers are kept, and to which the general public can go to inspect the registers and file information with the Registrar for registration in the register.

4. *File* is used to refer to a collection of information.

He's a well-known terrorist; the CIA have a large file on him.

We keep all that information on file.

File as a verb can have two meanings:

(a) to put documents in a certain place

Those documents should be filed under the name of the plaintiff.

(b) to make a formal legal accusation, request, complaint or claim.

Mr and Mrs Wade filed the adoption papers in July 2005.

LETTER-WRITING

Following the initial correspondence the parties have had about the different kinds of companies that Mr Wallis could set up, Mr Blake, his English lawyer, is writing to him to inform him of the steps necessary for the formation of a company in England. Mr Blake's letter is a very strange mixture of formal and informal. Pay attention to the words in bold and try to find a more formal equivalent for them.

The Fried Partnership
25 Charing Cross Road
London
England

Bruce Wallis, Esq.
127 Sunset Boulevard
Los Angeles
CA. 80332
U.S.A.

May 24, 2003

Dear Mr Wallis,

   Thanks *for your letter of 10th May* **about** *the formation of your companies in Europe. We* **think the way you trust us is great** *and agree that a private limited company is probably the best* **pick.**

   The steps involved in the formation of a private limited company in England **aren't** *very complicated. The procedure begins with* **writing** *the memorandum and articles of association. These documents must be* **left** *at the Registry of Companies together with a statutory declaration* **saying you have followed the Companies Act** *and a statement of* directors and secretaries. The **first one** must be signed by the solicitor **working on** the formation of the company or by the company secretary or a director. The **second one** must **have** the name, address, nationality and directorships of the secretary and directors, as well as the address of the registered office of the company and must be signed by the subscribers to the memorandum or **for them**.

As long as the Registrar is **happy with** **what the documents say**, he will, on payment of certain fees, **give out** a certificate of incorporation. He also has to publish **news about** the issue of the certificate of incorporation and of any non-cash assets acquired by the company from a subscriber. This **news** will be published in the London Gazette.

You should **know** that the procedure for the formation of a company is not necessarily **shared by** all European countries. In some Continental countries you might need **to do other things** such as **getting** a name certificate and a public deed of incorporation executed before a notary. You may also need authorisation from the relevant exchange control authorities for any foreign money **you're bringing in**.

We hope this information gives you a clear picture of what is required for the formation of a company in England. **In case** you have any further doubts, please **feel free** to contact us.

We look forward to hearing from you again in the near future.

Yours sincerely,

Rupert Blake

Mr Blake does not have a clear idea about the incorporation procedures for limited companies in other countries besides England. You must write to Mr Wallis with information about the procedure in your country.

EXERCISE

Match the concepts in the left-hand column with their definition in the right-hand column.

1. writ	(a) the word used when a holding in a company is expressed in terms of total value.
2. paid-up shares	(b) obligatory relinquishment of shares by a member when he does not pay after a call is made upon him.
3. stock	(c) the right of companies, which must be expressly given by their articles, to retain the title until the shares have been fully paid up.
4. shares	(d) a formal written command in the name of the sovereign, state or court.
5. lien on shares	(e) shares which have been fully paid up.

6. classes of shares	(f) a division of the company's equity capital, expressed in units, each unit having a nominal value.
7. forfeiture	(g) fixed number of members who must be present to make the proceedings of general meetings legally valid.
8. quorum	(h) different types of shares, each with a different legal right.

READING AND CLASSIFYING

A company's structure is governed by its MEMORANDUM OF ASSOCIATION and its ARTICLES OF ASSOCIATION.

The MEMORANDUM contains the most important details, and is of interest to outsiders who may wish to have dealings with the company.

The ARTICLES OF ASSOCIATION set out the regulations which govern the internal management of the company and are of interest mainly to the shareholders and directors.

Working with a partner, decide whether you would find the following information in the memorandum or in the articles of association, referring to the notes below.

1. Whether the company is a public or a private limited company.
2. If a company is authorised to convert its paid-up shares into stock or reconvert stock into paid-up shares of any denomination.
3. If a director is empowered to appoint an alternate director to act in his place in the event of his absence.
4. The name of the company.
5. The amount of a company's authorised capital.
6. What quorum is required for general meetings in order that business may be validly transacted.
7. If you want to know whether the company has been registered with the Registrar of Companies in Cardiff (for English and Welsh companies) or the Scottish Registrar of Companies in Edinburgh.
8. Who the subscribers to the company are.
9. Who is empowered to appoint and remove the company secretary.
10. What the objects of the company are.

NOTES

1. The memorandum must contain a clause stating that the company is to be a private limited company or a public limited company.
2. The articles of a company lay down the regulations concerning shares. In addition to the authorisation to convert paid-up shares into stock, the articles cover such headings as classes of shares, share certificates, lien on shares, calls on shares and forfeiture, transfer of shares, modification of share capital, and the purchase by the company of its own shares.

3. The articles set out provisions for the number of directors, alternate directors, their powers and their delegation, the appointment and retirement of directors, their disqualification and renewal, the remuneration and expenses of directors, the directors' gratuities and pensions.

4. The memorandum must state the name of the company with Ltd as the last word if the company is a private limited company, and plc if the company is a public limited company. If the company has its registered office in Wales, its memorandum and articles may be in Welsh and its name may terminate in Welsh, with cyf (Ltd) for a private limited company, and in the case of a public limited Company, ccc (plc).

5. The authorised or nominal capital of a company is set out in the memorandum. The clause must also specify the division of the share capital into shares of a fixed amount.

6. The articles of a company provide for the holding of general meetings and all the relevant provisions, such as notice, proceedings and voting of members.

7. The third clause of the memorandum must state whether the company's registered office is to be situated in England, Wales or Scotland. If the registered office is to be in England or Wales, registration is carried out by the Registrar of Companies in Cardiff, and in the case of Scotland by the Scottish Registrar of Companies in Edinburgh. The actual address is not set out in the memorandum but must be sent to the Registrar upon incorporation. The registered office is the official address, where legal documents, such as writs, official notices and other communications are to be formally served. It is also at this office that certain documents and registers must be available for inspection by shareholders and creditors of the company.

8. The memorandum contains an association clause stating that the persons signing the memorandum desire to be formed into a company and agree to take the share opposite their names.

9. The articles confer the power to appoint and remove the secretary. This power is usually conferred upon the board.

10. The memorandum must contain an objects clause. This sets out in the form of a list the activities which the company can undertake. If the company does business which is not included in the objects clause then any such transaction will be *ultra vires* at common law and consequently void. It is therefore of the utmost importance to decide upon the specific wording to cover the company's activities and to reflect these details in the objects clause. In practice, however, the objects are drafted in the widest terms so as to overcome the problem of *ultra vires*.

READING

Ultra Vires – In English law the doctrine of *ultra vires* used to be very important. It meant that a company could only carry out acts which were expressly or impliedly sanctioned by its objects, during the course of business. Any other acts were void and had to be ratified later by a special resolution of the members of the company, in order to take effect.

The original objective of the *ultra vires* doctrine was to protect the shareholders of the company against the acts of the directors. As business became more sophisticated, shareholders of companies were not so concerned about the kind of business entered into by the directors of a company so long as profits were made and a capital return arose in the form of dividends declared.

In time, the only persons really affected in practice by the doctrine were persons supplying goods and services to a company for a purpose which was not included in the company's objects clause. This doctrine is now ineffective as against third parties by virtue of s.35(1) of the Companies Act 1985, as amended by the Companies Act 1989, which provides as follows:

> "The validity of an act done by a company shall not be called into question on the ground of lack of capacity by reason of the fact that it is beyond the objects of the company stated in the memorandum of association."

The effect of this legislation has been to abolish the *ultra vires* doctrine as against innocent third parties dealing in good faith with a company, but to retain the doctrine for internal purposes covering the relations between the shareholders and the directors of a company.

Case Law: *Ashbury Railway Carriage and Iron Co v Riche* [1875] L.R. 7 H.L. 653

EXERCISE

1. Look back at the text on *ultra vires,* and choose the best meaning, in its context, of the following words:

1. sanctioned
   (a) authorised   (b) punished   (c) confirmed   (d) decreed
2. ratified
   (a) motivated   (b) confirmed   (c) recognised   (d) voted
3. so long as
   (a) until   (b) unless   (c) as far as   (d) provided
4. return
   (a) reply   (b) profit   (c) homecoming   (d) report
5. ineffective
   (a) fruitless   (b) inefficient   (c) inoperative   (d) impractical
6. by virtue of
   (a) as a result of   (b) because of   (c) resulting from   (d) under
7. amended
   (a) abandoned   (b) improved   (c) corrected   (d) bettered
8. ground
   (a) basis   (b) position   (c) point   (d) excuse
9. abolish
   (a) do in   (b) do up   (c) do away with   (d) do down
10. retain
    (a) keep in place   (b) secure the services of   (c) not forget   (d) continue to have

SUMMARY WRITING

Complete the following paragraph about the *ultra vires* doctrine. You may refer to the text if necessary.

Under the *ultra vires* doctrine, if a company _____ acts which were not _____ , it had to ratify these acts by _____ . Originally the doctrine existed to protect shareholders, but shareholders later became more _____ than _____ . The only persons affected by the doctrine were _____ but the two Companies Acts have rendered _____ . Now the doctrine is retained to _____ .

POINTS TO REMEMBER

1. *to serve a notice/a writ on/upon somebody*
This is a formal expression which means to notify somebody in writing of some formal event, such as a legal action, a general meeting or a demand for payment.
2. *"This power is usually conferred upon the board"*
Confer is used both passively and actively in formal English to mean to grant or to give an honour or power.
The Chancellor of the University conferred an honorary degree upon the King of Spain.
3. *hold* and *celebrate*
We *celebrate* a special joyous occasion by doing something, whereas we *hold* more ordinary events, such as a meeting.
4. *of importance to ... of interest to ...*
A more formal way of saying *This is very important for me* is *This is of the utmost importance to me.* Similarly, you can say *This may be of interest to you* instead of *This may be interesting to you.*

EXERCISES

1. Finish the following sentences in the most appropriate way.

(a) His total debts _____

(b) If we cannot meet our mortgage payments _____

(c) A limited company has perpetual succession, regardless _____

(d) A partnership is automatically dissolved upon _____

(e) A quick and easy way of setting up a company is _____

(f) All writs and official notices are served upon a company at _____

(g) In order for the proceedings of a general meeting to be valid, there _____

(h) The power to appoint and remove a secretary is usually _____
_____

(i) As the articles of association have an inherent contractual nature _____
_____

(j) Whereas the memorandum is mainly aimed at outsiders, the articles are of _
_____

2. Complete the grid.

VERB	NOUN	ADJECTIVE	PERSONAL NOUN
repossess			████████
	mortgage		
	succession		
		corporate	
	registration		
authorise			████████
subscribe			
	remuneration		
ratify			
dissolve			
confiscate			
			convert

3. Would you use *hold* or *celebrate* in the context of the following events?

a referendum; an exam; Mass; a meeting; your birthday; a trial; the Olympic Games; a victory in the Olympic Games; elections; your wedding anniversary; a hearing; an opinion.

_____

BLANK-FILLING

_____

Complete the following description of the articles of association by putting one word in each gap. The first letter of each word has been provided.
The articles of association have an inherent contractual nature by v_____ of s.14 of the Companies Act 1985. This section p_____ the following:

    S_____ to the provisions of the Act the memorandum and the articles when registered b_____ the company and its m_____ to the same e_____ as if they respectively had been s_____ and s_____ by each m_____ , and contained covenants on the part of each m_____ to observe all the p_____ of the memorandum and of the articles.

Companies may d_____ up their own individual articles or may adopt Table A. This table s_____ out the standard r_____ for the management of the commonest type of registered company, the p_____ or p_____ company limited by s_____ 8 of the Companies Act 1985. B_____ virtue o_____ this Act, the Secretary of State is e_____ to make, by m_____ of statutory instrument, regulations specifying forms of memorandum and forms of articles to cover the different kinds of registered companies.

POINTS TO REMEMBER:

The following words are easily confused.

1. *request* and *require*

(a) *We are sending you the information you requested.* (asked for)
   Mr Rennie requested Mr Lane to acknowledge receipt of the £6,000.
   The public is kindly requested not to take photographs of the exhibits.

(b) *We are sending you the information you require.* (need)
   A company is required to state its objects in the memorandum.

The nominal forms are *request* and *requirement*.

At the request of our clients we have drawn up a licensing agreement.

One of the requirements for converting a private company into a public limited company is for the general meeting of the company so to resolve by a special resolution.

2. *entitle* and *empower*

(a) Entitle: *Members of a company are not entitled to take part in its management, unless they are elected to the board of directors.*

Entitle always involves a right.

All citizens over 18 are entitled to vote.

(b) Empower: *By virtue of this Act, the Secretary of State is empowered to make regulations.*

Empower involves power to do things because one is in an authoritative position.

The board of directors is empowered to appoint a company secretary.

3. *company/firm/society*

(a) The word *society* has two meanings.
   First, it refers to the organisation of community life.
   The values of our society are rapidly changing.
   Secondly, it refers to a group of people who have come together for a particular purpose.
   the Drama Society/the Royal Society for the Prevention of Cruelty to Animals/the Society of Jesus

(b) When people form an organisation for business purposes we use the word *company*, or *business*, not *society*. Strictly speaking, the word *firm* refers to a partnership, whereas *company* refers to a limited company. However, English-speaking laymen do not usually make this distinction.

READING

A promoter of a company is always very concerned about the extent of his personal liability. Below you will find the facts of a case involving personal liability related to the formation of a company.

Case: *Phonogram Ltd v Lane* [1982] Q.B. 938

Facts: In 1973 a group of musicians decided to form a pop group called "Cheap Mean and Nasty", and a company called Fragile Management Ltd to run the group.

Prior to the formation of the company, Phonogram Ltd, part of the Hemdale Group, agreed to pay £12,000 towards financing the pop group, £6,000 of which was actually paid for the group's first album.

This transaction had been negotiated by Brian Lane on behalf of Fragile Management Ltd and by Roland Rennie on behalf of Phonogram Ltd.

The following letter sent from Mr Rennie to Mr Lane on July 4, 1973 was an essential part of the deal.

> "*In regard to the contract now being completed between Phonogram Ltd and Fragile Management Ltd concerning recordings of a group . . . with a provisional title of 'Cheap, Mean and Nasty', and further to our conversation of this morning. I send you herewith our cheque for £6,000 in anticipation of a contract signing, this being the initial payment for the initial LP called for in the contract. In the unlikely event that we fail to complete within, say, one month, you will undertake to pay us the £6,000 . . . For good order's sake, Brian, I should be appreciative if you could sign the attached copy of this letter and return it to me so that I can keep our accounts people informed of what is happening.*"

Mr Lane signed the letter "for and on behalf of Fragile Management Ltd". The cheque was sent and deposited in the account of Jelly Music Ltd, another subsidiary of the Hemdale Group, one of whose directors was Mr Lane. It transpired that the group never performed under Fragile Management Ltd as the latter was never formed, and the £6,000 was never repaid.

Following the court of first instance's ruling that Mr Lane was not personally liable on the contract, the Court of Appeal was asked to decide who was liable to repay the £6,000.

SUMMARY WRITING

Complete the following summary with information from the facts of the case.

In 1973 Roland Rennie, acting on _____, negotiated a deal with Brian Lane, acting on _____ _____ , in which Phonogram Ltd committed itself to _____ . Before a contract was actually signed, _____ . On receipt of this cheque, Mr Lane signed _____ _____ using the words "for and on behalf of Fragile Management Ltd". The money was deposited _____ , because Fragile Management Ltd _____ . When the £6,000 was never repaid, an action _____ .

DISCUSSION

Before reading the ruling, discuss what the result of a similar case would be in your country.

READING COMPREHENSION

Ruling: The Court of Appeal held Mr Lane personally liable on the contract.

The court's first observation was that Fragile Management Ltd could not be sued because it never came into existence.

Lord Denning went on to quote what is now s.36(c) of the Companies Act 1985, which states:

> "Where a contract purports to be made by a company, or by a person as agent for a company, at a time when the company has not been formed, then subject to any agreement to the contrary the contract has effect as one entered into by the person purporting to act for the company or as agent for it and he is personally liable on the contract accordingly."

Lord Denning took the view that Mr Lane had made the contract on behalf of Fragile Management Ltd at a time when the company had not been formed, and he purported to make it on behalf of the company and was thus personally liable for it.

Lane's counsel had argued that Directive 68/151, upon which s.36(c) is based, states that its provisions are limited to companies in course of formation and, therefore, could not be applied in this case as Fragile Management Ltd had never commenced the incorporation process.

Lord Denning's rejection of this submission was based on Art.189 of the Treaty of Rome, which states:

> "A Directive shall be binding, as to the result to be achieved, upon each member State to which it is addressed, but shall leave to the national authorities the choice of form and method."

Lord Denning construed this article to say that an English court abides by the statute which implemented the Directive and that statute did not limit its provisions to companies in formation.

The court further decided that the form in which the contract was made, either as an agent as in the case of "for and on behalf of the company" or merely signing the company's name and subscribing one's own name, did not matter and would not affect the personal liability of the person signing.

In the court of first instance it had been contended that the words "subject to any agreement to the contrary" could be used as the basis of the argument that a person who signs "for and on behalf of the company", as agent, is saying in effect that he does not intend to be liable.

As regards this point Lord Denning said:

"If there was an express agreement that the man who was signing was not to be liable, the section would not apply. But, unless there is a clear exclusion of personal liability, (the section) should be given its full effect. It means that in all cases such as the present, where a person purports to contract on behalf of a company not yet formed, then however he expresses his signature he himself is personally liable on the contract."

Now choose the best alternative to answer the following questions.

1. Lord Denning held that a person who entered into a contract as an agent for a company prior to the formation of that company was personally liable on the contract

    (a)   once the incorporation process had begun

    (b)   regardless of whether or not that company was in course of formation.

    (c)   only if the company is eventually incorporated.

2. As regards Directive 68/151, Lord Denning held that:

    (a)   it was not applicable in this case as Fragile had never been in course of incorporation.

    (b)   it had no binding effect on the English court.

    (c)   the English court was only bound by the statute which was implemented to bring about the ultimate objective of the directive.

3. Lord Denning held that the words "for and on behalf of the company"

    (a)   could not be construed as an implied exclusion of personal liability.

    (b)   clearly indicated the person signing below was acting as an agent for the company and would never be held personally liable for the contract.

    (c)   gave rise to a construction which would not be the case had the person signed the company name and then added his/her own name.

EXERCISE

Without looking back at the text, see if you can remember how the following were expressed in a more formal way.

1. *Before the company was formed,* an agreement had been reached.

2. This *business deal* had been negotiated by Brian Lane.

3. *Following up* our telephone conversation of this morning, I am sending you the contract.

4. *It isn't very likely* that we *won't* complete the deal, but you will *promise* to pay the £6,000.

5. The copy was signed *as it was supposed to be.*

6. The £6,000 was *put into* Jelly Music's bank account.

7. It *turned out* that Mr Lane was a director of the other company.

8. The court of first instance *decided* that Mr Lane *should pay back* the £6,000.

9. Mr Lane had *deliberately given the impression that he was making* the contract *for* the company.

10. Fragile Management Ltd had *never even started to get incorporated*.

11. An English court must *follow* the statute which implemented the directive.

TEXT COMPLETION

Below you will find an incomplete version of a conversation between Mr Blake and a lawyer from another country. Both of them are attending an international conference on the incorporation of companies. Act out the conversation by filling in the gaps.

Lawyer: That was an interesting talk, wasn't it?

Blake: Yes, it was. And I especially enjoyed the part on promoters. It reminded me of a case I handled in England in 1982. You see, it was quite a nasty case involving a pop group ...

Lawyer: Oh, do tell me about it. I find case law fascinating.

Blake: Well, you see, these musicians _____

_____

_____

Lawyer: How interesting. What was the ruling?

Blake: _____

_____

And you can see how informative the talk was for me because I was so mixed up in it. Tell me, where do promoters stand under the law in your country?

Lawyer: _____

_____

Blake: Ah, I see. That clears up quite a lot, but what about renting premises?

Lawyer: _____

_____

Blake: Oh, I see. And do they have to pay for the company to be set up?

Lawyer: I'm sorry, what do you mean? The costs of incorporation?

Blake: Yes, the expenses of registration.

Lawyer: _____

Blake: Ah yes. Well, thank you very much, Mr ... er ...? What is your name, by the way? What you say is very interesting.

Lawyer: My name's _____. Delighted to meet you.

Blake: Mine's Rupert Blake. It's a pleasure for me too. Oh, look! Everyone's moving back towards the conference room. We'd better head on in too. Have you

finished your coffee?
Lawyer: Look, here's my card. Could you possibly fax me a copy of the facts of the case you mentioned? I found it very interesting.

POINTS TO REMEMBER
1. *"The contract has effect as one entered into by the person purporting to act for the company."*
Effect can be used in various ways related to contracts, laws, regulations, etc.
The new regulation has been in effect since January 1 of this year.
put into effect
Once we have signed the agreement we shall have to work on putting it into effect.
take effect/go into effect/come into effect
His appointment to the board of directors will take effect on March 1, 2005.
with immediate effect/with effect from
The board has passed a resolution with effect from April 25.
2. *"Its provisions are limited to companies in course of formation.*
in the course of/in due course = during/after a period of time
The company was incorporated in the course of three weeks.
course of action = one of the things you can do in a specific situation.
In this situation the company has two courses of action: close down a factory or reduce the staff in all existing factories.
3. *An English court abides by the statute which implemented the Directive.*
Abide by is a formal phrasal verb which means to remain faithful to, to obey, to act upon and in law is used in connection with terms, laws and regulations.
We also use it as an adjective: *a law-abiding citizen.*

EXERCISES

1. Read each of the following situations and for each write a sentence using one of the following phrasal verbs. Some will have to be used more than once.

set out/set up/draw up/lay down/abide by

(a) In the USA most drivers take the speed limit on highways very seriously. However, in many European countries drivers seem to pay no attention to the limit.

(b) On the last page of the contract you will find a list of prices and minimum orders.

(c) We advise you to consult a lawyer before you write the company's memorandum and articles.

    (d) Considering his entrepreneurial abilities, I wouldn't be surprised if he decided to start his own company.

    (e) Below I have listed the steps established in the Companies Act 1985 for registering a company.

2. Fill the spaces in the following sentences with ONE suitable preposition.

    (a) We have had to mortgage the premises _____ a building society.
    (b) I have a large stake _____ the company.
    (c) Fifty per cent of our share capital is paid _____ .
    (d) A limited company is an entity separate _____ its members.
    (e) We have complied _____ the registration procedures _____ the Companies Act.
    (f) There is a limit _____ 20 members; membership is limited _____ 20.
    (g) Please advise us as _____ the most suitable kind of company for this venture.
    (h) We would like to register our company _____ the name of Teddy Bears Ltd.
    (i) Our articles authorise us to convert our paid-up shares _____ stock.
    (j) The court found him liable _____ the contract.
    (k) He sold his company to Hoffmann-La Roche _____ return _____ a seat on the Board.
    (l) The documents must be sent to the Registrar _____ incorporation.
    (m) When registered, the articles of a company bind each member _____ the same extent as if each member had signed them.
    (n) He acted _____ behalf _____ his client.
    (o) She sold her house _____ a profit.

BLANK-FILLING

Complete the following paragraph on agency by putting ONE word in each space.

Agency is the relationship which arises when two parties agree that one – the agent – will _____ (1) work or services for and _____ (2) the control of the other – the principal. By entering into a principal-agent relationship, a principal _____ (3) the agent to act _____ (4) his or her behalf, by _____ (5) negotiations, by entering into _____ (6), and buying and selling goods and property. In such business, the agent may legally _____ (7) the principal, and the latter becomes _____ (8) to third parties involved, just as _____ (9) the principal had himself been engaged in the _____ (10).

CROSSWORD FOUR

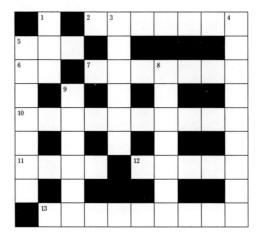

Across

2. Member of a law firm.
5. Cash on delivery.
6. either ... _____.
7. *Salomon v Salomon* is a
   _____ case.
10. Agents work on behalf of their
    _____.
11. Everything and everybody is called by a
    _____.
12. The Registrar will _____ a
    certificate of incorporation.
13. These people launch a company.

Down

1. In return _____.
3. When one person negotiates or works on
   behalf of another, their relationship is one
   of _____.
4. Books kept in the Registrar's office.
5. They formed a _____ so as to
   avoid unlimited liability.
8. Mr. Lane was keen to _____
   the cheque in the bank.
9. More resistant, stronger.

Chapter Two

THE LIFE OF A COMPANY

READING

From *The Rag Trade Press*, May 6, 1999:

PRETTYWOMAN TO GO PUBLIC?

Rumour has it that we will soon see Prettywoman listed on the Stock Exchange. For the past few years the company has been registering spectacular profits on its trading account, but it is now showing signs of outgrowing its market. Arthur Young, the chairman, is known to be keen to expand into other E.U. countries. Such an expansion would require a corresponding expansion of capital, which analysts reckon is beyond the family's means. Sources close to the company feel that at tomorrow's general meeting a resolution is likely to be passed authorising a change in the status of the company. Once it goes public, Prettywoman will be able to raise all the capital it needs.

POINTS TO REMEMBER

1. *"Prettywoman will be able to raise all the capital it needs"*
raise – raised – raised
rise – rose – risen
It is vital to learn how to use these two very important verbs correctly: *rise* is intransitive; that is, it cannot be followed by a direct object. For example:
They all rose when the judge entered the courtroom.
Inflation has risen by five per cent.
"raise" is transitive; that is, it MUST be followed by a direct object. For example:
They need to raise £2m for their expansion project.
The Government has undertaken not to raise income tax.
2. *"Prettywoman was showing signs of outgrowing its markets."*
Several verbs can be formed with the prefix "out-", which generally gives the meaning of going further, faster, longer, etc.
"outperform" "outmarch", etc. Can you think of any others?
3. *... analysts reckon ...*
The verb *reckon* used to mean "count up, calculate" but the modern derived meaning is "estimate, think".
According to my reckoning, there were 500 people at the dinner.
I reckon I'll have finished in half an hour.

4. ... *he is known to be keen to expand* ...
There is a small difference of meaning between "to be keen to do something" and "to be keen on doing something"
The former is limited to interest in performing an action just once, whereas the latter indicates a more general interest or liking. Compare:
They are keen to visit that museum.
They are keen on visiting that museum.
In which of the two sentences do we understand that they have not yet visited the museum?

EXERCISE

Add the prefix "out-" to the verbs in the following list in order to complete each sentence in an appropriate way. Be careful to use the correct tense.

perform	live	bid
sell	weigh	number
grow	wit	

1. Look at all our rivals' fans: they must _____ us by ten to one.
2. We'll never get as big a share of the market as Copo; they _____ every single other brand.
3. It is very possible that you will _____ your husband, Mrs Jones. Even so, it is highly advisable to make a will.
4. Now that I'm in my last year I'm beginning to feel that I've _____ this university mentally. I need wider horizons.
5. In Aesop's fable, the fox _____ the crow and got the grapes from it.
6. Look at Microsoft's shares: they've risen two points above the average every week this year. They're _____ all other securities.
7. Vodafone _____ Telecom Italia for the control of Deutsch Telecom.
8. What you've just said, Sonia, is very important. It _____ any other consideration raised so far.

READ AND ORDER

In order for a private company to alter its status and to become public, the procedures laid down in ss.43–48 of the Companies Act 1985 must be complied with.
Put these steps in the correct order.

(a) The Registrar of Companies will issue the company with a new certificate of incorporation.
(b) The memorandum and articles of association must be altered.
(c) A special resolution to re-register the company as a public company will be passed.
(d) An application on a form signed by a director or the secretary of the company for re-registration will be sent to the Registrar of Companies.

(e) The Registrar of Companies will examine the application to check that it has complied with all the necessary statutory requirements applicable for the re-registration of the company.

(f) A general meeting of the company will be called.

READ AND MATCH

If Prettywoman goes public, its accountants will have to become used to dealing with the different kinds of share capital listed below. Match the definitions with the types of share capital.

1. Paid-up share capital	(a) It is the part of a company's authorised share capital which has been issued to shareholders.
2. Authorised/nominal share capital	(b) It is the sum of the money which the holders of the company's shares have been asked to pay.
3. Reserve capital	(c) It is the total amount of money that has been paid to date for a company's shares.
4. Issued capital	(d) This represents the total nominal value of shares which a company is allowed to issue. It is usually set out in the company's memorandum, and can be increased or reduced.
5. Called-up share capital	(e) Some companies leave a part of their uncalled-up share capital as a fund for the payment of creditors if it should go into liquidation.

Now that you know what issued share capital and called-up share capital are, what do you think unissued and uncalled-up share capital are?

EXERCISE

Rewrite the following sentences, using the word in brackets, so that the new sentence means exactly the same as the original.

1. If the director is removed, a meeting will be convened to appoint another. (event)

2. The articles state that the material interests of directors must be disclosed. (provide for)

3. The board is empowered to remove the secretary. (conferred)

4. The shareholders have decided to re-register the company as a public company. (resolution)

5. Bill Fence has financed this venture. (backing)

6. I've been appointed to the board of directors as of May 1. (effect)

7. We knew perfectly well that the secretary had failed to notify the members. (aware)

WRITING – SENTENCE EXPANSION

Was *The Rag Trade Press* misinformed?
   Analysts have been informed by Prettywoman that it is merely interested in raising temporary finance in the form of debentures.

   Expand the following sentences so that they are both meaningful and grammatical.
1. debentures/ distinguished/ share capital/ in that/ loan/ company.

2. secured/ either/ charge/ specific assets/ or/ floating charge/ all the assets.

3. debentures/ redeemable/ irredeemable/

4. redeemable/ repayable/ specified date/ usually/ issued/ when/ the need/ finance/ temporary/ and when/ interest rates/ likely fall.

5. irredeemable/ not repayable/ until/ company/ wound up/ or/ fails/ pay/ interest due.

6. usually/ issued/ interest rates/ low/ likely/ rise.

7. although/ debentures/ carry/ no voting rights,/ interest/ must/ pay/ whether/ not/ profits.

READ AND PUT INTO CATEGORIES

The Rag Trade Press had a well-informed reporter because three months later a prospectus for Prettywoman's shares was published in the financial press.
   Prettywoman's prospectus was for ordinary shares. However, there is another common kind of share. What is it?
   Here is a list of rights usually attached to shares. Which would be attached to each class?

   (a) preferential treatment when dividends are declared.
   (b) option on rights issues.

(c)   cumulative dividend – payment of dividend can be carried forward from one year to the next.
(d)   priority in the return of their capital investment.
(e)   voting rights in general meetings.
(f)   unfixed dividends.
(g)   a fixed rate of return.
(h)   known as equity share capital.

1. Ordinary shares   2. _____ shares

A third kind of share is known as deferred. Unlike an ordinary share, it is not at all common. It gives the holder the right to participate in the residue of the distributed profit, after the payment of a dividend to the ordinary shareholders. Thus ordinary shares have preference in dividends and in liquidation over deferred shares. Consequently, if these shares exist they will in fact constitute the equity share capital of the company. If deferred shares are issued they are not called until a later date. This kind of share may often carry what are called heavy voting rights to reflect the risk attached to it and may on the liquidation of the company participate in the division of the surplus assets to a greater degree than the ordinary shareholders. Investors these days do not like deferred shares for obvious reasons, and thus it is unusual for companies to issue them nowadays.

WRITING

Now write a comparison between ordinary shares, preference shares and debentures, indicating the advantages and disadvantages of each for the investor.
Remember: (a) the language of contrast: *although, whereas, like, unlike, in contrast, on the other hand, etc.*
(b) the language of cause and result: *consequently, because, lead to, arise from, result in, etc.*

(Introduction):
Companies may raise capital by issuing shares or debentures. While both are a means of financing the company, there are some differences.
(Paragraph One):
The main advantage of ordinary shares ....
(Paragraph Two)
Preference shares, in contrast, ...
(Paragraph Three)
Debentures can be distinguished from ....
(Conclusion)
In short, the kind of investment you should choose depends on ....

DISCUSSION

Arthur and Jean Young, with 10 per cent of the equity capital each, are *members* of Prettywoman. Decide with a partner whether the following are to be considered members of their respective companies:

(a) Arthur Young inherited 10,000 shares in Boots on the death of his father.

(b) Mitsubishi bought a 1 per cent stake in M.G.M. studios on the New York Stock Exchange.

(c) Martha Wallis, Bruce Wallis' sister, acquired 20 bearer shares in Kodak this morning.

(d) Arthur Young's father-in-law is a subscriber to Hill-Lane plc, a cement company.

(e) Brian Lane owned 5,000 shares in the Bradford Banking Co Ltd, which were forfeited by a resolution of the board of directors.

(f) Jean Young made an application to GlaxoSmithKline for 8,000 shares, and, having paid 25 per cent of their nominal value, was duly allotted them.

READ AND MATCH

Membership can be acquired in the following four ways. Read the explanation and decide by which of the four ways the parties in the above exercise became members.

(1) by subscribing the memorandum when a company is registered. The founder members are the persons who sign or subscribe the memorandum of association. They are said to become members on subscription.

(2) by taking a transfer of shares from an existing member.

(3) by allotment. This is where a person makes an application for shares under a prospectus or offer for sale to the public.

(4) by transmission, which arises on the death or bankruptcy of an existing member.

POINTS TO REMEMBER

1. *One has to resort to case law for guidance.*

resort to is a general English word which means to turn to, or go to for help, often when all else has failed. It is normally followed by a noun.

2. allot / allocate

When companies make a new share issue, they allot (distribute officially) shares among the people who apply for them. Companies allocate (assign or devote) funds to their different departments – marketing, administration, etc.

3. Bearer share certificates

Instead of share certificates some public companies issue share warrants which entitle the bearers of the warrants to the shares. They can be transferred to other people by handing over the warrant without any special transfer instrument, and so they are like any negotiable instrument, such as cheques. Unless the company's articles prohibit it, the holder of a share warrant may surrender it to the company and have his shares registered in his name in the register of members, whereupon he will be issued with a share certificate to cover those shares.

READING

Directors

As we have already seen, the members of a company are entitled to vote at general meetings. One of the items on which a resolution can be passed is the appointment, removal, or maintenance of the directors in their position. Sometimes the directors too are members of a company; this depends on what is laid down in the articles of association.

By law, a public company registered in England must have at least two directors, whereas one will suffice in a private company. Apart from these stipulations, the number of directors is regulated by the articles.

An executive director of an English company is both an officer and agent of the company. The courts have imposed two basic duties upon directors; a fiduciary duty and a duty of care. Neither duty is covered in detail by statute law, and consequently one has to resort to case law for guidance.

READ AND DISCUSS

Below are two cases involving fiduciary duty, which *Black's Law Dictionary* defines as follows:

> "A duty to act for someone else's benefit, while subordinating one's personal interest to that of the other person. It is the highest standard of duty implied by the law."

Partner A read the first case and Partner B the second. Each partner should report the facts of the case to her/his partner and discuss what you think the judgment should be and why.

(A) *Industrial Development Consultants Ltd v Cooley* [1972] 2 All E.R. 162

The defendant, a well-known architect, was managing director of a company called Industrial Development Consultants, which offered a consultancy service to gas boards. IDC (Industrial Development Consultants) were very keen to do business with the Eastern Gas Board, which was about to build four gas depots. The consultancy service contract connected with this construction was worth a lot of money. The defendant negotiated the contract on behalf of IDC, but the Eastern Gas Board stated that it was unwilling to hire a firm of consultants. Thus the architect was presented with the possibility of obtaining the contract just for himself, and so he pretended to be ill. Having been informed of the defendant's illness, IDC, which was of the opinion that he was on the point of a nervous breakdown, agreed to terminate his contract of employment on very short notice. The defendant did not wait long before making moves which resulted in the Eastern Gas Board offering him the contract for the four depots. IDC sued the defendant for the profits that he would make on the consultancy work during the construction of the four depots.

(B) *Regal (Hastings) Ltd v Gulliver (1942)* [1967] 2 A.C. 134

Regal (Hastings) Ltd owned a cinema, but the directors wished to buy two more with a view to selling the company as a going concern. The Regal company formed a subsidiary so that the latter could buy the two cinemas. In order to provide the subsidiary with sufficient paid up capital to make the purchase, Regal's directors bought some of the shares in the subsidiary themselves. In this way the subsidiary company had enough funds to purchase the two cinemas. Later, the directors, instead of selling the company as planned, sold their shares in the subsidiary along with the shares they had in the parent company, Regal. The sale of their shares realised a substantial profit for them. The new owners of Regal discovered this and Regal brought an action against the former directors to recover the profit they had made on the sale of the shares.

Now turn to p.108 and read the summary decision in each case. Do they correspond to what you thought?

BLANK FILLING

Read about fiduciary duty and fill in each blank with one word.

A director must always act *bona fide* for the b_____ of a company as a whole. As seen in the judgments, a director must a_____ to the company for any profit he may make in the c_____ of his dealings with the company's property. This accountability arises from the m_____ fact that a director makes a profit from his privileged k_____ ; it is not a q_____ of loss to the company. If a director does not d_____ a profit made in such a way, it would a_____ to what is known as insider dealing, which can be a criminal o_____. Insider dealing means dealing in the s_____ of a company for the purpose of private g_____ by a person who has i_____ information about those s_____ which would affect their price if it were generally known. The insider dealing l_____ in England is very complex. The Company Securities (Insider Dealing) A_____ of 1985 does not employ the word "insider" but "individual connected with a company". T_____ the legislation is clearly directed towards directors and other employees of a company.

READING

Duty of Care

In addition to his fiduciary duties, a director also owes a duty of care to the company not to act negligently in managing its affairs.

Discuss what this duty of care may entail.

How high a standard should be upheld by the courts?

The following is a leading case on the duty of care. Read the facts of the case and give your opinion of the judgment.

Case Law: *Re City Equitable Fire Insurance Company Ltd* [1925] Ch. 407.

The chairman of City Equitable Fire Insurance Company had a substantial stake in a firm which owed a large debt to the former company. Not wishing the debt to be noticed on City Equitable's balance sheet, he committed fraud by pretending to have bought Treasury Bonds shortly before the end of the accounting period and to have sold Equitable's just after the audit. In this way, the other company's debts were reduced on City Equity's balance sheet by means of increasing the gilt-edged securities which were shown as assets. The other directors of the insurance company appear to have left the management of its business almost entirely in the hands of the chairman, and due to their lack of care he was able to commit his frauds more easily.

Held, *inter alia*

1. A director need not exhibit in the performance of his duties a greater degree of skill than may reasonably be expected from a person of his knowledge and experience.

2. A director is not bound to give continuous attention to the affairs of his company. His duties are of an intermittent nature to be performed at periodical board meetings, and at meetings of any committee of the board upon which he happens to be placed. He is not, however, bound to attend all such meetings, though he ought to attend whenever, in the circumstances, he is reasonably able to do so.

3. In respect of all duties that, having regard to the exigencies of business, and the articles of association, may properly be left to some other person, a director is, in the absence of grounds for suspicion, justified in trusting that person to perform such duties honestly.

READ AND MATCH

Re City Equitable Fire Insurance Company Ltd [1925] Ch 407 contains specific items of vocabulary connected with finance. Match the items in the left-hand column with their definitions in the right-hand column.

1. Treasury Bonds	(a) something such as a building or machinery that has value and that may be sold to pay a debt.
2. accounting period	(b) stock, especially that offered by the Government, that is considered to be safe. Although the rate of interest is small, the stock is very unlikely to fail.
3. audit	(c) a statement, which appears in the company report, of a company's financial position on a particular date.
4. balance sheet	(d) an official examination of a company's accounts, usually carried out once a year by a firm of outside accountants.
5. gilt-edged securities	(e) a piece of paper in which the Government promises to pay back with interest the money which has been invested.
6. assets	(f) another way of referring to a company's financial year.

(A) *Industrial Development Consultants Ltd v Cooley* [1972] 2 All E.R. 162

Held that the defendant had acted in breach of duty and must account to IDC for the profit made as a consequence of entering into the contract with the Gas Board.

(B) *Regal (Hastings) Ltd v Gulliver (1942)* [1967] 2 A.C. 134

Held by the House of Lords – that the former directors must account to the Regal Company for the profit because they made their profit only through the knowledge they had as directors of the company.

Case Law: *Cranleigh Precision Engineering Ltd v Bryant and Another* [1965] 1 W.L.R. 1293; *Bishopsgate Investment Management Ltd (In liquidation) v Maxwell (No.2)* [1994] 1 All E.R. 261

POINTS TO REMEMBER
1. *"A director must account ... for any profit ... "*
The phrasal verb *account for* has two meanings:
   i. explain when something comes about.
When travelling for the company make sure you get receipts for everything because you'll have to account for all your expenses.
   ii. represent.
Small domestic appliances account for 20 per cent of our product range.
2. *"his dealings with the company property."*
Deal (dealt). You deal with someone or something.
The book deals with commercial law.
Treat is used with an adverb or adverbial phrase to indicate the manner in which a subject or person is handled.
Clients should always be treated respectfully.
As you entered into the contract under undue influence, it will be treated as void.
3. *If a director does not disclose a profit ...*
Disclose means to make publicly known, and is used for abstract matters such as a secret or information.
He made a surprising disclosure about his past.

EXERCISES

1. You are probably familiar with other forms of *account*. Fill in the blanks with the correct form of *account* or an expression using *account*.

    (a)   I have just opened a savings _____ in Citibank.
    (b)   He wants some day to be a CPA (Certified Public _____), so he is now studying.

(c) A director will be held _____ for any transaction he carries out on behalf of the company.

(d) He has had to submit _____ of his expenditure.

(e) Many things must be _____ for when deciding to change the articles of a company.

2. Complete the following grid.

VERB	ABSTRACT NOUN	PERSONAL NOUN
inherit		
	application	
vote		
		accountant
	issue	
	participation	
finance		
	offence	
represent		
	liquidation	

3. Complete the following sentences by using both appropriate language and concepts.

(a) In our firm there are 5,000 male employees but only 1,000 female employees. The men out- _____

(b) If a company cannot pay the dividends on preference shares in a financial year, those dividends may be _____

(c) If a shareholder fails to pay up when called upon to do so, the other shareholders may pass a resolution to _____

(d) Debentures are distinguished from shares in _____

(e) Before registering a company as a public limited company, the Registrar ____ _____

(f) In my country the Red Cross usually raises funds by _____

(g) I know there are disadvantages in registering our company but I strongly feel we should do so. The limited liability it offers its members out- _____

(h) If we are unable to carry out our plans for expansion with the funds we have, we may have to resort _____

(i) Called-up share capital is _____

(j) If a director makes a profit in the course of his duties, he must _____

SUBSTITUTION

The Powers of Directors

Read the following paragraph and substitute each of the words in **bold** with one of the more formal words in the list below.

laid down	in this respect	convene	remove
vested in	provided	exercise	pass a resolution
disapprove of	delegate	acts in a dual capacity	provide for
alter	granted	appoint	

The directors' powers are usually **put** in the articles of association of the company. These powers are **given** to the directors and only they may **use** them. Consequently, the shareholders of the company cannot control the actions of the directors **as long as** these are within the scope of the powers **given to** them. If the shareholders **do not like** the director's actions, they may **call** a meeting to **make a decision** to **change** the articles to restrict the powers of the directors or to **get rid of** any particular director. A director may not **give** his powers to somebody else. The directors may **hire** a managing director if the articles **talk about** such an appointment. It is usual for the managing director to have a contract of employment setting out his powers and duties and terms of employment, and **like this** he **has a double role** as a director and as an employee.

WRITING

Write two paragraphs summarising first the duties and then the powers of a director of a company in England compared with those of a director in your country.

Try to include the language of contrasts seen in Part One.

1.

2.

BLANK FILLING

The company secretary

Choose the best alternative from the list to complete the following description of the appointment of a company secretary.

In _____ (1) with s.283(1) of the Companies Act 1985 every company has to have a secretary. Table A, art. 99 _____ (2) that this officer is to be _____ (3) by the company's directors on such conditions _____ (4) they consider appropriate and that the faculty to _____ (5) the secretary is to be _____ (6) in the directors. A company has to keep details at its registered office (similar _____ (7) those kept for directors) of its company secretary (s.290 of the Companies Act 1985). It also has to send details of its secretary to the Registrar of Companies who must also be _____ (8) of any change of appointment.

A _____ (9) director of a company cannot also be the company's secretary (s.283(2) of the Companies Act 1985). _____ (10), in companies with more than one director, a director may be authorised by the board to act in the place of a _____ (11) appointed secretary; the director may so act _____ (12) a function which needs the presence of both the director and secretary is not _____ (13) by one person acting as both the director and secretary.

In a public company the secretary must be a suitably qualified person, either by having _____ (14) the directors of the company regard as the necessary experience to carry out the secretary's _____ (15) or by having professionally recognised qualifications (s.286 of the Companies Act 1985).

1. (a) agreement
   (b) relation
   (c) accordance
   (d) accord

2. (a) states
   (b) lays
   (c) speaks
   (d) supplies

3. (a) asked
   (b) made
   (c) appointed
   (d) voted

4. (a) that
   (b) than
   (c) so
   (d) as

5. (a) remove
   (b) retire
   (c) resign
   (d) leave

6. (a) invested
   (b) given
   (c) vested
   (d) laid

7. (a) than
   (b) that
   (c) to
   (d) at

8. (a) noticed
   (b) notified
   (c) supplied
   (d) provided

9. (a) alone
   (b) single
   (c) sole
   (d) singular

10. (a) Therefore
    (b) Although
    (c) Because
    (d) However

11. (a) formally
    (b) formerly
    (c) former
    (d) formal

12. (a) although
    (b) in case
    (c) providing
    (d) in the event that

13. (a) carried
    (b) performed
    (c) conducted
    (d) made

14. (a) that
    (b) which
    (c) those
    (d) what

15. (a) works
    (b) functions
    (c) labours
    (d) employment

READING

The directors are required by law to draw up a balance sheet and a profit and loss account for the previous financial year, and to submit them to the annual general meeting of the company for its approval. These annual accounts must provide a "true and fair" view of the finances of the company and must be inspected by an independent firm of auditors, whose report must also be submitted to the meeting. It is normal practice for these details to be included in one document, called the company report.

The balance sheet sets out the capital and reserves of the company. It indicates the state and the use made of the shareholders' investment, and is not designed to provide an accurate idea of the company's net worth. It is drawn up as of the last day of the financial year described in the profit and loss account. The size of the company determines whether an abridged form of its assets and liabilities may be presented or whether a more complete breakdown is required.

The profit and loss account sets out the company's profits and losses during the previous financial year. As in the case of the balance sheet, it must be drawn up in accordance with a certain format. Furthermore, in both cases additional disclosures or explanations may be necessary in the form of notes to the accounts in order to fulfil the requirement that the annual accounts should provide a "true and fair" view of the company.

FILL IN THE BLANKS

The following tables show Prettywoman's balance sheet and profit and loss account for the financial year ended May 31, 2004. Complete the tables by putting in the correct name beside each missing entry. Choose your answers from the following list.

Turnover	Net assets
Shareholders' funds	Operating profit
Cash at bank and in hand	Profit and loss account
Called-up share capital	Dividends
Profit on ordinary activities before taxation	Total assets less current liabilities
Provisions for liabilities and charges	Profit for the year
Current assets	Fixed assets
	Net current assets

CONSOLIDATED PROFIT AND LOSS ACCOUNT
for the year ended May 31, 2004

	1996 £000	1995 £000
(1)	14,972	11,268
Cost of sales	(9,051)	(7,994)
Gross profit	5,921	3,274
Distribution costs	(1,456)	(1,086)
Administrative costs	(1,792)	(1,147)
(2)	2,673	1,041
Interest receivable	201	319
Interest payable	(697)	(481)
(3)	2,177	879
Taxation	(546)	(186)
Profit on ordinary activities after taxation	1,631	693
Minority equity interests	(3)	(2)
Extraordinary item	(29)	–
(4)	1,599	691
(5)	(897)	(412)
Transfer of reserves	(702)	(279)
Earnings per share	21.7p	9.2p

CONSOLIDATED BALANCE SHEET
as at May 31, 2004

	£000	£000
Tangible assets	3,012	2,922
Investments	517	584
(6)	3,529	3,506
Stocks	2,574	2,012
Debtors	1,902	1,839
(7)	2,160	1,293
(8)	6,636	5,144
Creditors – amounts falling due within one year	(3,989)	(3,107)
(9)	2,647	2,037
(10)	6,176	5,543
Creditors – amounts falling due after one year	(2,248)	(2,096)
(11)	(61)	(75)
Minority interests	(47)	(21)
(12)	3,820	3,351
Capital and reserves		
(13)	963	959
Share premium account	701	650
Revaluation account	328	325
(14)	702	279
(15)	2,694	2,213

READ AND REPORT

Meetings

Working in pairs, Partner A should read about the legal procedures of general meetings and be able to explain them to B. B should read about the different kinds of meetings and explain them to A.

A. It is necessary to consider the legal as distinct from the secretarial aspects of company meetings.

1. Quorums

In order for business to be validly transacted at a meeting, a minimum number of persons, known as a quorum, must be present. This number may be laid down in the articles, but in the absence of such a provision two members present in person, or by proxy, will constitute a quorum. In the event of single member companies one member present in person or by proxy constitutes a quorum.

2. Proxy

Every shareholder with voting rights is entitled to appoint a proxy, who has the same right as the member to speak at the meeting and to vote on a resolution on a show of hands or on a poll. Proxies need not be members of the company, but they must have attained their majority. The instrument appointing a proxy is correctly known as a proxy form, but is often referred to as a proxy.

3. Resolutions

There are three kinds of resolutions: special, extraordinary and ordinary. All three require notice served on the shareholders, and the proposed resolutions must be set out clearly in the agenda for the meeting. Sometimes the articles require a seconder for a resolution.

4. Voting

All voting must be carried out by a show of hands unless the articles otherwise provide. Each member therefore has only one vote, irrespective of the number of shares he holds. A member who holds proxies for other members may be counted once only. It is the chairman's duty to count the show of hands. Members may however demand a poll as the size of members' shareholdings is disregarded in a show of hands. It is usual for the articles to provide that on a poll each member has one vote for each share he holds. The chairman has to fix the time and place for the poll to be held.

B. There are three broad types of meeting which are attended by members of a company:

1. Annual general meeting

Section 366 of the Companies Act 1985 requires every company in each calender year to hold a general meeting as its annual general meeting. There must not be more than 15 months between meetings. Notification of the annual general meeting must be served on the members at least 21 days in advance.

The business which is usually transacted at the annual general meeting includes declaring a dividend, the consideration of the accounts, balance sheets and directors' and auditors' reports, the election of directors and the appointment and remuneration of auditors.

In fact, any other business on the agenda may also be transacted at the annual general meeting but in practice it is usual to convene an extraordinary general meeting to deal with business other than the business normally transacted at the annual general meeting.

As an exception, private companies may dispense with annual general meetings by what is called "elective resolution". This is made possible by the Companies Act 1989 and if an elective resolution is passed the election has effect for the year in which it is made and later years.

2. Extraordinary general meeting

All general meetings other than the annual general meeting are known as extraordinary general meetings and the board of directors may convene such a meeting whenever they wish by giving 14 days' advance notice.

Section 368 of the Companies Act provides that the directors must convene an extraordinary general meeting at the request of members holding not less than one tenth of the paid-up capital carrying the right to vote.

The business transacted at an extraordinary general meeting is anything other than the usual business of the annual general meeting, for example, the alteration of the articles.

3. Class Meetings

At times, a meeting of a particular class of shareholders is held and these are known as class meetings. At such a meeting, the holders of the remainder of the company shares have no right to be present.

The business transacted at this meeting is usually to consider a variation of class rights.

READ AND DECIDE

Sometimes it is not very wise to believe everything you read in newspapers. Look at the following excerpts from articles in the business press about Prettywoman and, basing your decisions on what you have just read, decide whether the reporters knew what they were talking about or not.

"A pressure group of shareholders of a rival group Uglyman p.l.c., who are aiming to destabilise Prettywoman with a view to making a hostile take-over bid, are trying to create a division in Prettywoman by seeking to present resolutions which are not on the agenda."

"The A.G.M. was called exclusively to approve the accounts of the previous financial year, ended 31 May 2004."

"The reduced turnout for Prettywoman's A.G.M. was put down to the fact that the Chairman, Arthur Young, only gave twenty-four hours' notice to the shareholders."

"The chairman of Prettywoman, Arthur Young, nearly fainted when a surprise proposal was made for his removal because he was suspected of misappropriation of the company's money, insider dealing and breach of fiduciary duty."

"A proposal was made to reject the accounts and to appoint a committee of investigation from among the shareholders to liaise with the auditors and to report back to the next shareholders' meeting."

"Shortly after the A.G.M., held in November, 2004, one of the members of the Board of Directors resigned, and Arthur Young convened a second A.G.M. so that shareholders could approve the appointment of a new director."

"An extraordinary general meeting has been called at the request of the Uglyman shareholders, who hold 20% of Prettywoman's ordinary shares."

"The preference shareholders have called a class meeting to plan their strategy for defeating a possible hostile bid by Uglyman. To the consternation of the chairman of the meeting, Uglyman shareholders were present and outnumbered the preference shareholders."

POINTS TO REMEMBER

1. *"The business transacted at the A.G.M. includes declaring a dividend ..."*
The verb *include* is a useful way to express a partial list of items, and avoid such awkward expressions as "etc." or "and so on".

2. *dispense with* is a formal phrasal verb which in a legal context often means *waive the requirement of*
The negative adjective *indispensable*, meaning *absolutely necessary*, is often used in formal English.
Bread is an indispensable part of the Western diet.
His signature to the deed is indispensable.

3. Notice the use of prepositions after the following verbs:
(a) *attend / attend to*
He was unable to attend the board meeting. (be present at)
The matter is of the utmost urgency. You will have to attend to it at once. (deal with)
(b) *approve / approve of*
The shareholders approved the accounts for the preceding year. (formally give approval)
I don't approve of the way the chairman handled the matter. (have a good opinion of)
(c) *pay / pay for*
Before I take out another loan, I must pay my outstanding debts.
(pay money, pay debts)
The company cannot afford to pay for the construction of another warehouse. (pay (money) in exchange for something)

EXERCISES

---

1. Add the correct prefix to the following words in order to make them negative:

stabilise	paid	wise
approve	partial	regard
usual	correctly	able
respective	limited	valid

2. Complete the following sentences by using a form of the word in brackets.

(a) The company was refused registration because its purposes were _____. (law)

(b) A director should never forget his _____ to the shareholders. (account)

(c) There is a special exchange for the shares of small companies, which are generally _____. (list)

(d) Some of the shareholders feel that the managing director has been _____. (neglect)

(e) The votes cast in favour of the resolution _____ the votes against by three to one. (number)

(f) He was removed from office on the grounds of _____ of company funds. (appropriate)

(g) _____ trading became an offence under the Companies' Securities Act (_____ Dealing) 1985. (side)

(h) The first step in winding up a company is the _____ of its liabilities. (charge)

(i) He paid quite a high fee for their _____ services. (consult)

(j) The tendency nowadays is for multinationals to _____ their structure. (size)

3. Rewrite the following sentences, using the word in brackets, so that the new sentence means the same as the original.

(a) Mr Wallis became a member of the company when he subscribed the memorandum. (upon)

_____

(b) Prettywoman's shares will soon get an official quotation on the London Stock Exchange. (listed)

_____

(c) The directors must convene an extraordinary general meeting when members holding not less than one-tenth of the paid-up capital ask for one. (the request)

_____

(d) All the members entitled to attend an AGM must be notified in writing at least 21 days in advance. (notice)

_____

(e) He will have to explain how he made a profit on that transaction. (account)

_____

(f) We plan to continue with the business when the partnership is dissolved. (regardless)

_____

_____

DISCUSSION

Read the two situations and decide with a partner what can or should be done. Then look at the probable outcome on p.121.

(a) You own 1.5 per cent of ABC plc's stock. You and a number of other shareholders believe that the management is paying Ms Z, the chairman's personal secretary and suspected mistress, an excessively high salary. The

117

chairman and Ms Z are known to go on "business trips" to the Bahamas and New York at the company's expense. What course of action can be taken to protect the shareholders' interests?

(b) The managing director of Ironsteels plc, an antique car company, is asked by the company to attend an auction. He is directed to bid up to, but no further than, £75,000 for a 1931 Rolls Royce. The bidding goes up to £95,000 and then the managing director buys the car for himself at £99,000. Is his action proper?

READING

Read the minutes of the 2004 annual general meeting which were duly entered in Prettywoman's minute book after the chairman had signed them. Which of the newspaper articles quoted on pp.115–116 correspond to the minutes?

PRETTYWOMAN P.L.C.

MINUTES OF THE ANNUAL GENERAL MEETING HELD ON NOVEMBER 14, 2004 AT 11 A.M. IN THE SUSSEX ROOMS, EBURY STREET, LONDON S.W.3

DIRECTORS PRESENT: A. MacDonald; D. Mitchell; L. Oldcastle; M. Stewart; J. White; A. Young; J. Young.

CHAIRMAN: Mr A. Young was elected Chairman for the purposes of the Meeting.

The following resolutions were adopted:

(1) The accounts for the financial year ended August 31, 1997 were adopted.

(2) It was agreed that the firm of Anthony Andersfield, Chartered Accountants, should perform the audit for the current financial year.

(3) The chairman's report was presented and approved.

(4) D. Mitchell stood down, and M. Goodbody was appointed in his place.

(5) It was agreed that as Prettywoman's results had been excellent, each director should receive a bonus of £20,000.

(6) A dividend of 9p per share was approved.

There being no further business to discuss, the chairman adjourned the meeting.

READING

On October 15, 2004, Bruce Wallis constituted the Home Ranch Café as a private limited company in your country. Acting upon the recommendations of the local branch of The Fried Partnership he has appointed you secretary. As Bruce Wallis does not speak your language, all the business transacted at the meeting must be reported to him in English. The date fixed for the 2007 shareholders' annual general meeting is approaching, and you have drawn up the following notice of meeting along with a proxy form to send to all the English-speaking members of the company.

THE HOME RANCH CAFE LTD

NOTICE OF MEETING

Notice is hereby given that the Annual General Meeting of the **Home Ranch Café Ltd** will be held at the Palace Hotel, Capital City on Tuesday March 17, 2007 at 11 a.m. for the following purposes:

1. to approve the balance sheet, profit and loss account, directors' and auditors' reports for the year ended October 15, 2006.
2. to re-elect Mr B. Wallis as a director.
3. to re-elect Mr H. Grint as a director.
4. to re-appoint and fix the remuneration of the retiring auditors.
5. to declare a dividend for the financial year ended October 15, 2006.
6. that subject to and in accordance with article 22 of the company's articles of association Ms Martha Wallis be removed from the office of director.
7. to transact such other business as may be properly transacted at an annual general meeting.

By order of the Board

Secretary

FORM FILLING

You are a member of the Home Ranch Café, but you cannot attend the Annual General Meeting. Fill in the proxy form as you think appropriate.

THE HOME RANCH CAFE LIMITED

Form of proxy

I

....
(*block capitals, please*)
of
....
being a member of The Home Ranch Café Ltd, hereby appoint the chairman of the meeting or
.... of
....
as my proxy to vote in my name and on my behalf at the second annual general meeting of the company to be held on the seventeenth day of March next or at any adjournment thereof. I desire my proxy to vote on the resolutions proposed to be submitted as follows:

Ordinary Resolutions

Resolution One (Directors' reports and auditors' accounts)	FOR/AGAINST
Resolution Two (Re-election of Mr B. Wallis)	FOR/AGAINST
Resolution Three (Re-election of Mr H. Grint)	FOR/AGAINST
Resolution Four (Re-appointment of auditors)	FOR/AGAINST
Resolution Five (Approval of dividend)	FOR/AGAINST
Resolution Six (Removal of Ms Wallis)	FOR/AGAINST

Please delete FOR or AGAINST as the case may be. In default of instruction the proxy will vote or abstain at his discretion.

Dated this   day of   two thousand and seven.
Title

....

Please use block capitals
Name

....

First names

....

Address

....

No. of shares held

....

Usual signature ....

WRITING

Bruce Wallis was able to go to the meeting and consequently did not use the proxy form. However, your job is not yet finished. You have to prepare the minutes of the meeting in English for all the English-speaking shareholders. Base your work on the Prettywoman minutes. If you are aware of any differences in the way minutes are written in your own country, you should adapt them accordingly. (*Note*: Martha Wallis was not removed)

EXERCISE

Complete the following phrasal verbs with a suitable word.

1. The objects clause sets _____ the activities a company can undertake.
2. Although it is a small company, he takes _____ well over $5,000 a month.
3. He fears his house may be repossessed as his debts are mounting _____ .

4. The procedure for converting a private company into a public one is laid _____ in the Companies Act.
5. Less than 4 per cent of the shareholders turned _____ for the meeting.
6. Things went badly last year but now the business finally appears to be taking _____ .
7. We hope to take _____ several new workers for the summer.
8. We lost quite a bit of money in the first quarter, but we hope to break _____ this quarter.
9. Office supplies account _____ 25 per cent of our sales.
10. The board has decided to dispense _____ your services.

ANSWER TO DISCUSSION ON PAGES 117–118

(a) Your objections to Ms Z's salary are only based on hearsay. Your first step should be to take the matter up with the board of directors. At the same time you could request the holding of an extraordinary general meeting to consider the situation. If improper payments are in fact discovered, the company may be able to sue, and the directors may force the chairman to account for the misappropriation of funds.

(b) The managing director has probably not acted in breach of duty, as he was not authorised to exceed £75,000. Had he bought it for less and for himself he would have been in breach. If he had purchased the car for the company at a higher price, he would have exceeded his authority, and the company might either have called for him to make up the difference, or merely reprimand him. So he was implicitly authorised to buy the car for himself.

Case Law: *Foss v Harbottle* [1843] 2 Hare 43

PUT IN ORDER

The words and phrases in bold are in the wrong place in the paragraph. Put each in its correct place in the text so as to make a coherent paragraph.

The Annual return

When **its officers** have been approved by **the Registrar of Companies** at the A.G.M., they must be annexed, along with the directors' and auditors' report, to **the shareholders**, which must be filed with **the members**. The return must also include details about the directors and members of the company and particulars about **a criminal offence**. Failure to comply with **incorporation** is **the share capital** and the company in default and each of **the annual return** become liable to **the annual accounts**. The law requires the public to have access to information on **the requirements**, officers and finances of each company granted the privilege of **a fine**.

CROSSWORD FIVE

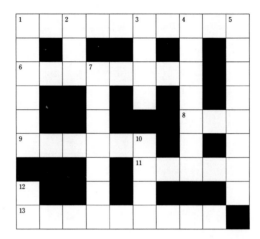

Across

1. A person in charge of the accounts of a company.
6. Ordinarily shareholders are _____ to vote at general meetings.
8. Excessively.
9. The positive side of the balance sheet.
11. The case was one of _____ influence, because of the defendant's position.
13. These securities are very safe. (4–5).

Down

1. The list of items that are to be discussed at a meeting.
2. To trim or reduce.
3. _____ and void.
4. The accounts of the company have been _____ this year.
5. The income from the sales a company makes.
7. The beneficiaries of a will _____ the testator's estate.
10. The company _____ the managing director for breach of duty.
12. For example, in Latin.

CHAPTER THREE

THE DEATH OF A COMPANY

READING

This article appeared in *The Rag Trade Press* for January 19, 2005.

UGLYMAN TO WIN PRETTYWOMAN?

The fate of Prettywoman plc will be decided at tomorrow's Extraordinary General Meeting, called at the request of Uglyman, which controls 20 per cent of Prettywoman's ordinary shares. John McLeary, chairman of Uglyman, is confident that the offer of 145 pence per ordinary share will be accepted by Prettywoman's shareholders, but Arthur Young, founder and chairman of Prettywoman, is known to be totally against the takeover. He feels that the company's results for last year more than justify a rejection of the bid, and plans further expansion. So tomorrow's Meeting is expected to produce a lot of sparks from both sides.

POINTS TO REMEMBER

1. *Arthur is known to be totally against the takeover.*
Notice this personalized impersonal passive, frequently found in formal, and not-so-formal English. Another way of saying this would be:
It is known that Arthur Young is totally against the takeover.
Look at similar examples using different tenses:
The two sides are said to have reached agreement.
The earthquake is thought to have killed two thousand people.
The defendant was held to have acted negligently.
What other example can you find in the text?
2. *A takeover bid.* Here the word *bid* means *offer* and comes from the world of auctions. The irregular verb has various forms, but when it means *offer* it is conjugated *bid, bid, bid.* It is used in similar ways to the verb *offer.*
£500,000 was bid for that house.
They were bid £500,000 for their house.
3. *Fate* has a similar meaning to *destiny* but is not to be confused with *destination* (the final point of a journey)
The port of destination of the goods is Singapore.
Nobody knows what destiny has in store for them.

READING

Uglyman's takeover bid was turned down by Prettywoman's shareholders, but six months later they received the following letter.

𝔙𝔘𝔏𝔗𝔘𝔕ℜℰ 𝔭𝔩𝔠

This is an important document and needs your immediate attention.

February 14, 2005

Dear Shareholder,

You probably know that your company, Prettywoman plc, is badly in need of a face-lift, which can only be supplied with the financial backing of a much larger group.

Vulture plc can supply that backing and make Prettywoman smile again. You, Prettywoman's shareholders, will also smile when you hear that we are offering 375 pence per ordinary share.

This is an unbeatable offer that you will find very difficult to reject. Have you honestly any good reasons for rejecting it? So don't hesitate: send in your acceptance right away and put a smile on your own – and Prettywoman's – faces.

Yours sincerely,

Henry Pecker
Chairman

One month later, the shareholders received the following letter.

PRETTYWOMAN PLC

This document is important and requires your immediate attention. Before taking any action it is recommended that you seek financial advice from your stockbroker, bank manager, solicitor, accountant or other professional adviser. If you have sold or no longer hold any shares in Prettywoman plc, please send this document to the stockbroker through whom the sale was effected for transmission to the purchaser or transferee.

March 10, 2005

Dear Shareholder,

A bone to pick?

The letter which you have recently received from Vulture plc is worth your careful attention.

Nothing can conceal the fact that Prettywoman plc is at a critical point in its development: we either sink or swim, with the support of Vulture plc.

All this may seem confusing to you because at the extraordinary general meeting held to consider the Uglyman offer, I argued vigorously against acceptance. This was because I genuinely felt, and still feel, that Prettywoman was worth far more than the paltry 145 pence per share that was offered by Uglyman.

However, my stance on the present bid differs considerably. First of all, Vulture has given guarantees that the future of Prettywoman is assured, and, secondly, the bid is, in my view, one that is extremely difficult to reject.

So it has come as a surprise to me to learn that, four weeks into the bid, Vulture has received acceptances covering only 0.8 per cent of Prettywoman's shares, a lower percentage at this stage than for the Uglyman bid.

You still have two weeks in which to make up your minds. Consider carefully: do you honestly think you will receive a better offer than 375 pence per share?

Perhaps I really shall have a bone to pick with you in the future.

Yours sincerely,

Arthur Young
Chairman

READ AND DISCUSS

Vulture's bid was accepted by the majority of Prettywoman's shareholders. Which company became the purchaser and which the vendor?

Look at the following list of some of the steps to be taken by both companies' lawyers in order to effect a legal takeover. Which steps need to be taken by the purchaser's lawyers, which by the vendor's, and which steps need to be taken by both?

(a) Ensure that all necessary information about the company has been obtained.
(b) Draft the acquisition agreement.
(c) Carry out the re-organisation of the share capital.
(d) Hand over the share transfers and other relevant certificates.
(e) Hand over the resignation documents of the directors, secretary and auditors.
(f) Hand over the seal and statutory books of the company.
(g) Hand over banker's draft or cheque for the purchase price of the company.
(h) Hand over certificates of allotment of the shares or other securities which may be offered as consideration.
(i) Prepare all the necessary forms to be filed with the Registrar of Companies.
(j) Prepare press announcements.

READING

A short article appeared in *Money and Finance* for October 11, 2005.

VULTURE FINDS MEAGRE PICKINGS

Doubts have been cast on the wisdom of the recent acquisition of Prettywoman plc by the well-known holding company Vulture plc. It appears that the price paid by Vulture – 375 pence per ordinary share – grossly overestimated the market value of Prettywoman's assets. Michael Hawkesworth, financial director of Vulture, has already tendered his resignation and the company's accountants, Cruncher and Chewer, have been asked to submit a full report. Meanwhile, Arthur Young, former chairman of Prettywoman, is being accused by the accountants of feeding them false and misleading financial data, thus contributing to the inflated share price.

DISCUSSION

Two interesting legal problems can be found in the events reported in the preceding article. Read the problems and discuss with a partner what the legal consequences, if any, would be in your country.

1. It appears that the accountants, Cruncher and Chewer, have miscalculated the value of Prettywoman plc. Can they be held liable if Vulture takes them to court?
2. All indications are that Arthur Young did inflate the value of the assets for his own benefit as a major shareholder. What can Vulture do about it and what bearing would it have on the accountants' position?

Then turn to p.130 to find out what the likely outcome would be in England.

EXERCISES

1. Vocabulary. Are the following pairs of words true opposites? Explain the differences if you think they are not.

closure	disclosure
doubtful	doubtless
appear	disappear
security	insecurity
appoint	disappoint
relevant	irrelevant
respect	disrespect
action	inaction

2. Rewrite the following sentences in a style suitable for legal documents, using the word given in brackets.

(a) If you don't tell the proxy what to do, he will vote or not as he thinks best. (default)

(b) If the meeting is put off to another day, the proxy vote will still be valid. (adjournment)

(c) Because of the court case, the director has offered to resign. (resignation)

(d) If I were you, I'd try to get advice. (recommended)

(e) You must contact the solicitor who made the sale. (whom)

3. With a partner, orally comment on each of the following situations using reject/ rejection, refuse/refusal or deny/denial.

    (a) The board of directors accused Arthur Young of failing to disclose a profit he made using information he had obtained in the course of his duties as managing director. Mr. Young said that it was not true.
    (b) Uglyman plc's attractive offer to Prettywoman's shareholders was turned down.
    (c) Although the board of directors has recommended the implementation of a downsizing scheme, the managing director has stated that he will not, under any terms, implement such a policy.

READING

Read the following letter from Bruce Wallis' U.S. attorney

The Fried Partnership
Mr William J. Gehert   *Attorneys-at-Law*
1575 Beverley Hills Avenue   *2102 Long Beach*
                                                 CA 2100

June 22, 2007

Dear Mr Gehert,

As was painfully obvious at the last annual general meeting, there is considerable dissension within the company as to the best policy to adopt regarding the company's position in Europe.

You will be well aware that we have subsidiary companies in four European countries, namely Britain, France, Germany and Holland, with five Cafés in Britain (London, Manchester, Birmingham, Edinburgh and Cardiff), two each in France (Paris and Orleans), Germany (Frankfurt and Hamburg) and one in Spain (Marbella). You will also be aware that these companies are not doing as well as initially expected.

The interim results for the six months ended April 15, 2002 have just become available, and show that the company's subsidiaries in Europe, especially in Britain and France, are in a precarious financial position. Given the seriousness of the situation, Mr Wallis has instructed me to write to all the shareholders to inform them of the company's crisis.

This letter does not constitute formal notice of the liquidation. Its aim is merely to give all shareholders ample time to reflect and to come to a decision regarding the subsidiaries in Europe. An extraordinary general meeting will shortly be called to reach a decision on this, and you will be hearing from the company.

Sincerely yours,

Tom Ford,
Attorney-at-Law

TEXT COMPLETION

Choose the best alternative to complete the following passage:

> When a company is in danger of *failing/breaking/going bankrupt*, an insolvency practitioner may be appointed by the company itself or by a *creditor/debtor/supplier*. To *jeopardise/save/safeguard* the general public by *ensuring/assuring/insuring* that the people who take *on/in/over* companies as insolvency practitioners are *suitably/enough/fairly* qualified, the Insolvency Act 1986 *ensures/provides/enacts* that they must be members of a recognised professional *society/corporation/body* and be *authorised/let/stipulated* by the *laws/rules/commandments* of that *society/ corporation/body*. Frequently insolvency practitioners are members of the Institute of Chartered Accountants in England and Wales, but whatever the body, it must have *got/obtained/applied* the recognition of the Department of Trade and Industry.

READ AND MATCH

The three most important kinds of insolvency practitioners are liquidators, administrators and administrative receivers. The following three paragraphs describe the duties and position of each. Name the insolvency practitioner in each case.

1. The person may either be appointed by ordinary resolution of the members of a company, commonly known as a members' voluntary winding-up, or by a court order in compulsory liquidation. He is not a general agent, but can continue the business for the sole purpose of winding it up to the best advantage of all concerned. His duties are to realise the company's assets in order to distribute the remaining assets to satisfy the company's creditors and pay himself and the company's creditors in a fixed order of priority.
2. This kind of insolvency practitioner must be appointed by a court order following a petition either by the members of a company, the directors or a creditor. He is an agent of the company, and once his appointment has been made by court order the company cannot be put into liquidation. He has wide powers to deal with assets which are subject to a charge. These powers enable him to find purchasers for those assets as part of a rescue package for the company. The principle duty of this insolvency practitioner is to prepare a plan for the implementation of an administration order, and he has three months in which to do this, unless the period is extended by the court.

3. Banks often appoint this sort of insolvency practitioner when a company is unable to pay back its overdraft. He is normally appointed out of court and is an agent of the company, but is personally liable on any new contracts he enters into on behalf of the company. His duty consists of taking income from the business itself or from the sale of assets in order to pay his own fees, and the preferential creditors in a fixed order, and then the secured creditor who appointed him.

Discuss who are the counterparts of these insolvency practitioners in your country.

WRITING

This is the outline of a letter from Rupert Blake to Mr Gehert announcing the imminent winding-up of the Home Ranch Café's English subsidiary.

Expand the following sentences so that they are both meaningful and grammatical.

Mr William J. Gehert
1575 Beverley Hills Avenue
C.A. 28000
USA

The Fried Partnership
25 Charing Cross Road
London

16th October, 2007

Dear Mr Gehert,

regret / inform you / that / 10th October / administrative receiver / appoint / Home Ranch Café Ltd.
this / due/ company's inability / pay / debenture / called for / bank. People's Bank/ empowered / under / terms / debenture / appoint / receiver / non-compliance / demand for payment.
unfortunately / company's financial position / show / impossible / continue trading. probable liquidator / called in / wind up / company. doubtful whether / surplus assets / remain / distribute / members of the company.
I / very pleased / answer / questions / regarding / matter. Please feel free / contact / any time.

Yours sincerely,

Rupert Blake

READING

Read the following case and then answer the questions.

Griffiths v Secretary of State for Social Services [1973] 3 All E.R. 1184

A part-time administrative receiver was appointed out of court to a company by its debenture holders when it defaulted on its interest payments. The plaintiff was the managing director of the company and, as he had a service agreement, was thus treated as one of the company's employees. The plaintiff did not resign immediately but waited until four weeks after the appointment of the administrative receiver before he tendered his resignation. The issue in dispute concerned the plaintiff's national insurance position, as it was not clear whether his contract of employment ended when the administrative receiver was appointed or when he in fact resigned. The Court of Appeal held that the plaintiff had been employed until the company had accepted his resignation. Contracts of employment continue despite the out-of-court appointment of an administrative receiver. However, there are three cases where an employee's contract may be terminated: firstly, if the employee's function is incompatible with that of the administrative receiver; secondly, if the company is sold at the same moment as the appointment, and thirdly, if the administrative receiver enters into a new contract of employment with the employee.

Now decide whether the following statements are true or false. If they are false, write the correct statement in the space provided.

1. The company made a mistake when calculating its interest payments.

2. Mr Griffiths handed in a letter of resignation four weeks before the administrative receiver was appointed.

3. The court held that the administrative receiver's appointment resulted in the termination of Mr Griffiths' contract.

4. In some cases the appointment of an administrative receiver can lead to the termination of employees' contracts.

5. An administrative receiver has the power to enter into new contracts of employment.

ANSWER TO DISCUSSION ON PAGE 126

1. The accountants are under a duty to act honestly and to exercise reasonable skill, care and caution. As long ago as 1896, the High Court said that an auditor is "a watchdog but not a bloodhound", and that an auditor is not bound to be a detective. A valuation of shares is not an easy task for any accountant, and there are many factors involved. If there has been a gross miscalculation of the assets, then it would seem that the accountants may have acted negligently. Whether or not they would be held liable by the court would depend upon all the circumstances.
2. The members of Vulture may call an Extraordinary General Meeting to force the company to take proceedings for negligence against Cruncher and Chewer. However, the accountants when carrying out an audit have to rely upon officers of the company to provide them with accurate financial information. So long as the information appears to be *bona fide* the accountants can be expected to rely on it. Assuming it can be shown that Arthur Young did mislead the accountants, this would effectively let them off the hook, and Vulture, on behalf of its members, would look to Arthur Young to recover damages.

DISCUSS AND PUT IN ORDER

The following is a list of the people the liquidator has to pay when he realises a company's assets in the course of winding up a company.

What do you think the order of precedence would be?

(a) preferential debts – including employees' taxes and national insurance (social security) contributions, VAT (Value Added Tax) and Corporation Tax, wages and salaries, contributions to state pension schemes.
(b) members of the company according to their rights at winding-up.
(c) ordinary unsecured creditors.
(d) his own fees and expenses.
(e) holders of floating charges.
(f) interest on debts since the date the winding-up process commenced.

Is this order similar in your country?

POINTS TO REMEMBER

1. *A company is unable to repay its overdraft.*

over- and *under-* are frequently used as prefixes. As they imply, *over-* normally has the meaning of *too much*, and *under-* that of *too little*.

There are delays in the High Court because it is understaffed.

In some cases, however, these prefixes give the root words a completely new meaning, for example, *undertake*. Can you think of other words like this beginning with *over* or *under*?

2. *He tendered his resignation.*

We saw in the section on contracts that *to tender* means *to make a formal offer* to furnish goods or services.

That firm tendered for the construction of the new bridge.

It can also be used with *resignation* with the same meaning of *offer*.

3. *It defaulted on its interest payments.*

To *default* means to fail to pay, and is used widely in banking and business circles. The expression *to be in default* is also commonly used.

He was in default on the payment of the invoice.

Many defaults by debtor countries would spell ruin for the creditor nations.

4. The *interim* results ...

Under the Companies Act 1985 the directors must present to the members at the annual general meeting copies of the company's annual accounts for the previous financial year, the directors' report and the auditors' report on the accounts. English companies often circulate financial statements to shareholders on a quarterly or six-monthly basis to inform them of the company's progress and these are known as *interim results*.

The *interim dividend* is a payment on account of the dividend for the year as a whole, and will depend on the company's profit progress. Thus it is a partial distribution in advance of the company's profits.

EXERCISES

1. Prefixes "over" and "under"
(a) Put "over" or "under" before the following words. Which words can be preceded by both prefixes? Indicate the cases where the new word takes on a completely different meaning.

night	all	go	subscribed
draft	due	take	hear
charge	seas	graduate	ride
valued	throw	write	age
rule	power	lying	state

(b) Complete the following sentences with the correct form of one of the words in the above list.

    (i) That share issue was _____ and the company has to allot the shares on a first-come-first-served basis.

    (ii) Society in general disapproves of young people drinking too much. There are laws to discourage _____ drinking.

    (iii) The stockmarket is greatly _____ at present. I fear there may be a crash similar to Black Monday's.

    (iv) The interest payment on the debenture was _____, so the bank called in a receiver.

    (v) One of the _____ causes of the slowness of the civil process is the lack of an arbitration service.

    (vi) The Government has _____ a major revision of the Health Service.

2. Complete the following sentences so as to make them correct both legally and grammatically. You may have to consult the previous chapter.

    (i) As a managing director is both a director and an employee, he acts _____
_____

    (ii) The powers of a director cannot _____
_____

    (iii) The company report normally _____
_____

    (iv) The company's profits and losses are set _____
_____

    (v) A minimum number of persons, known as a quorum, must be present at a meeting in order _____
_____

    (vi) If the company wants to conduct other business than that normally on the agenda at annual general meetings, it can _____
_____

    (vii) When a company receives a hostile takeover bid, its shareholders often receive a letter from the board urging _____
_____

    (viii) The shareholders of a company can accept a takeover bid either _____
_____

3. Word building.
Make abstract nouns from the following words.

receiver	appoint	insolvent	secure
member	allot	arbitrator	accept
approve	accountant	transferee	chairman

READ AND CHOOSE

Read the list of steps that must be taken in the final stages of the voluntary winding up of a company. Only four are correct; the rest are inappropriate.

(a) A meeting of the board of directors is called.
(b) An administrative receiver is appointed.
(c) A meeting of the company and its creditors is called.
(d) A rescue plan is approved by the creditors.
(e) The liquidator presents his accounts of the winding-up to the members.
(f) All the directors of the company tender their resignation.
(g) The liquidator files a copy of the accounts with the Registrar of Companies.
(h) The liquidator becomes the new chairman of the company.
(i) Three months later the company is dissolved.

DISCUSSION

Are the four steps that you have chosen from the list in the previous exercise applicable in your country, and, if so, in what circumstances?

BLANK FILLING

Complete the following text by inserting one suitable word into each blank space. The first letter of each word has been given.

The Home Ranch Café Ltd has decided to w_____ u_____ its English o_____ , as it is u_____ to satisfy its c_____ , and has serious c_____-f_____ problems. The company has presented a petition to the C_____ for an order for the a_____ of a l_____ to realise the a_____ and pay off the c_____ , any s_____ funds being d_____ among the s_____ . When the company's affairs are w_____ u_____ , the C_____ will make an order d_____ the company. The l_____ will register the order with the Registrar of Companies and the company will be r_____ from the r_____ .

CROSSWORD SIX

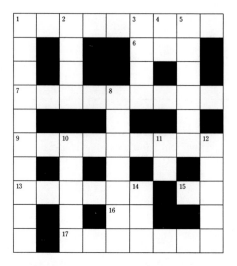

Across

1. A loan secured on the assets of a company.
6. Did you _____ to study very hard when you were at university?
7. The _____ Act, 1985.
9. Say something in an exaggerated way.
13. Not smooth, not flat.
15. I insist that my wishes _____ obeyed!
16. _____ City Equitable Fire Insurance Co Ltd [1925] Ch. 407.
17. Give evidence in court.

Down

1. The act of making a secret or documents public.
2. A period of rapid economic growth.
3. Each director in _____ gave his approval.
4. The United States.
5. The opposite of accept.
8. Replies.
10. The act of choosing a representative by means of a poll.
11. *Anno Domini.*
12. _____ step has been taken to try to rescue this company.
14. I want my computer to be linked to the Inter_____.

DESCRIPTION OF CASES

Alexander Brogden and Others v The Directors of the Metropolitan Railway Company
[1877] 2 H.L. 666

Brogden had for some years supplied the Metropolitan Railway Company with coal on an informal basis with no agreement. At last, Brogden suggested that the parties should enter into a formal contract. After their respective agents had met, the terms of agreement were drawn up by the agent representing the Metropolitan Railway Company, and sent to Brogden. Brogden filled up certain parts of the document which had been left in blank, and introduced the name of a person who was to act as an arbitrator in the case of any differences between the parties, wrote "approved" at the end, and signed it in his own name. The document was returned to the agent of the Metropolitan Railway Company, who put it in his desk, and nothing further was done in the way of a formal execution of the document by the parties. Both parties continued for some time acting in accordance with the arrangements mentioned in the document, and coal was supplied and paid for. When complaints were made of inexactness in the supply of the coal, according to the terms of the document by the Metropolitan Railway Company, excuses and explanations were given by Brogden, and a reference was made in correspondence to the "contract". Matters then continued as before until disagreements arose and Brogden denied that there was any contract binding him in the matter. HELD: by the House of Lords that these facts, and the actual conduct of the parties, established the existence of a contract, and as there had been a clear breach of it, Brogden must be held liable upon it. A contract had come into existence the moment the company ordered the first load of coal in accordance with the written terms. (*See* p.35)

Allcard v Skinner [1887] 36 Ch.D. 145

In June, 1868 the plaintiff was introduced by the Reverend D. Nihill, her spiritual director and confessor, to the defendant who was the lady superior of a Protestant institution known as "The Sisters of the Poor". This institution had been founded by the Reverend D. Nihill and the defendant, and was a voluntary association of ladies who resided together and devoted themselves to works of charity under the direction of the defendant.

The plaintiff became an associate of the sisterhood, and in 1871, having passed through the grades of postulant and novice, she became a professed member of the sisterhood and bound herself to observe, *inter alia*, the rules of poverty, chastity, and obedience, by which the sisterhood was regulated. These rules were drawn up by the Reverend D. Nihill, and were made known to the plaintiff when she became an associate.

The rule of poverty required the member to give up all her property, either to her relatives, or to the poor, or to the sisterhood itself. But, the forms in the schedule to the rule were in favour of the sisterhood, and provided that property made over to the lady superior should be held by her in trust for the general purposes of the sisterhood. The rule of obedience required the member to regard the voice of her superior as the voice of God. The rules also enjoined that no sister should seek advice of any extern without the superior's leave.

Shortly after becoming a member, the plaintiff made a will bequeathing all her property to the defendant. In 1872 and in 1874, having come into possession of considerable property, the plaintiff transferred large sums of money and shares to the defendant. In May, 1879, the plaintiff left the sisterhood and immediately revoked her will. However, she made no demand for the return of her property until 1885, when she commenced an action against the defendant claiming the return of her property on the ground that it had been made over by her while acting under the paramount and undue influence of the defendant, and without any independent and separate advice.

HELD: that although the plaintiff had voluntarily and while she had independent advice entered the sisterhood with the intention of devoting her fortune to it, yet as at the time when she made the gifts she was subject to the influence of the defendant and the Reverend D. Nihill, and to the rules of the sisterhood, she would have been entitled on leaving the sisterhood to claim the restitution of such part of the property as was still in the hands of the defendant, but not of such part as had been expended on the purposes of the sisterhood while she remained in it; however, the plaintiff's claim was barred because of her delay in bringing proceedings. (*See* p.24)

Arab Bank Ltd v Barclays Bank (Dominion, Colonial and Overseas) [1954] A.C. 495

In 1939 the appellant bank, having its registered office in Jerusalem, entered into a contract of current account with the Jerusalem branch of the respondent bank, which had its registered office in England. Palestine was British mandated territory until the mandate expired at midnight on May 14, 1948, and simultaneously with the termination of the mandate the Provisional Council of State and Provisional Government of the State of Israel were constituted. Immediately the mandate ended war broke out between Israel and the Arab States and, by reason of hostilities in Jerusalem further performance of the contract became impossible.

The respondent bank's branch had closed on the previous day and did not reopen until July, 1948. From the date of the termination of the mandate the appellant bank's premises were situated in Arab-controlled territory and the respondent bank's premises in Israeli territory.

In October, 1950, the appellant bank sued the respondent bank for repayment of the amount standing to its credit as money had and received to its use, on the ground that the contract had been frustrated by the outbreak of war. The respondent bank had paid the amount of the credit balance to the Custodian of the Property of Absentees appointed under the legislation of the State of Israel.

HELD: that the right to be paid the credit balance survived the outbreak of war, remaining in existence subject to the suspension of the appellant bank's right to recover it. Being locally situated in Israel, it became subject to the legislation of that State and vested in the Custodian of the Property of Absentees, and was not not recoverable by the appellant bank from the respondent bank. (*See* p.21)

Archbolds (Freightage) Ltd v S. Spanglett Ltd [1961] 1 Q.B. 374

The parties entered into a contract whereby the defendants agreed to carry by road 200 crates of whisky owned by a third party. The vehicle which was used had a C licence, which meant that they could carry their own goods but not the goods of others, for payment. The Road and Rail Traffic Act 1933 prohibited the use of goods vehicles on a road when carrying goods for others for reward except with an A licence. When the contract was made, the defendants knew that a vehicle with a C licence would be used but the plaintiffs had no idea. While the goods were being transported, they were stolen due to the driver's negligence, and the plaintiffs claimed damages for breach of contract and negligence. The defendants pleaded illegality.

HELD: by the Court of Appeal that the contract was *ex facie* legal, and the plaintiffs' claim for damages succeeded because they were unaware that the vehicle to be used only had a C licence.

Ashbury Railway Carriage and Iron Co v Riche [1875] L.R. 7 H.L. 653

The company purchased a concession for the construction of a railway system in Belgium and entered into a contract to finance Riche to build a railway line. The objects of the company included the manufacture and sale of railway wagons and other railway plant and carrying on the business of mechanical engineers and general contractors. Riche started the work and the company made payments in accordance with the terms of the contract. Later, the company ran into financial difficulties and the shareholders attempted to get the directors to assume liability for the company's contract in a personal capacity and to indemnify the shareholders. The directors then repudiated the contract on behalf of the company and Riche sued the company for breach of contract.

HELD: by the House of Lords, which applied a restrictive construction of the Companies Act 1862, that any matter not expressly or impliedly authorised by a company's objects clause must be taken to have been forbidden. Although the objects clause permitted the company to act as general contractors, this could not be extended to permit the company to engage in business as finance agents. (*See* p.88)

Att-Gen v Lindi St Clair (Personal Services) Ltd [1981] 2 Co. Law 69

When Miss St Clair's accountants received a letter from the Inland Revenue stating that prostitution was considered to be a trade, they advised her to register a company. After rejecting several names, the Registrar finally accepted the name of Lindi St Clair (Personal Services) Ltd, but the Attorney-General took proceedings against this decision, contending that the company should not have been registered as its objects were for sexually immoral purposes and thus against public policy.

HELD: that the company was indeed illegal and that the registration should be quashed. (*See* p.83)

Bainbridge v Firmstone [1838] Ad. & E. 743

The plaintiff, at the request of the defendant, consented to allow the defendant to weigh two boilers of great value which belonged to the plaintiff. The defendant promised that he would, within a reasonable time after the weighing was effected, return the boilers in as perfect and complete condition and fit for use as they were at the time that the plaintiff gave his consent. After weighing the boilers, the defendant took them to pieces and refused and neglected to return the two boilers to the plaintiff in their original state and condition. The plaintiff sued the defendant for damages. The defendant argued that the plaintiff had given no consideration to support the promise to return the boilers in their original state and condition. (See p.13)

Per Lord Denman C.J.:

> "It seems to me that the declaration is well enough. The defendant had some reason for wishing to weigh the boilers, and he could do so only by obtaining permission from the plaintiff, which he did obtain by promising to return them in good condition. We need not enquire what benefit he expected to derive. The plaintiff might have given or refused leave."

Per Patteson J.:

> "The consideration is, that the plaintiff, at the defendant's request, had consented to allow the defendant to weigh the boilers. I suppose the defendant thought he had some benefit; at any rate, there is a detriment to the plaintiff from his parting with the possession for even so short a time."

HELD: that the plaintiff's consent given at the defendants' request amounted to consideration and the defendants' promise was therefore binding, and the plaintiff's claim succeeded.

Balfour v Balfour [1919] 2 K.B. 571

The defendant was a colonial civil servant stationed in Ceylon (Sri Lanka). In November 1915, he returned to England on leave with his wife. In August 1916 the defendant returned alone to Ceylon because his wife's doctor had advised her that her health would not stand up to a further period of service abroad. From Ceylon the defendant wrote to his wife suggesting that they should remain living apart. The wife then took divorce proceedings and in 1918 obtained a decree nisi. In the divorce proceedings the wife alleged that the defendant, before returning to Ceylon, had agreed orally to pay her £30 each month in consideration for her agreeing not to call upon him for further maintenance. The wife sued the defendant because he failed to abide by the agreement, and she sought to enforce the agreement against him.

HELD: that there was no intention to create legal relations. It was a domestic agreement between husband and wife and the wife's claim failed, as it was not an enforceable agreement. (*See* p.17)

Bettini v Gye [1876] 1 Q.B.D. 183

The plaintiff, an Italian singer, was hired to sing in theatre and at concerts from March 30, until July 13, 1875, for the whole of the season. The contract stipulated that he should arrive six days before the commencement of the engagement in order to take part in rehearsals. The plaintiff was ill and arrived only three days before the start of the engagement and the defendant sought to terminate the contract.

HELD: that the rehearsal clause was a subsidiary part of the contract and was not a condition and that while the defendant could claim compensation for any loss he had incurred, he could not treat the contract as discharged. (*See* p.43)

Bigg and Another v Boyd Gibbins Ltd [1971] 1 W.L.R. 913

During negotiations for the proposed sale of property by the plaintiffs to the defendants the plaintiffs wrote stating: "For a quick sale I would accept £26,000 . . ." and in their reply the defendants wrote: "I accept your offer" and asked the plaintiffs to contact the defendants' solicitors. The plaintiffs wrote informing the defendants that they were placing the matter with their solicitors and that they were pleased that the defendants "are purchasing the property". On application by the plaintiffs for summary judgment Pennycuick V-C held that on the plain construction of the letters there was a concluded contract and ordered specific performance.

HELD: dismissing the appeal, that the correspondence constituted a binding contract for the sale and purchase of the property so that the plaintiffs were entitled to an order for specific performance. (*See* p.9)

Bishopsgate Investment Management Ltd (In liquidation) v Maxwell (No.2) [1994] 1 All E.R. 261

The plaintiff company brought proceedings against the defendant who was a director of the company, for breach of his fiduciary duty in signing various stock transfers whereby shares held by the company as trustee of a number of pension funds were transferred for no consideration to another company controlling his father's private interests. The defendant was also a director of that other company.

The plaintiff company's articles of association required the stock transfers to be signed by two directors, or by one director and the secretary. The transfers were not authorised by the board of directors. The defendant made no inquiry about the transactions and signed the transfers because his brother and co-director had done so.

The plaintiffs took proceedings against the defendant and obtained summary judgment against him for damages to be assessed and an order for an interim payment of £500,000. The defendant appealed against the summary judgment on the ground that the plaintiffs had failed to show that they had suffered any loss as a result of his breach of duty since they had not demonstrated that if the defendant had made proper inquiries, they would have prevented the loss. The defendant also sought leave to appeal against the order for an interim payment on the grounds, *inter alia*, that there was insufficient evidence of the damage suffered by the plaintiffs and that the judge had given insufficient consideration to the evidence that the defendant could not pay £500,000.

HELD: that the defendant was in breach of his duty because he had given away company assets for no consideration to a private family company of which he was a director. The cause of action was constituted not by the failure to make inquiries but by the improper transfer which had caused the company loss and the necessary causal connection had therefore been established. Accordingly, the appeal against the order for summary judgment was dismissed. (*See* p.108)

British Steel Corp v Cleveland Bridge and Engineering Co Ltd [1984] 1 All E.R. 504

The defendants successfully tendered for the fabrication of steel work in the construction of a building. The design required steel beams to be joined to a steel frame by means of steel nodes. The plaintiffs were iron and steel manufacturers and were approached by the defendants to produce a variety of cast-steel nodes for the project. The plaintiffs prepared an estimated price based on incomplete information and sent it to the defendants by telex on February 9, 1979. After further discussions as to the appropriate specifications and technical requirements, the defendants sent a letter of intent to the plaintiffs on February 21, which (i) recorded the defendants' intention to enter into a contract with the plaintiffs for the supply of cast-steel nodes at the prices itemised in the telex of February 9, (ii) proposed that the contract be on the defendants' standard form, which provided for unlimited liability on the part of the plaintiffs in the event of consequential loss due to late delivery, and (iii) requested the plaintiffs to commence work immediately "pending the preparation and issuing to you of the official form of sub-contract." The plaintiffs would not have agreed to the defendants' standard form of contract and intended to submit a formal quotation once they had the requisite information.

The plaintiffs did not reply to the letter of intent since they expected a formal order to follow shortly and instead they went ahead with the manufacture of the nodes. The defendants then indicated for the first time that they required delivery in a particular sequence. There were further discussions as to the proper specifications to be met in the manufacture but no final agreement was reached. The specifications were then changed extensively by the defendants after the first castings proved to be unsatisfactory.

On May 16 the plaintiffs sent the defendants a formal quotation on their standard form quoting a significantly higher price with delivery dates to be agreed. The defendants rejected the quotation and again changed the specifications. The plaintiffs went ahead with the manufacture and delivery of the nodes and eventually, at a meeting between the parties on August 1, they reached provisional agreement on the basis of the quotation given on May 16, but they were unable to agree on other contract terms such as progress payments and liability for loss arising from late delivery. By December 28 all but one of the nodes had been delivered, delivery of the remaining node being held up until April 11, 1980 due to an industrial dispute at the plaintiff's plant. The defendants refused to make any interim or final payment for the nodes and instead sent a written claim to the plaintiffs for damages for late delivery or delivery of the nodes out of sequence. The amount claimed far exceeded the quoted price. The plaintiffs thereupon sued for the value of the nodes on a *quantum meruit*, contending, *inter alia*, that no binding contract had been entered into. The defendants counterclaimed for damages for breach of contract for late delivery and delivery out of sequence, and claimed a right of set-off, contending, *inter alia*, that a binding contract had been created by the various documents, especially the letter of intent, and by the plaintiffs' conduct with the manufacture of the nodes.

HELD: that a contract could come into existence following a letter of intent, either by the letter forming the basis of an ordinary executory contract, under which each party assumed reciprocal obligations to the other, or under a unilateral contract (*i.e.* an "if" contract), whereby the letter amounted to a standing offer which would result in a binding contract if acted on by the offeree before it lapsed or was validly withdrawn. On the facts an executory contract had not been created by the plaintiffs acceding to the defendants' request in the letter of intent that they begin work on the nodes pending the issue of a formal sub-contract, since at that stage the parties were still negotiating over material contractual terms such as price and delivery dates and it was therefore impossible to say what those terms were. Accordingly, the plaintiffs were entitled to succeed on their claim and the defendants failed in their counterclaim and set-off. (*See* p.9)

Carlill v Carbolic Smoke Ball Co [1893] 1 Q.B. 256

The defendants were the proprietors of a medical preparation called "The Carbolic Smoke Ball", which was intended to protect the consumer against influenza. The defendants issued an advertisement in a newspaper in which they offered to pay £100 to anyone who contracted 'flu after having used one of their smoke balls in a specified manner and for a specified period. They also stated that they had deposited £1,000 with a bank as a sign of their good faith. The plaintiff read the advertisement and purchased a Carbolic Smoke Ball. She used it following the instructions for two weeks but caught 'flu.

The plaintiff brought an action to recover the sum of £100 offered in the advertisement by the defendants.

HELD: that the advertisement was an offer to the whole world, and by analogy with reward cases, it was possible to make such an offer. Using the inhalant three times a day for two weeks was sufficient consideration. The facts established a contract by the defendants to pay the plaintiff £100 in the event which had happened. (*See* pp.9, 31)

Cehave NV v Bremer Handelsgesellschaft mbH The Hansa Nord [1976] 1 Q.B. 44

By contract of sale in September 1970, German sellers agreed to sell to Dutch buyers 12,000 tons of U.S. citrus pulp pellets c.i.f. Rotterdam for use as animal feed. The contract incorporated the trade association term "shipment to be made in good condition". Following the buyers' payment of the price of £100,000 and receipt of the shipping documents, a shipment on the *Hansa Nord* with 1,260 tons of pellets in no.1 hold and 2,053 tons in no.2 hold, arrived in Rotterdam on May 21, 1971, by which time the market price of citrus pulp pellets had fallen. On May 22 discharge of the pellets commenced. Much of the cargo in No. 1 hold was found to be damaged, while the goods in no.2 hold were in substantially good condition. On May 24 the buyers rejected the whole cargo from both holds and claimed repayment of the price on the ground that the shipment was not made in good condition. The sellers rejected this claim. The entire cargo was sold to an importer on June 2 for £30,000, and the importer on the same day resold it to the buyers for the same sum. The buyers then used the entire cargo to manufacture cattle food by using smaller percentages in their compound feeds than would be normal with sound goods.

HELD: by the Court of Appeal that the term "shipment to be made in good condition" was not a condition any breach of which entitled the buyers to reject the goods, but an intermediate stipulation which gave no right to reject unless the breach went to the root of the contract; that since the whole cargo was used for its intended purpose as animal feed, the breach did not go to the root of the contract and the buyers, though entitled to damages, were not entitled to reject. (*See* p.42)

Re City Equitable Fire Insurance Co Ltd [1925] Ch. 407

Fraud was committed by the chairman of the company because he purported to buy Treasury Bonds just before the end of the company's accounting period and sold them shortly after the audit. The chairman had an interest in another company which was a debtor of City Equitable, and by the purchase of Treasury Bonds this debt was considerably reduced on the balance sheet as there was an increase in the number of gilt-edged securities shown as assets.

HELD: that the auditors were not liable as this was only one item in a very large audit. In the *obiter dicta* the judge laid down the duties of care and skill of directors, because it appeared that in this case the other directors had left the running of the company almost entirely to the chairman, who was thus able to perpetrate his frauds more easily. The judge explained the extent of a director's duty of skill and care in the following way:

1. A director need not exhibit in the performance of his duties a greater degree of skill than may reasonably be expected from a person of his knowledge and experience.
2. A director is not bound to give continuous attention to the affairs of his company. His duties are of an intermittent nature to be performed at periodical board

meetings, and at meetings of any committee of the board upon which he happens to be placed. He is not, however, bound to attend all such meetings, though he ought to attend whenever, in the circumstances, he is reasonably able to do so.

3. In respect of all duties that, having regard to the exigencies of business, and the articles of association, may properly be left to some other official, a director is, in the absence of grounds for suspicion, justified in trusting that official to perform such duties honestly. (*See* pp.106, 107)

Clarion Ltd v National Provident Institution [2000] 2 All E.R. 265

The plaintiff, Clarion Ltd (C. Ltd) was a company providing management services. It advised trustees of various pension schemes to invest in a particular policy issued by the defendant NPI. Under the terms of this policy, investors were permitted to switch their investments from units in one fund to units in another fund. C. Ltd, which had an agency with NPI for the introduction of business, alleged that it had reached an agreement with the latter for a special block switching arrangement, applying a system of historic pricing to the switching of investments. Such a system was more commercially advantageous to C. Ltd and the trustees, than forward pricing, which was the method NPI claimed was its standard practice in relation to switching. C. Ltd and the trustees brought proceedings against NPI alleging that NPI had wrongfully terminated the agreement. NPI denied the existence of such an agreement, but alternatively contended that it believed it was only entering into an administrative arrangement and that it had not appreciated that the agreement could or would be used to enable C. Ltd to exercise its switching opportunities with the benefit of historic pricing. NPI therefore contended that it was entitled to avoid and rescind the contract in equity on the grounds of mistake going to the subject matter of the agreement.

HELD: that save for those special cases where equity might be prepared to relieve a party from an unconscionable bargain, it was ordinarily no part of the function of equity to allow a party to escape from a bad bargain. The jurisdiction of equity did not therefore extend to relieving a party from his contract when the nature of the mistake went not to the contract's subject matter or terms, but only to its commercial consequences and effect. In this case the alleged mistake did not relate to the terms of the contract but merely to its potential for commercial exploitation. This could not be characterised as a mistake relating to the subject matter of the contract. Accordingly, NPI was not entitled to rescind the alleged agreement on the grounds of mistake. (*See* p.23)

Cranleigh Precision Engineering Ltd v Bryant [1965] 1 W.L.R. 1293

The defendant had been the managing director of the plaintiff company for some years, and was an inventor of considerable ability. The company manufactured an above-ground swimming pool with two unique features, invented by the defendant.

On December 3, 1962, heads of agreement were drawn up whereby, *inter alia*, the defendant was to transfer to the company all patents, and registered designs and any such applications in connection with goods manufactured and sold by the company, subject to the payment of a royalty to the defendant of one-half per cent, and the defendant and the company were to enter into a service agreement, whereby the defendant would be appointed managing director at a salary of £1,250 per annum and was to agree that all inventions or patents he might make or obtain should belong to the company.

In March 1962, the plaintiff's patent agents informed the defendant on behalf of the plaintiffs, of a rival patent known as the Bischoff patent, relating to a similar swimming pool to the one marketed by the plaintiffs, although lacking the two unique features. The defendant never disclosed this information to his other directors.

In August 1963, the defendant gave notice terminating his employment with the plaintiffs. Thereafter, he transferred his services to another company belonging to his own family. While still employed by the plaintiffs, the defendant had introduced the manufacture of the swimming pool to his own company, and had also diverted an order for one of their pools from the plaintiffs to his family company. In October, 1963, he obtained an assignment of the Bischoff patent.

The plaintiffs brought an action for, *inter alia*, injunctions to restrain the defendant and his family company from making use of or disclosing information regarding the plaintiffs' swimming pools, and damages for the defendant's breach of duty as managing director. HELD: that the knowledge concerning the two unique features of the plaintiffs' swimming pools was a trade secret and confidential; that the defendant had acquired that knowledge as the plaintiffs' managing director and in confidence; and that, having sought to use it, since he left the plaintiffs to his own advantage, he was in breach of his duty of confidence and therefore, both he and his family company should be restrained from taking advantage of that breach; that the defendant was in breach of his duty in concealing the existence of the Bischoff patent and in breach of confidence in making use of the information to his family company's advantage. (*See* p.108)

Craven-Ellis v Canons Ltd [1936] 2 K.B. 403

The plaintiff was appointed managing director of the defendant company by a contract in writing and under the company's seal, by a resolution of the board of directors. The articles of association imposed a share qualification on the directors, none of whom ever obtained it. The plaintiff sued for his salary under the contract, and, alternatively, for reasonable remuneration on a *quantum meruit* basis, for work carried out in quasi-contract.

HELD: that the plaintiff's claim on the contract failed, because under the articles of association his appointment could not be valid due to his failure to take up his qualification shares. Moreover the contract was invalid as none of the signatories had obtained the necessary share qualification to enable them to act as directors. His claim in quasi-contract succeeded, as he had performed services for the company at its request. (*See* p.10)

Currie and Others v Misa [1875] L.R. 10 Ex. 153

An action was brought by the plaintiffs, who were bankers carrying on business in London under the firm name of Glyn, Mills, Currie & Co, against the defendant who was a wholesale wine merchant carrying on business in London and in Jerez, Spain, to recover the sum of £1,999 3s. and interest thereon in respect of a cheque issued by the defendant and dishonoured by him.

On February 14, 1873, the defendant issued his cheque for the payment of the amount in question directed to Messrs Barnetts, Hoares, Hanburys, & Lloyd, bankers, requiring them to pay the amount to F. de Lizardi & Co or bearer. The plaintiffs became the bearers of the cheque which was duly presented for payment and was dishonoured. The defendant was given notice of the dishonour, but did not pay the amount of the cheque.

Inter alia, the defendant denied that the plaintiffs had become the bearers of the cheque, and argued that there was never any consideration for the making or the payment of the cheque, and that F. de Lizardi & Co merely delivered the cheque to the plaintiffs to hold as the agents of and on account of F. de Lizardi & Co and not as the bearers or transferees thereof; that when the cheque was presented for payment to the defendant and dishonoured by him, the plaintiffs had notice that there never was any consideration for the making or the payment of the cheque by the defendant, and the plaintiffs became the bearers of the cheque and held it without having given any consideration for it; that the defendant was induced to draw the cheque and to deliver it to F. de Lizardi & Co by the fraud of F. de Lizardi & Co, and that the plaintiffs were the bearers of the cheque and held it without giving any consideration for it.

HELD: that the title of a creditor to a negotiable security given to him on account of a pre-existing debt, and received by him *bona fide* and without notice of any infirmity of title on the part of the debtor, is indefeasible, whether that security be payable at a future time or on demand. (*See* p.12)

Curtis v Chemical Cleaning and Dyeing Co [1951] 1 K.B. 805

The plaintiff took a white satin wedding dress with beads and sequins to the defendants' shop for cleaning. She was asked to sign a receipt which contained the following clause: "This or these articles are accepted on condition that the company is not liable for any damage howsoever arising or delay." When giving evidence, the plaintiff said that when she was requested to sign the document, she asked the reason for having to do so. She said that the assistant explained that it was because the defendants would not accept liability for certain specified risks, including the risk of damage by or to the beads and sequins with which the dress was trimmed. The plaintiff told the court that she did not read the receipt before she signed it. The dress was returned stained and the plaintiff sued for damages. The company relied on the clause.

HELD: that the company could not rely on the condition contained in the receipt as an exemption clause because the assistant had innocently misrepresented the effect of the document which misled the plaintiff and induced her to sign the receipt. (*See* p.23)

Davis Contractors Ltd v Fareham Urban District Council [1956] A.C. 696

The plaintiff contracted to construct 78 houses for the defendant in a period of eight months at a price of £92,000. This is what is called a fixed price contract. As a consequence of bad weather and labour shortages, not due to the fault of either party, the construction work took 22 months to complete and cost £17,000 more. There was no clause in the contract to cover this. The plaintiff alleged that the weather and the labour shortages, which were unforeseen, had frustrated the contract, and tried to recover the additional cost of £17,000 by way of *quantum meruit*. *Quantum meruit* means "as much as he has earned".

HELD: by the House of Lords, that the contract had not been frustrated. The fact that without the fault of either party, there had been an unexpected turn of events, which rendered the contract more onerous than had been contemplated, was not a ground for relieving the contractors of the obligation which they had undertaken and allowing them to recover on the basis of a *quantum meruit*. (*See* p.66)

Entores v Miles Far East Corp [1955] 2 Q.B. 327

The plaintiff company in London made an offer by Telex to the agents in Holland of the defendant corporation, whose headquarters were in New York, for the purchase of a quantity of copper cathodes, and their offer was duly accepted by a communication received on the plaintiffs' Telex machine in London.

The defendants failed to perform the contract and consequently the plaintiffs sought to sue them. However, there was a procedural problem because the defendants' registered office was in New York, and notice of the writ had to be served on them there. The Supreme Court allows service out of the jurisdiction only when the contract is made within the jurisdiction, and the defendants alleged that the contract was made in Holland when acceptance was typed on to the Telex machine there. The plaintiffs therefore applied to the court for leave to serve notice of a writ on the defendants in New York claiming damages for breach of the contract so made.

HELD: that although where a contract is made by post acceptance is complete as soon as the letter of acceptance is put into the post box, where a contract is made by instantaneous communication, *e.g.* by a telephone, the contract is complete only when the acceptance is received by the offeror, since generally an acceptance must be notified to the offeror to make a binding contract; and that, since communications by Telex were virtually instantaneous, the contract in this case was made in London, and accordingly it was a proper case for service out of the jurisdiction. (*See* p.16)

Foss v Harbottle [1843] 2 Hare 43

Two shareholders of a company incorporated by Act of Parliament brought proceedings on their own behalf and also on behalf of all the other shareholders, except the defendants, against the five directors (three of whom had become bankrupt), and against another shareholder who was not a director, and the solicitor and architect of the company. The plaintiffs alleged that the defendants had carried out various fraudulent and illegal transactions in relation to the company's property which had been misappropriated; that there were insufficient qualified directors to constitute a board; that the company had no office, or secretary; that in these circumstances the plaintiffs had no power to seize the property from the defendants or to wind up the company; the plaintiffs sought an order whereby the defendants should make good the loss and damage to the company, and that a receiver should be appointed.

HELD: that upon the facts stated, the continued existence of a board of directors *de facto* must be intended, and that the possibility of convening a general meeting of shareholders capable of controlling the acts of the existing board was not excluded, and that there was nothing to prevent the company from obtaining redress in its corporate character in respect of the matters complained of; the plaintiffs' claim was dismissed.

G. Percy Trentham Ltd v Archital Luxfer Ltd [1993] 1 Lloyd's Rep. (CA) 25.

Trentham were building and civil engineering contractors and were engaged as main contractors by Municipal Mutual Insurance Ltd to design and build industrial units in two phases. An agreement dated February 2, 1984 (the main contract) governed phase one. An agreement dated December 18, 1984 (the supplemental agreement) governed phase two. The work for both phases included the design, supply and installation of aluminium window walling, doors, screens and windows (window works).

Archital carried on business as manufacturers, suppliers and installers of aluminium window walling, doors, screens and windows, and it was common ground that Archital undertook for Trentham the window works in phases one and two and that Trentham paid Archital for carrying out the window works.

Trentham contended that two separate sub-contracts, one covering phase one window works and the other phase two window works came into existence. Trentham alleged that there were defects in the window works in both phases one and two and claimed damages for breach of contract.

Archital denied that the dealings between the parties ever resulted in the conclusion of binding sub-contracts and denied or did not admit the alleged defects.

HELD: at first instance, that Trentham had established that the two contracts were concluded.

Archital appealed.

HELD: that (1) with regard to phase one, where a transaction was fully performed the arguments that there was no evidence on which the judge could find that a contract was proved was implausible; a contract could be concluded by conduct;

(2) in the negotiations and during the performance of phase one of the work all obstacles to the formation of a contract were removed; it was not a case where there was a continuing stipulation that a contract would only come into existence if a written agreement was concluded; plainly the parties intended to enter into binding contractual relations; the exchanges and the carrying out of what was agreed in those exchanges supported the view that there was a course of dealing which on Trentham's side created a right to performance of the work by Archital and on Archital's side a right to be paid on an agreed basis; a contract came into existence during performance; it impliedly governed pre-contractual performance and a binding contract was concluded in respect of phase one;

(3) since a contract was concluded in respect of phase one, the submission by Archital that during negotiations for phase two the parties were mistakenly of the view that a contract had been made in respect of phase one would be rejected; the exchanges regarding phase two and what was done in respect of that transaction left the court in no doubt that the trial judge came to the right conclusion and the appeal was dismissed. (*See* p.5)

Great Peace Shipping Ltd v Tsavliris Salvage (International) Ltd [2002] 2 Lloyd's Rep. 653 (CA)

The defendant entered into a contract to hire the plaintiff's vessel called the *Great Peace* in order to assist a vessel in difficulties called the *Cape Providence*, in the South Indian Ocean on her way with a cargo of iron ore from Brazil to China. At the time they made the agreement, both parties mistakenly believed that the *Great Peace* was close to the *Cape Providence*. The hire was to be for a minimum of five days and the purpose of the charter was to escort and stand by the *Cape Providence* for the purpose of saving life. The contract gave an express right to cancel, subject to a cancellation fee of five days' hire. However, there was a fundamental mistake resulting from misleading information as to the position of both vessels, which were, in fact, 410 miles away from each other. Once the parties discovered their mistake and found a closer vessel which could assist the *Cape Providence*, the defendant repudiated the contract and refused to pay the minimum five days' hire. The plaintiff brought an action for payment of the cancellation fee or for wrongful repudiation of the contract of hire. The defendant asked for the contract to be rescinded on the ground of common mistake. The trial judge gave judgment for the plaintiff, and the defendant appealed.

HELD: dismissing the appeal, that there was no jurisdiction in equity to grant rescission of a contract on the ground of common mistake where that contract was valid and enforceable on ordinary principles of common law. (*See* p.23)

Griffiths v Secretary of State for Social Services [1973] 3 All E.R. 1184

A part-time administrative receiver was appointed out of court to a company by its debenture holders when it defaulted on its interest payments. The plaintiff was the managing director of the company and, as he had a service agreement, was thus treated as one of the company's employees. The plaintiff did not resign immediately but waited until four weeks after the appointment of the administrative receiver before he tendered his resignation. The issue in dispute concerned the plaintiff's national insurance position, as it was not clear whether his contract of employment ended when the administrative receiver was appointed or when he in fact resigned.

HELD: by the Court of Appeal that the plaintiff had been employed until the company had accepted his resignation and that contracts of employment continue notwithstanding the out of court appointment of an administrative receiver. However, the court considered there are three cases where an employee's contract may be terminated: firstly, if the employee's function is incompatible with that of the administrative receiver; secondly, if the company is sold at the same moment as the administrative receiver is appointed, and thirdly, if the administrative receiver enters into a new contract of employment with the employee. (*See* p.129)

Hadley and Another v Baxendale [1854] 9 Exch. 341

The defendants unduly delayed delivery of a mill shaft to the plaintiffs' mill. The mill was out of action for a considerable time. The plaintiffs did not tell the defendants that the lack of the shaft would mean closing the mill. The plaintiffs claimed damages for loss of profit due to the delay. The defendants argued that the alleged loss was too remote and they were not liable.

HELD: that the plaintiffs could recover damages against the defendants for the delay in delivery, but not for the loss of profits occasioned by the closure of the mill, as there was no way the defendants could have foreseen that their delay would mean the closure of the mill. By this decision, damage is not too remote if the damage is the natural consequence of the breach, and is something that should have been foreseen by the defendant when making the contract. (*See* p.69)

Harris v Nickerson [1873] L.R. 8 Q.B. 286

The defendant was an auctioneer who advertised a sale by auction in London newspapers, to be held at the town of Bury St Edmunds. Among the lots advertised for sale was certain office furniture. The plaintiff was commissioned by a client to attend the auction to bid for and purchase the office furniture. The plaintiff duly travelled to Bury St Edmunds to attend the auction sale. On his arrival he discovered that the defendant had withdrawn the office furniture from the sale.

The plaintiff brought an action against the defendant to recover his expenses of attending the auction and damages for the loss of his time. At first instance, before the

Judge of the City of London Court, the court gave judgment for the plaintiff, and the defendant appealed.

In giving his judgment in favour of the defendant, Blackburn J. said:

> "I think the appellant is right, and the Judge of the City of London Court was wrong. The facts of the case are simple. Part of the articles catalogued and advertised for sale by the defendant on certain days were withdrawn without notice, and were not put up for sale. The plaintiff says, and the judge has found as a fact, that the plaintiff was damaged thereby to the amount claimed. The defendant has been held liable on the ground that by advertising he entered into a contract with the plaintiff that all the goods in the catalogue would be put up for sale and sold to the highest bidder. In the first place, if this were so, it would be very inconvenient; on the same principle every shopkeeper who advertises goods for sale must never shut up his shop; and every theatrical manager would be responsible to the world if his doors were closed. This would be monstrously inconvenient, and would require strong authority to make us act upon it; but no such authority has been found."

HELD: that the plaintiff had no right of action as the advertisement did not amount to an offer, and was only an invitation to treat.

Harvey v Facey [1893] A.C. 552

The plaintiff sent the following telegram to the defendant: "Will you sell us Bumper Hall Pen? Telegraph lowest cash price." The defendant telegraphed in reply: "Lowest price for Bumper Hall Pen £900." The plaintiff then telegraphed: "We agree to buy Bumper Hall Pen for £900 asked by you. Please send us your title deed in order that we may get early possession." The defendant did not reply. The Supreme Court of Jamaica granted the plaintiff a decree of specific performance of the contract.

HELD: on appeal to the Judicial Committee of the Privy Council, that the defendant's telegram was not an offer, but an invitation to treat, telling the plaintiff the lowest price that he would accept for the land. (*See* p.28)

Hong Kong Fir Shipping Co Ltd v Kawasaki Kisen Kaisha Ltd [1962] 2 Q.B. 26

The plaintiffs chartered a ship to the defendants for 24 months from Liverpool in February 1957. However, when the defendants took delivery, they found that there were not enough mechanics in the engine-room to maintain the very old engines. The plaintiffs admitted that the ship was not suitable for ordinary cargo service and that it was unseaworthy, and thus that one of the terms of the contract had been broken. The ship was delayed for five weeks due to engine trouble on a voyage to Osaka and there was a further delay of fifteen weeks at Osaka because the engine-room staff had been too incompetent to maintain the machinery properly. It was not until September 1958 that the ship was finally deemed seaworthy. In the meantime, the defendants had repudiated the charterparty in June 1957 and the plaintiffs sued for breach of contract and claimed damages for wrongful repudiation of the charterparty.

HELD: by the Court of Appeal that the breach of contract on the part of the plaintiffs entitled the defendants to claim damages but not to treat the contract as discharged. The plaintiffs had broken a warranty but not a condition, and although delay had arisen from the breakdowns and the repairs, these were not so serious as to frustrate the commercial object of the charterparty. (*See* p.42)

Industrial Development Consultants v Cooley Ltd [1972] 2 All E.R. 162

The defendant was an architect and a director of Industrial Development Consultants (IDC), a consultancy company. A very big contract with the Eastern Gas Board was being negotiated by the defendant on behalf of IDC, but it became plain that the Gas Board did not wish to make a contract with the firm of consultants but with the defendant personally. As a result of this offer, the defendant alleged that he was close to a nervous breakdown in order to terminate his employment with IDC. A short time afterwards he obtained the Eastern Gas Board contract for himself, and IDC sued him for the profits he would make from the new contract.

HELD: that the defendant had acted in breach of duty and must account to IDC for the profit made as a consequence of entering into the contract with the Gas Board. (*See* pp.105, 108)

John Lee & Son (Grantham) Ltd and Others v Railway Executive [1949] 2 All E.R. 581

Goods stored in a railway warehouse let to a tenant were damaged by fire and the tenant brought an action against the Railway Executive alleging that the accident was due to their negligence because a spark or other combustible material ejected from their railway engine had caused the fire. The Railway Executive set up a clause in the tenancy agreement providing that: "The tenant shall be responsible for and shall release and indemnify the company and their servants and agents from and against all liability for personal injury (whether fatal or otherwise) loss of or damage to property and any other loss damage costs and expenses however caused or incurred (whether by the act or neglect of the company or their servants or agents or not) which but for the tenancy hereby created or anything done pursuant to the provisions hereof would not have arisen."

HELD: that the words "which but for the tenancy hereby created ... would not have arisen" were confined to liabilities which arose by reason of the relationship of landlord and tenant; the fact that the tenant was occupying the warehouse under an agreement from the Railway Executive was immaterial to the allegation in the present case of negligence; and the tenant, therefore, could not be called on to release or indemnify the Railway Executive in the event of negligence being established. (*See* p.5)

John Price v Easton [1833] 4 B. & Ad. 433

A certain William Price owed the plaintiff John Price the sum of £13, being the balance of a larger sum due for the price of a wooden carriage sold and delivered to him. The defendant promised William Price that if he did certain work for him, he would pay the sum of £13 to the plaintiff. William Price did work for the defendant and in fact earned a large sum of money which he left with the defendant, but the defendant failed to pay the plaintiff the sum of £13.

Per Lord Denman C.J.:

"I think the declaration cannot be supported as it does not show any consideration for the promise moving from the plaintiff to the defendant."

HELD: that the plaintiff's claim failed because no consideration had passed from him to the defendant, and the plaintiff could not sue the defendant. (*See* p.14)

Joseph Constantine Steamship Line Ltd v Imperial Smelting Corp Ltd [1942] A.C. 154

On the day before a chartered ship was due to load her cargo an explosion of such violence occurred in her auxiliary boiler that the performance of the charterparty became impossible. The charterers claimed damages, alleging that the owners had broken the charterparty by their failure to load the cargo. The owners contended that the contract was frustrated by the destructive consequences of the explosion. The cause of the explosion could not be ascertained.

HELD: by the House of Lords that, since the charterers were unable to prove that the explosion was caused by the neglect or default of the owners, the defence of frustration succeeded and the contract was discharged. (*See* p.66)

J. Spurling Ltd v Bradshaw [1956] 1 W.L.R. 461, 466

The defendant had used the warehouse the plaintiffs owned for many years. One delivery he stored in their warehouse was a consignment of eight barrels of orange juice. He received a document from the plaintiffs which acknowledged receipt of the barrels and referred to clauses printed on the back. One clause exempted the plaintiffs from "any loss or damage occasioned by the negligence, wrongful act or default of themselves or their servants". The defendant later collected the barrels from the store but they were empty. He therefore refused to pay the storage charges and the plaintiffs sued him. The defendants counter-claimed for negligence and the plaintiffs pleaded the exemption clause. The defendant admitted that in his previous dealing with the plaintiffs he had often received similar documents but that he had never taken the trouble to read them.

HELD: that the defendant was bound by the clause and was therefore liable for breach. (*See* p.46)

Krell v Henry [1903] 2 K.B. 740

By a contract in writing the defendant hired a flat from the plaintiff for two days to view the coronation procession of King Edward VII. The King became ill and his illness caused the postponement of the coronation procession.

HELD: that the defendant should be excused from paying rent for the room, because both parties had regarded the holding of the procession on the date planned as basic to the enforcement of the contract. (*See* p.66)

Re McArdle [1951] Ch. 669

Mr McArdle and his wife lived in a house which formed part of the estate of his father in which he and his brother and a sister had a beneficial interest, expectant on the death of their mother, who was the tenant for life. In the years 1943 and 1944 his wife paid the sum of £488 for improvements and decorations to the property. In 1945, after the work had been completed, the beneficiaries, including Mr McArdle, signed a document addressed to his wife which stated "In consideration of your carrying out certain alterations and improvements to the property, we the beneficiaries under the will (of their father) hereby agree that the executors ... shall repay to you from the said estate, when so distributed, the sum of £488 in settlement of the amount spent on the improvements." Later, in 1945, the tenant for life died and the daughter-in-law claimed payment of the sum of £488.

HELD: that the improvement had been carried out before the document was executed. The consideration was past and the promise could not be enforced. (*See* p.14)

Mitchell (George) (Chesterhall) Ltd v Finney Lock Seeds Ltd [1983] 1 All E.R. 108

The plaintiffs bought 30lb of cabbage seed from the seed merchants Finney Lock Seeds Ltd. However, the seed proved to be defective because the cabbages when they grew had no heart and their leaves turned inwards. The seed had cost £201.60, but the plaintiffs lost £61,000, the cost of a year's production from the 63 acres planted. They had no insurance cover on the crop. The defendants claimed that they were not liable because of an exclusion clause on the back of their invoice which limited their liability to the cost of the seed or its replacement.

HELD: by the Court of Appeal that although the words of the exclusion clause did effectively limit the defendants' liability, the clause was not reasonable as the parties were not of equal bargaining power. The exclusion clause had been inserted by the defendants in their invoice without any negotiation with the plaintiffs. The seriousness of the mistake was a result of negligence on the part of the seed merchants and under s.6 (3) of the Unfair Contract Terms Act 1977, it was not fair and reasonable to allow them to rely on the clause to limit their responsibility. (*See* p.45)

Panatown Ltd v Alfred McAlpine Construction Ltd [2000] 4 All E.R. 97

The defendant (building contractor) entered into a contract with the claimant (employer) to design and construct a building on a site owned by U Ltd, a company in the same group as the employer. On the same day, and pursuant to an obligation under that contract, the contractor executed a deed in favour of U Ltd, giving the latter a direct remedy against it for any failure to exercise reasonable skill, care and attention in respect of any matter within the scope of the contractor's responsibilities under the building contract. Subsequently the employer brought arbitration proceedings against the contractor seeking the recovery of damages for delay and defective work. In its defence, the contractor contended that the employer was not entitled to recover substantial damages under the building contract since it had no proprietary interest in the site and had therefore suffered no loss. That contention was rejected by the arbitrator on the hearing of the preliminary issue, but his decision was reversed by the judge. On the employer's appeal, the Court of Appeal held that the case fell within an established exception to the rule that a party could only recover substantial damages for his own loss, namely that which allowed a contracting party, who had not himself suffered any loss as a result of a breach of contract, to recover damages on behalf of a third party who had suffered such a loss. Accordingly, the employer's appeal was allowed, and the contractor appealed to the House of Lords.

HELD: that where a contractor was in breach of a contract with the employer to construct a building for a third party, the employer could not recover substantial damages on behalf of the third party if it had been intended that the latter should have a direct cause of action against the contractor to the exclusion of any substantial claim by the employer. Such a case fell outside the scope of the exception to the rule that a claimant could only recover damages for a loss which he himself had suffered. The appeal was allowed. (*See* p.5)

Pao On and Others v Lau Yiu Long and Others [1980] A.C. 614

The plaintiffs were the owners of the issued share capital of a private company whose principal asset was a building under construction. The defendants were the majority shareholders of a public company, which wished to acquire the building. In order to achieve their objective, in February, 1973, the defendants entered into an agreement with the plaintiffs to purchase their shares in the private company. The parties agreed that no money was to pass, and that the price of the shares was to be satisfied by issuing shares in the public company to the plaintiffs. The plaintiffs undertook to retain 60 per cent of their newly acquired shares until after April 30, 1974, so as not to depress the market for the shares. The plaintiffs and the defendants agreed orally that the plaintiffs should be protected against any loss from a possible fall in the value of the shares between the acquisition date and April 30, 1974. The parties then entered into a second agreement whereby the defendants agreed to buy back 60 per cent of the allotted shares at a guaranteed price of $2.50 a share on or before April 30, 1974, thus protecting the plaintiffs against a loss, should the value of those shares fall below that price.

In April, 1973, the plaintiffs realised that this second agreement, while protecting them from any loss, would not allow them to make a profit on those shares, if the share price rose above the guaranteed buy-back price. Consequently, the plaintiffs refused to complete the terms of the first agreement unless the defendants cancelled the second agreement and replaced it by a guarantee in the form of an indemnity.

The defendants feared that if the completion of the terms of the first agreement did not take place, or if there was any delay arising from litigation, there would be a loss of public confidence in the company, to its detriment. The defendants in these circumstances decided to accede to the plaintiffs' demands, and a contract of guarantee was executed.

Thereafter, the share price dropped, and the plaintiffs sought to rely on the contract of indemnity. The defendants refused to indemnify them, and the plaintiffs successfully brought an action based on the indemnity in the High Court of Hong Kong. On appeal, the decision was reversed, and the plaintiffs appealed to the Judicial Committee of the Privy Council in London.

HELD: allowing the appeal, that the consideration was the promise by the plaintiff not to sell 60 per cent of their allotted shares until after April 30, 1974. Although the promise was made before the indemnity was given, the arrangement had been made at the defendants' request, and with the object of protecting the plaintiffs against a loss; that although the defendants had been subjected to commercial pressure, the facts disclosed that they had not been coerced into the contract of guarantee and, therefore, the contract was not voidable on the ground of duress; that, in the absence of duress, public policy did not require a contract negotiated at arm's length to be invalidated because a party had either threatened to repudiate an existing contractual obligation or had unfairly used his dominant bargaining position in negotiating the agreement and that, therefore, the defendants, having failed to show that the contract of guarantee was either invalid or voidable, were bound by its terms. (*See* p.24)

Parker v South Eastern Railway Co [1877] 2 C.P.D. 416

On the deposit of articles at the cloak-room at a railway station, a charge of 2d. was made for each, and the depositor received a ticket, on the face of which were printed the times of opening and closing the cloak-room and the words "See Back" and on the back there was a notice that the company would not be responsible for any package exceeding £10. There was a notice containing the same condition hung up in the cloak-room.

The plaintiff deposited his bag, the value of which exceeded £10, in the defendants' cloak-room, paid 2d., and was given a ticket. The bag was either lost or stolen, and the plaintiff brought an action claiming the value of the bag. The plaintiff argued that he had taken the ticket without reading it, as he thought it was only a receipt for the sum of 2d. which he had paid to deposit his bag, or was evidence that the defendants had received his bag for deposit. He said he had not seen the notice hung up in the cloak-room.

HELD: that the trial judge had misdirected the jury inasmuch as the plaintiff could be under no obligation to read the condition, and the jury should have been asked whether the defendants did what was reasonably sufficient to give the plaintiff notice of the condition. The trial judge had left the following questions for the jury: 1. Did the plaintiff read or was he aware of the special condition upon which the article was deposited? 2. Was the plaintiff, under the circumstances, under any obligation, in the exercise of reasonable and proper caution, to read or to make himself aware of the condition? The jury had answered both questions in the negative, and the trial judge had entered judgment for the defendants. A new trial was ordered.

This leading case is an authority for the proposition that an exclusion clause will never be enforced unless adequate notice of it has been given to the other party. (*See* p.46)

Parkinson v College of Ambulance Ltd and Harrison [1925] 2 K.B. 1

Mr Harrison, the second defendant, was the secretary of the defendant company, which was a charity. He fraudulently represented to the plaintiff that he was in a position to nominate persons to be given titles. He told the plaintiff that he or the charity could arrange for him to be given a knighthood if the plaintiff would make an adequate donation to the charity. After a certain amount of negotiations, the plaintiff paid £3,000 to the charity but did not receive a knighthood in return for his donation. The plaintiff brought an action to recover the £3,000 which he had paid to the charity.
HELD: that the agreement was contrary to public policy and illegal. Consequently, no relief could be granted to the plaintiff. (*See* p.13)

Pharmaceutical Society of Great Britain v Boots Cash Chemist Southern Ltd [1952] 2 Q.B. 795

The defendants' shop at Edgware consisted of a single room adapted to the "self-service" system. In that room was a "chemist's department", under the control of a registered pharmacist, in which various drugs and proprietary medicines, included, or containing substances included, in Pt 1 of the Poisons List compiled under s.17(1) of the Pharmacy and Poisons Act 1933, but not in Sch.1 to the Poisons Rules 1949, were displayed on shelves in packages or other containers with the price marked on each. A customer on entering the room was given a basket and then selected the articles that he wished to buy from the shelves, put them in the basket and took them to the cashier's desk at one of the two exits. The cashier scrutinised the articles, stated the total price and received the money; and the pharmacist in control of the department supervised that part of every transaction involving the sale of a drug which took place at the cash desk and was authorised to prevent the removal of any drug from the premises.

An action was brought by the plaintiffs alleging that the provisions of s.18 of the Act requiring the sale of poisons included in Pt 1 of the Poisons List to be effected by or under the supervision of a registered pharmacist were infringed by the defendants.
HELD: that the display of the articles on the shelves, though coupled with an invitation to the customer to select and take any that he wished to buy from the shelves, did not amount to an offer by the defendants to sell, but merely to an invitation to the customer to make an offer to buy; and that offer was made and accepted at the cashier's desk and the sale was therefore effected under the supervision of a registered pharmacist, as required by the Act. (*See* p.15)

Phonogram Ltd v Lane [1982] Q.B. 938

It was agreed that a company called Fragile Management Ltd should be formed to manage a pop group. Phonogram Ltd was to provide £12,000 for the financing of the group. £6,000 of this was paid to Fragile Management Ltd towards the group's first album which was never made. A letter was written from Phonogram's negotiator, Roland Rennie, to Brian Lane, who had negotiated on behalf of Fragile Management Ltd. The letter read *"In regard to the contract now being completed between Phonogram Ltd and Fragile Management Ltd concerning recordings of a group ... and further to our conversation of this morning, I send you herewith our cheque for £6,000 in anticipation of a contract signing, this being the initial payment for the initial LP called for in the contract. In the unlikely event that we fail to complete within, say, one month, you will undertake to pay us the £6,000 ... For good order's sake, Brian, I should be appreciative if you could sign the attached copy of this letter and return it to me so that I can keep our accounts people informed of what is happening."* Brian Lane signed the copy of the letter and added "for and on behalf of Fragile Management Ltd" after his name, and then paid the money into the account of Jelly Music Ltd of which he was a director. Phonogram Ltd sued for the recovery of the £6,000.

HELD: that Brian Lane was personally liable on the contract as he had purported to make the contract on behalf of Fragile Management Ltd even though the company had not been formed. (*See* p.92)

Photo Production Ltd v Securicor Transport Ltd [1980] A.C. 827

The plaintiffs contracted with the defendants for the provision of a night patrol service for their factory of four visits a night. The main perils which the parties had in mind were fire and theft. The contract was on the defendants' printed form incorporating standard conditions which, *inter alia*, provided:

"Under no circumstances shall the company be responsible for any injurious act or default by any employee of the company unless such act or default could have been foreseen and avoided by the exercise of due diligence on the part of the company as his employer; nor, in any event, shall the company be held responsible for: (a) Any loss suffered by the customer through ... fire or any other cause, except insofar as such loss is solely attributable to the negligence of the company's employees acting within the course of their employment."

Condition 2 limited the defendants' potential liability under the terms of the contract, "or at common law".

On a Sunday night one of the defendants' employees entered the factory on duty patrol and then lit a fire which burned down the factory. The plaintiffs claimed damages particularised at over £648,000, based on breach of contract and/or negligence. The trial judge rejected allegations against the defendants of want of care and failure to use due diligence as employers, and held that condition 1 of the contract excluded them from responsibility for their employee's act in setting fire to the factory, and that the doctrine of fundamental breach did not prevent judgment being given for the defendants. The Court of Appeal reversed the trial judge's decision, and the defendants appealed to the House of Lords.

HELD: allowing the appeal that the doctrine of fundamental breach by virtue of which the termination of a contract brought it, and with it, any exclusion clause to an end was not good law; the question of whether and to what extent an exclusion clause was to be applied to any breach of contract was a matter of construction of the contract; that normally when the parties were bargaining on equal terms they should be free to apportion the risks as they thought fit; and that the words of the exclusion clause were clear and on their true construction covered deliberate acts as well as negligence so as to relieve the defendants from responsibility for their breach of the implied duty to operate with due regard to the safety of the premises. (*See* p.45)

Poussard v Spiers & Pond [1876] 1 Q.B.D. 410

The plaintiff, an actress, was hired to play the leading part in a French operetta for its whole run. However, although she attended several rehearsals, she fell ill, failed to attend the final rehearsals and was unable to take up her part until a week after the operetta's run had started. In the meantime, the producers had found a substitute as it was uncertain how long the plaintiff's illness might continue and refused to let the actress take up her part. The plaintiff brought an action for wrongful dismissal.
HELD: that the plaintiff's inability to perform on the opening night and subsequent performances went to the root of the matter, and the defendants were justified in rescinding the contract. (*See* p.42)

Regal (Hastings) Ltd v Gulliver (1942) [1967] 2 A.C. 134

Regal (Hastings) Ltd owned a cinema, but the directors wished to buy two more with a view to selling the company as a going concern. The Regal company formed a subsidiary so that the latter could buy the two cinemas. In order to provide the subsidiary with sufficient paid up capital to make the purchase, Regal's directors bought some of the shares in the subsidiary themselves. Thus the subsidiary company was able to purchase the two cinemas. Later, the directors, instead of selling the company as planned, sold their shares in the subsidiary along with the shares they had in the parent company, Regal. The sale of their shares realised a substantial profit for them. However, the new owners of Regal became aware of this fact and caused Regal to bring an action against its previous directors in order to recover the profit made on the shares.
HELD: by the House of Lords that the former directors must account to the Regal Company for the profit because they made their profit only through the knowledge they had as directors of the company. (*See* pp.106, 108)

Rose and Frank Co v J. R. Crompton and Brothers Ltd [1925] A.C. 445

In 1913, the plaintiffs, who were a US corporation, entered into an agreement with the defendants, who were an English company, whereby the plaintiffs were appointed the sole US agents of the defendants. The agreement contained the following clause:
> "This arrangement is not entered into nor is this memorandum written, as a formal or legal agreement, and shall not be subject to legal jurisdiction in the Law Courts of either the United States of America or England, but it is only a definite expression and record of the purpose and intention of the three parties concerned to which they each honourably pledge themselves with the fullest confidence, based on past business with each other, that it will be carried through by each of the three parties with mutual loyalty and friendly co-operation."

The agreement was for a period of three years with an option to extend the period. The agreement was extended to March 1920. In 1919 the defendants terminated the agreement without any notice and refused to execute orders received before their termination of the agreement. The plaintiffs sued for breach of contract and for non-delivery of the goods for which orders had already been placed.
HELD: that the 1913 agreement was not binding on the parties because of the "honour" clause, but that as the agreement had been acted upon by the defendants' acceptance of

orders, those orders only were binding contracts of sale, as the orders had been accepted and delivery was therefore legally required. (*See* p.17)

Salomon v Salomon & Co Ltd [1897] A.C. 22

When his boot and leather business was doing well, Aaron Salomon incorporated a limited company in order to take the business over. He himself, his wife and five of his children signed the memorandum of association. The members of his family subscribed one share each and the plaintiff was paid £39,000 for the business. The terms of the payment agreed were as follows: £10,000 in the form of debentures, 20,000 shares of £1 each and the remainder in cash. Unfortunately the company did not do well, and Mr Salomon obtained an outside loan for £5,000. The lender caused a liquidator to be appointed as the company was unable to service the loan, and Mr Salomon claimed that as a debenture-holder he was entitled to be repaid before the unsecured trade creditors. However, the unsecured creditors alleged that Mr Salomon's company had been incorporated for fraudulent purposes and that he was personally liable on the debts.
HELD: that the company was a separate and distinct person from Mr Salomon and that his debentures were valid. There was no fraud involved in the company's incorporation. (*See* pp.72, 75)

Shirlaw v Southern Foundries (1926) Ltd [1940] A.C. 701

The plaintiff who was already a director, was appointed managing director of the defendant company by an agreement dated December 21, 1933, for a period of 10 years. Article 91 of the company's articles of association provided that a managing director should, "subject to the provisions of any contract between him and the company, be subject to the same provisions as to ... removal as the other directors of the company and if he cease to hold the office of director he shall *ipso facto* and immediately cease to be a managing director."

In 1935 another company, Federated Foundries Ltd acquired all the shares of the defendant company, and by a special resolution the articles of association were abrogated and new articles adopted. These empowered the company to remove any director, and made a managing director's appointment subject to termination if he ceased to be a director.

On March 27, 1937, the company served notice upon the plaintiff removing him from the office of director, and thereupon treated him as ceasing to be managing director.

The plaintiff commenced proceedings claiming damages against the company for wrongful repudiation of the agreement.
HELD: on appeal to the House of Lords, that it was an implied term of the agreement of December 21, 1933, that the company should not remove the plaintiff from his position as director during the term of years for which he was appointed managing director, and that the company was in breach of the agreement, and the plaintiff was entitled to the damages awarded by the trial judge. (*See* p.40)

Spencer and Others v Harding and Others [1870] L.R. 5 C.P. 561

The defendants sent the plaintiffs and others engaged in the wholesale trade a circular inviting submissions of tenders to purchase goods listed and described in the advertisement as being of a value of £2,503, and to be sold at a discount in one lot. The rest of the advertisement consisted of a statement of the circumstances under which the tenders would be opened, and that the stock books might be inspected.

A tender was submitted by the plaintiffs, and although it was the highest, it was not accepted. The plaintiffs contended that the advertisement was equivalent to a promise by the defendants to accept the highest tender.

HELD: that the circular was merely an invitation to submit offers, and was not an offer, and the defendants were under no obligation to accept any tender, not even the highest one. There was no promise, either express or implied, to accept the highest tender.

Spice Girls Ltd v Aprilia World Service BV, *The Times*, April 5, 2000

The Spice Girls entered into a contract with Aprilia whereby they, through their company Spice Girls Ltd, participated in making a film which advertised and promoted a product of Aprilia to be called "Spice Sonic Scooters". They also provided logos and pictures of all five Spice Girls and Aprilia entered into the agreement on that basis. However, the Group had failed to disclose that Geri Halliwell intended to leave the Group, a fact of which they were aware when they entered into the agreement with Aprilia. Aprilia claimed against Spice Girls Ltd for damages in misrepresentation by conduct.

HELD: that the participation of the Group in making the film constituted a representation by conduct of an intention of the Group that it would not break up during the term of the advertising contract, and that it was a continuing representation which the Group had a duty to correct when it was untrue, and these representations by conduct were such as to be likely to induce a person to enter the agreement. (*See* p.24)

Taylor v Caldwell [1863] 122 E.R. 309

The plaintiff entered into a contract with the defendant whereby the defendant agreed to let the plaintiff have the use of a music hall and gardens in order to hold a series of four concerts. Prior to holding the first of the concerts, the music hall was destroyed by fire, through no fault of either party, and the concerts could not be given. The plaintiff claimed damages for breach of contract, and to recover wasted advertising expenses in respect of the concerts.

HELD: that the contract was impossible to perform and the defendant was not liable; the continuation of the contract was subject to an implied condition that the parties would be excused performance thereof if the subject matter of the contract was destroyed through no fault of theirs. (*See* pp.50, 66)

Taylor v Webb [1937] 2 K.B. 283

In this case, there was a lease of a house. The parties to such a lease are called the lessor and lessee or landlord and tenant. The tenant sub-let the house to a sub-tenant and by doing this he created a further lease called an under-lease or sub-lease. When this arises the original lease is called a head lease and the parties are called the head-lessor and the head-lessee. The parties to the under-lease are called the under-lessor or sub-lessor and the under-lessee or sub-lessee. The under-lease may also be referred to as a sub-lease and the the parties may also be referred to as the sub-landlord and sub-tenant.

The sub-lease of the house contained a covenant (a promise in a deed) by the sub-lessor in the following terms: "To keep the outside walls and roofs in good and tenantable repair as and so far only as is required to be done by them under the head-lease." In the sub-lease, the sub-lessee covenanted (promised) to pay the rent to the sub-lessor. In the head-lease, the head-lessor covenanted to keep the premises "in good and tenantable repair (destruction or damage by fire and fair wear and tear excepted)". HELD: that the express covenant by the sub-lessee to pay the rent and the covenant by the sub-lessor to keep the outside walls and roofs in repair were independent covenants; a tenant's covenant in a lease to pay the rent to the landlord is completely independent of the landlord's covenant to repair the premises. So, just because the landlord refuses or fails to keep his promise to repair the premises, this does not justify the tenant not paying the rent, as the two promises are divisible and quite separate. (*See* p.9)

Thomas v Thomas [1842] 2 Q.B. 851

The plaintiff's husband had expressed informally to her the wish that if she survived him, she should have the use of their house. In his will the husband appointed his brothers executors and the will made no mention of the testator's wish that his wife should have the use of their house. The executors were aware of the testator's wish and therefore agreed to allow the widow to occupy the house in consideration of the payment of £1 per annum and upon the condition that she remained unmarried, and that she kept the house in good and tenantable repair. The plaintiff remained in possession of the house until the death of one of the executors. The surviving executor then evicted the plaintiff, and she sued him for breach of contract.
HELD: that the promises to keep the house in repair and the payment of £1 constituted good consideration moving from the widow and she was entitled to remain in the house; that consideration need not be adequate and that the promises made by the plaintiff had some value in the eyes of the law. (*See* p.12)

Thornton v Shoe Lane Parking Ltd [1971] 2 Q.B. 163

The plaintiff drove his car into a new automatic car park. He had not been there before. A notice on the outside gave the charges and stated that all cars were "parked at owner's risk". A traffic light on the entrance lane showed red and a machine produced a ticket when the car had drawn up beside it. The plaintiff took the ticket and, the light having turned green, he drove on into the garage where his car was parked by mechanical means. On the plaintiff's return to collect his car, there was an accident and he was severely injured. The plaintiff claimed damages from the defendant garage. The defendants contended, *inter alia*, that the ticket incorporated a condition exempting them from liability. The ticket stated the arrival time of the car and that it was to be presented when the car was claimed. In the bottom left hand corner in small print it was said to be "issued subject to conditions ... displayed on the premises". On a pillar opposite the ticket machine it was stated that the garage would not be liable for any injury to the customer occurring when his car was on the premises. The trial judge held that both parties were fifty per cent to blame for the accident, and the defendants appealed. HELD: dismissing the appeal, that since the plaintiff did not know of the exemption condition and the defendants had not done what was reasonably sufficient to bring it to his notice it did not exempt them from liability. (*See* p.45)

GLOSSARY OF LEGAL TERMS

A

Ab initio: from Latin, from the beginning. A term used in contract law to indicate that a contract is of no effect right from its formation. *The contract is void ab initio.*

Abstain: (v) to refrain from doing something. *He abstained from voting in the general election.*

Abuse: the misuse or improper use of a law, practice, regulation or legal process. *His abuse of his position as director led to a call for his resignation.*

Acceptance: consent, assent or approval. The acceptance of an offer to create a contract must be unqualified and may be either by word of mouth or by conduct. An assent to all the terms of an offer.

Acceptor: the person who accepts an offer.

Accord and satisfaction: the substitution and performance of a new set of obligations under a contract, by means of which the parties in question are released from their original obligations. An *accord and satisfaction* is frequently used in the settlement of a disputed debt. The agreement is the accord and the consideration is the satisfaction.

Account to: (v) to send a detailed statement to another person showing how money belonging to that person has been spent and what the situation of indebtedness is as between the parties. A solicitor must account to his client for any provision of funds paid over towards costs and disbursements.

Accrue: (v) to accumulate or to be added to something. *Interest accrues to capital.*

Accusatorial: Accusatorial or adversarial procedure is the system used in most common law countries. Under this system, the parties to a dispute have the primary responsibility for finding and presenting the evidence to the court. The judge does not investigate the facts.

Acquiescence: consent which is expressed or implied from conduct. A mere gesture, like the nod of a head, can mean acquiescence to an offer.

Act of God: an accident or event which arises independently of human intervention and which is entirely due to natural causes, *e.g.* an earthquake.

Act on: (v) to carry out, base your actions on something or comply with someone's wishes. *He acted on his client's instructions.*

Action: the formal exercise of a right to sue for what is due. A cause of action. It has been defined as "a factual situation the existence of which entitles a person to obtain a remedy against another person". *Your distributor may have a cause of action against you if you have not included a force majeure clause in your contract.*

Administrator: a person to whom the administration of the estate of a deceased person is entrusted by the court, which issues letters of administration authorising the administrator to act in cases where the deceased left no will.

Advocacy: the skills of an advocate. The ability to plead on behalf of a client before the court and present arguments which in civil cases are reflected in the pleadings. *Barristers are trained in advocacy.*

Affirm: (v) to confirm a judgment, for example where an appellate court confirms the judgment of the court below it. To make a solemn declaration instead of taking an oath. *He chose to affirm that his testimony was true, rather than take an oath, because of his religious convictions.*

Agency: the relationship of principal and agent, where the principal is bound by contracts entered into by the agent with third parties. *A power of attorney gives rise to an agency agreement.*

Agenda: the list of items to be discussed at a business meeting either at a meeting of the directors of a company or at a shareholders meeting. *The Agenda of general meetings is sent in advance to shareholders so that they know the business to be discussed at the meeting.*

Agent: a person who is employed to act on behalf of another person who is known as his principal. The work of an agent is to bring his principal into contractual relations with third parties.

Aggrieved party: a party who has a cause or reason to complain about the conduct of another party. It has been defined as "A man who has suffered a legal grievance, a man against whom a decision has been pronounced which has wrongfully deprived him of something, or which has wrongfully refused him something, or wrongfully affected his title to something." *The aggrieved party may decide to bring legal action against the airline for negligence.*

Agreement: contract, bargain. From the Latin *aggregatio mentium*. A consensus of minds, or evidence of such consensus, in spoken or written form relating to anything done or to be done.

Alien: this is defined at common law as a subject of a foreign state, who was not born within the allegiance of the Crown, and by statute law as a person who is neither a Commonwealth Citizen, nor a British Protected Person, nor a citizen of the Republic of Ireland.

Allegation: a statement of fact made in legal proceedings by a party who undertakes to prove it. *He made an allegation that the order had not been properly served upon his client.*

Allege: (v) to make an affirmation about something, to put an idea forward as an argument or excuse. *The witness alleged that the motorist was driving at 60mph.*

Allotment: the distribution of unissued shares in a limited company in exchange for a contribution of capital. An application may be made for unissued shares following the issue of a prospectus when a public company is floated or when a state-owned industry is privatised. *Ace Ltd will accept your application by sending you a letter of allotment informing you of the number of shares allotted to you.*

Anticipatory breach: a term which refers to the repudiation of a contract before the time for its performance. *ABC's fax informing you that they will not be able to fulfil your order in accordance with the terms established in the contract constitutes an anticipatory breach.*

Appeal: a proceeding taken to seek to rectify an erroneous decision of a court or tribunal by bringing it before a higher court. It has been defined as "the transference of a case from an inferior to a higher tribunal in the hope of reversing or modifying the decision of the former". *Upon appeal, his sentence was reduced from one of imprisonment to a fine.*

Appellant: the party who appeals a decision of the court.

Appellate jurisdiction: the power of a court to hear an appeal.

Apprenticeship: from the noun apprentice, a person who learns a trade or profession. Such a person enters into a contract of apprenticeship and binds himself to serve and learn for a fixed period of time from an employer who on his part covenants to teach the apprentice his trade or profession. *You will be expected to serve a period of apprenticeship, known as serving articles, before becoming a fully-fledged solicitor.*

Arbitrator: an independent person who is appointed by agreement between parties in dispute or by a court to hear and decide a dispute. The process is known as an arbitration, and the decision, known as the award, is binding on the parties.

Arrest: (v) to deprive a person of his liberty by some lawful authority in order to compel the person to appear before the court to answer a criminal charge. *The police arrested him for armed robbery.*

Assent: to agree, concur. *He assented to all the terms of the agreement.*

Assets: any object of value to its owner. Normally assets are understood to mean cash or anything which can be turned into cash and which has a realisable value. *Ace Ltd's assets are far greater than its debts.*

Assign, assignee: a person to whom an assignment or transfer of a contract is made. *John assigned his rights under the distribution contract to Mary, who became his assign.*

Association clause: a clause in the memorandum of association of a company in which the subscribers to the memorandum declare their wish to be formed into a company and agree to take the number of shares recorded against their names.

Attorney General: the Chief Law Officer of the Crown who represents the Crown in legal proceedings and in some more important prosecutions. He is a member of the House of Commons with ministerial responsibility for certain Crown departments. He may be a member of the Cabinet but need not necessarily be so.

Auction: this is a method of sale whereby the public is invited to make competing offers to purchase something, such as a painting or an antique.

Audit: a detailed inspection of a company's accounts by outside accountants usually in connection with the preparation of the annual accounts of the company at the year end.

Authorised capital: the total amount of capital which a company is authorised to issue by its memorandum of association. It is also called nominal or registered capital. *The issued capital of a company is not necessarily the total amount of authorised capital.*

Avoid: (v) to evade obligations under a contract by making it null and void. *The contract was avoided on the grounds of duress.*

B

Balance sheet: one of the principal statements comprising the accounts of a company and which shows the financial state of a company at a particular date, normally the last day of the accounting period. It has three main headings: assets, liabilities, and capital.

Bankruptcy: the legal procedures related to insolvency under the the Insolvency Act of 1986. The state of a person who is unable to pay his debts and against whom a bankruptcy order has been made by the Court.

Bar: (v) (p./p.p. barred) to bar a claim. To

block, stop or prevent a claim going forward. Something which nullifies an action or claim. *Because he waited too long before making his claim, it was barred through lapse of time.*

Bargain: consensus, agreement, contract. *A bargain was struck by the parties who entered into a binding contract.* (v) to negotiate *In the process of plea bargaining the accused usually bargains for a lighter sentence.*

Beneficial interest: the equitable interest of a beneficiary. *If land is held by X in trust for Y, X is said to have the legal estate, and Y the beneficial interest.*

Beneficiary: a person who is entitled to something for his own benefit. *Mrs Smith was left money under the will of her aunt, and is therefore a beneficiary.*

Benefit: advantage, gain. Used in the context of consideration. *The courts have traditionally defined consideration in terms of a dichotomy of benefit to the promisor, who makes the promise or detriment to the promisee, to whom the promise is made.*

Bilateral: two sides; affecting two parties. *A bilateral agreement is one in which the two parties are under a reciprocal or mutual obligation towards each other.*

Bill of exchange: an unconditional order in writing, addressed by one person to another, signed by the person giving it, requiring the person to whom it is addressed to pay on demand, or at a fixed or determinable future time a certain sum in money to or to the order of a specified person or to bearer.

Binding: present participle of *bind* (v). See *bound*. Obligatory. Used very frequently in case law in the context of a precedent. *A precedent is generally binding and must be followed by the courts. A valid contract is binding on the parties thereto.*

Boilerplate clauses: These are clauses which deal with the way in which a contract operates, and are to be found in nearly all commercial contracts. They contain the essential terms which protect the contract and make it work. Hence the reference to the steel plating which covers and protects the hull of a ship.

Bound: the past participle of *bind*. See *binding*. *As a minor, he is not bound by this contract.*

Breach: the infringing or violation of a right, duty or law. *Miss Jones brought an action for breach of contract.*

Burden of proof: the obligation of proving facts. The evidence which satisfies the court as to the truth of a fact. Generally, the burden of proof lies on the party who asserts the truth of the issue in dispute. In civil cases the court comes to a decision on the balance of probabilities. In a criminal case, the prosecution must prove its case against the accused beyond all reasonable doubt.

Bystander: spectator; somebody physically present at the scene of an action. *Although Miss Clark was in the shop at the time of the theft, she was just an innocent bystander.*

C

Capacity: the legal competence to enter into and be bound by the terms of a contract. *Minors possess a limited capacity to contract.*

Cartel: an association of independent companies formed to regulate the price and conditions of sale of the goods or services they offer. Monopoly. *The setting* *up of cartels is restricted in the US antitrust laws.*

Certificate of incorporation: a certificate issued by the Registrar of Companies following the presentation and inspection of the memorandum and articles of association, confirming the official incorporation of the company.

Certiorari: from Latin, to be more fully informed of. This was formerly a writ directed to an inferior court ordering the proceedings to be transferred for review to a superior court. Since 1977 the system has been changed and now an application has to be made for a judicial review.

Chairman: the most senior officer in a company. He presides at meetings of the company and in particular at the annual general meeting and also at meetings of the board of directors.

Charter: (v) to hire a ship or an aircraft. *We're going to charter a plane to take our group to Alaska.*

Charterparty: a document by which a shipowner hires his ship to the hirer who is known as the charterer. *As the ship is not seaworthy, we are justified in repudiating the charterparty.*

Cheque: a bill of exchange drawn on a banker, payable on demand. *You must make out this cheque to Ace Ltd for the sum of £15,500.*

Claim: (v) to assert a right; to hold, insist, maintain. *He claimed that he was entitled to remuneration for the services he had performed.* (n) The assertion of a right, or a demand for a remedy by application to the court for relief.

Clause: a sentence or a paragraph in a contract. *This contract lacks a force majeure clause.*

Coercion: the use of moral or physical force in an attempt to interfere with the exercise of a person's free choice.

Common ground: something which is not disputed; frequently used in the context of litigation and negotiations; a matter on which the litigating parties are in agreement. *It was common ground between the parties that the contract was performed.*

Common law: the law of England formerly administered by the common law courts, as opposed to the system of law called equity which was administered by the court of Chancery. Since 1873, all courts administer common law and equity concurrently. It has been described as "the commonsense of the community, crystallised and formulated by our forefathers".

Company secretary: appointed by the board of directors. He is an officer of the company and every company must by law have a secretary. The sole director of a company may not also act as secretary of the company.

Condition: a term of a contract which is so fundamental to the contract itself that any breach allows the other party to choose to treat himself as discharged from future obligations under the contract and to sue for damages. Alternatively, he may choose not to terminate the contract but may sue for damages in respect of the other party's breach. *The actress's failure to appear on the opening night of the play constituted a breach of a condition, and her contract was terminated.*

Consent: compliance with or the deliberate approval of a course of action. *He gave his consent to a withdrawal of the court proceedings.*

Consideration: that which is actually given or accepted in return for a promise. *Waiving one's right to sue on a valid claim can constitute consideration.*

Consignment: a shipment or delivery of goods. *The consignment of spare parts we've been expecting from Ace Ltd has been held up at Customs.*

Construe: (v) to interpret something in a legal context. *One of the courts' tasks is to construe documents.*

Consultancy: a company will often call in expert advice and retain a firm or person to advise them under a consultancy agreement. The person whose services are retained in this way is known as a consultant. *As a lot of companies have trouble running their business, I want to set up a management consultancy.*

Contingency fee: an agreement reached between a lawyer and his client whereby no fee will be charged for the lawyer's services unless the claim is successful or is settled out of court. It is often based on a percentage of the damages.

Contract: a legally binding agreement or bargain; a promise or set of promises which the law will enforce. *We have entered into a contract with Ace Ltd.*

Convene: (v) to call, summon, assemble. *The chairman convened an extraordinary general meeting of the shareholders.*

Conviction: the act of finding a person guilty of an offence. *The prosecution's task is to secure a conviction.*

Copyright: a property right consisting of the exclusive right to print or otherwise reproduce a published literary work. See Copyright Designs and Patents Act 1988. "A property right (which is transmissible by assignment or will as personal property) which subsists in original literary, dramatic, musical or artistic works, sound recordings, films, broadcasts or cable programmes, and the typographical arrangement of published editions."

Corporation: a legal person which may be created by statute, by Royal Charter, by Act of Parliament, or by international treaty. The most common example to be found is a company, which is created by a statutory process under the Companies Acts. In this case a corporation is a separate legal entity, quite distinct from its members, and its basic features are that it has its own legal rights and duties, as well as perpetual succession. See *Salomon v Salomon & Co Ltd* [1897] A.C. 22.

Covenant: a promise or an agreement contained in a deed. *The lease contained many strict covenants.*

D

Damages: financial compensation awarded by a court for a loss suffered by the plaintiff in an action for breach of contract or tort. *The trial court awarded the plaintiff £4,000 in damages.*

Debenture: an instrument, usually in the form of a deed issued by a company or public body as evidence of a debt or as security for a loan of money at interest. It is the most usual kind of long-term loan taken by a company. A debenture contains a promise to pay the amount stated usually at a fixed date and most debentures provide for the payment of a fixed rate of interest. Debenture interest must be paid before a dividend is paid to the shareholders. *As the company was unable to repay the debenture on the date specified, the creditor called in a receiver.*

Debtor: a person who owes money to another person. The money owed is called a debt.

Decree nisi: a decree is a judgment or order of a court. A *Decree nisi* (from the Latin meaning "unless") is a conditional decree requiring something to be done before it can be made absolute.

Deed: a legal instrument which indicates that it is intended to be a deed and which must be validly executed as a deed. The person who executes the deed must sign it in the presence of a witness who must sign in his presence. *The transfer of ownership of real property is executed by means of a deed.*

Deem: (v) to consider as, believe, or to be treated as. This is used in documents and in particular by statutes to bring something within a certain term or expression. *Her case was deemed to fall outside the scope of the particular legislation.*

Default: (v) to fail in some duty to do something, to fail to act or to meet financial obligations. *Mexico defaulted on its loan repayments in 1994.*

Defence: see defendant. The defendant's answer to the plaintiff's claim is known as his defence. *The defendant's solicitors served the defence on the plaintiff's solicitors.*

Defendant: a person who is served with a writ of summons in legal proceedings, and against whom a claim is being made. The person who brings the claim, the claimant, is also known as the plaintiff, and the person claimed against is known as the defendant.

Defraud: (v) to deceive or cheat someone. It includes any act whereby somebody is unlawfully deprived of a belonging. *She was defrauded of her inheritance by the executors.*

Directive: a form of EU legislation. The Council and Commission of the EU may issue directives which are binding only as to the result to be achieved on member states.

Director: a person appointed to carry out the management of a company. There may be executive directors, *i.e.* full-time directors with service agreements or non-executive directors who are part-time and available on an advisory basis. The directors of a company collectively are known as the board of directors. A public company must have at least two directors but a private company need only have one.

Discharge: (v) release from an obligation. *The plaintiff claims that the defendant's breach of contract has discharged the plaintiff from his contractual obligations.*

Disclose: (v) to reveal, to make known. *Each party to a contract has to disclose all relevant facts concerning the subject matter*

of the contract. This is known as the obligation of disclosure.

Dismiss: (v) to reject or set aside; used (1) in employment law to terminate or bring to an end an employee's contract of employment; (2) when a court dismisses a claim or an appeal.

Disqualification: the act of depriving somebody of a right, a power or a privilege. *One of a number of penalties for dangerous driving is disqualification from holding a driving licence.*

Distributor: a party to a distribution agreement, who distributes the products under the terms of the agreement.

Dividend: the payment made to shareholders of a company from the profits made in the accounting year. If a dividend is declared, it means that the shareholders have agreed to a distribution of the profits at the annual general meeting and the dividend relating to the number of shares held by each shareholder is the payment of the profit distribution.

Document: something on which things are written, printed or inscribed, and which gives information. A paper which can be relied on as proof or evidence of something. See Civil Evidence Act 1968, which includes as a definition of a document the following: "any plan, map, graph or drawing, any photograph, and any disc, tape, soundtrack or other device in which sounds or other data (not being visual images) are embodied so as to be capable (with or without the aid of some other equipment) of being reproduced therefrom and any film, negative, tape or other device in which one or more visual images are embodied so as to be capable as aforesaid of being reproduced therefrom".

Donation: from Latin, *donatio*. A gift. There are two kinds of donations: *donatio inter vivos*, which is a gift between living persons, and *donatio mortis causa* which is a gift in contemplation of death. The person making the gift is called the donor and the recipient is called the donee.

Dumping: the selling of goods abroad at prices below their marginal cost, which implies that the seller is making a loss. *Norway is alleged to be dumping low-priced salmon in the European Union to the detriment of the Scottish salmon industry.*

Duress: actual violence or threats of violence to the person, including actual restraint by force, *e.g.* imprisonment. *When the plaintiff brought an action to enforce the contract, the defendant alleged he had signed the document under duress.*

E

Enact: (v) to turn a bill, which is draft legislation, into an act, which is the formally approved legislation; to enter a bill as an act in a public record. *The Criminal Justice Bill was enacted yesterday.*

Enforce: (v) compel obedience; impose or put into effect. *The terms of the contract were enforced by the court.* (noun: enforcement).

Enforceable: capable of being enforced. For example, a judgment, which is an order of the court and may be enforced against the defendant, or judgment debtor. *If a contract is properly formed, it will be enforceable by both parties.*

Equitable: fair and just; in accordance with the rules of equity. *When the common law remedy of damages is not adequate relief for breach of contract, the equitable remedy of specific performance may be ordered.*

Equity (1): from the Latin word *aequus* meaning fair. It is to be distinguished from common law. A system of rules and procedure which developed separately from common law and was administered in different courts. This system was evolved by the Court of Chancery in an attempt to remedy some of the defects of the system of common law, which was inflexible and had certain limitations which gave rise to unjust or unfair decisions.

Equity (2): a beneficial interest in an asset. Used often in the context of equity capital, the part of the share capital of a company owned by ordinary shareholders.

Essence: something intrinsic or essential; the essence of a contract means the essential, basic conditions, without which no contract would have been entered into. *The doctrine of commercial frustration will be applied only when the essence of a contract has been frustrated.*

Estate: an interest in land; the assets of a deceased person. *After all debts were paid, the deceased's estate was valued at £360,000.*

Exception: a saving clause in a contract or deed which prevents the coming into effect of something which would otherwise do so in its absence. *The insurance policy included an exception related to high risk sports.*

Exclusion clause: a clause which excludes or modifies an obligation that would otherwise arise under the contract by implication of law.

Execute: (v) sign, give effect to, carry out or enforce. *A will is executed by the testator. A court orders its judgment to be executed.*

Executor: a person named in a will and given the duty of administering the testator's estate on his death and carrying out the provisions of his will.

Executory contract: a contract which still has to be carried out; a contract which contains promises which are to be performed at a future date.

Exemption: freedom or exclusion from liability. *He obtained exemption from military service.*

Expansion of capital: increase of capital. *When a company increases its share capital, the company is said to be in expansion.*

Expectant: expecting. Used in relation to an heir. *An expectant heir is one who hopes to inherit property.*

Expectation: hope or prospect of inheriting property.

Expend: (v) (p. expended/p.p. expended) spend.

Express: clearly stated. *The contract contained an express promise.*

F

Fact: a circumstance or incident relevant to a contract or to a case. *Questions of fact are decided by a jury, and the judge decides questions of law.*

Fallacy: lack of logic or faulty reasoning in an argument. *Counsel for the defence is bound to point out the fallacy in this argument.*

False: untrue; deliberately wrong and intended to deceive. *He made a false statement of fact.* A statement although literally true may be false if it is used in order to convey a false impression.

Fiduciary relationship: a relationship between two or more persons involving trust or confidence. *As a fiduciary relationship existed between the two contracting parties, the burden of proof is on the defendant to prove that he did not exercise undue influence over my client, the defendant's son.*

Financial year: an accounting year or accounting reference period. Except in the case of a company's first accounting period which will be at least six but no more than 18 months in length, thereafter the accounting period must be 12 months. In England the financial year normally ends on March 31st but may end on any date chosen by the company.

Fine: a financial penalty. A sum of money ordered by the court to be paid to the Crown on conviction for an offence.

Floating charge: a kind of charge which can be created by companies to secure debentures. The court has described this kind of charge as ambulatory and it hovers over the property until some event occurs which causes it to settle and crystallise into a specific charge.

FOB: Free on board. The basis of an export contract where the seller pays the cost and insurance for sending the goods to the port of shipment and loading them on to the ship or aircraft. From that point, the buyer has to pay these charges. *Please quote us your prices FOB Boston.*

Forbearance: the act of refraining from enforcing a debt. *A forbearance to take legal action may be adequate consideration.*

Forfeit: (v) to lose something in consequence of having committed a wrong, whether a crime, fault or breach. *If shares have been forfeited by resolution of the board of directors (if the articles of association give such a power), the members involved are required to return the share certificate.*

Forfeiture: noun from forfeit.

Formal: a term used to describe a contract. *The parties entered into a formal contract for the sale of the house.*

Fraud: a false representation by means of a statement or conduct in order to gain a material advantage. Intentional deceit causing harm to another person. *He obtained the elderly couple's savings through fraud: he pretended to be running a high-interest offshore fund.*

Fraudulent: containing the intent to

167

defraud or deceive others. *The fund manager's behaviour was fraudulent because he lied about the assets of the fund in order to persuade potential clients to invest their money in it.*

Freehold: an estate or interest in land which is the most complete form of ownership of land. It is known as a legal estate in fee simple in possession.

Frustration: the termination of a contract caused by an unforeseen event which makes the performance of the contract impossible or illegal. It is also referred to as *force majeure*. An example would be the destruction of the subject matter of the contract. Frustration can be said to kill the contract and automatically to discharge the parties from any further obligations thereunder.

G

General Meeting: under the Company's (Tables A to F) Regulations 1985, all General Meetings other than Annual General Meetings are called extraordinary general meetings. The annual general meeting of a company is called to consider and pass the accounts for the preceding financial year.

Govern: (v) rule, regulate. *The terms governing the contract were very harsh.*

Gratuitous: given freely without any consideration. *A gratuitous promise is not considered to be a binding offer.*

Grounds: reasons. *He complained to the court on the grounds that the other party had presented false evidence.* By reason of the fact that ...; based on the fact that ...

Guardian: a person who is formally appointed by the court to look after the affairs of a person who is either lacking full legal capacity, or who is incapable of managing his own affairs.

Guilty: culpable or responsible. (1) the plea or formal statement offered by a person who is admitting that he has committed an offence of which he is accused. (2) the formal statement (verdict) offered by the court when the accused is found to have committed the offence.

H

Heir: beneficiary, next-of-kin. A person receiving, or legally entitled to receive, the estate of a deceased person.

Held: from the verb to hold. When a court decides a dispute before it, it gives judgment and in the reported facts of the case it is usual to refer to the judgment as "held by the court" followed by the details of the judgment.

I

Illegal: prohibited by law. *To give a false declaration of your income to the tax authorities is an illegal act.*

Implement: (v) to carry out, perform or put into effect. *He implemented the terms of the agreement.*

Implied, impliedly: suggested, or understood by implication or inference from the circumstances. *Frequently a promise to pay can be implied by the conduct of the parties, as in the case of a nod of the head.*

Imply: (v) to mean. An implied term of a contract is one which has not been expressly stated, but which the courts are prepared, or required by statute, to construe as such.

Incapacity: lack or absence of legal competence. *Contracts entered into under the influence of alcohol or drugs, depending on the degree of incapacity, may be voidable.*

Indemnity: agreement by one party to make good any loss or damage suffered by another party. Hence, indemnity insurance designed to compensate the holder of the insurance policy in the event that he suffers loss by the payment of money or by repair, replacement or reinstatement.

Induce: (v) to persuade a person by threat or promise to do something. *Ace Ltd has induced our managing director to break his contract with us in order to work with it by promising him benefits which we could never offer.*

Inducement: persuasion. *One element of consideration is that it is the inducement to a contract.*

Industrial dispute: trade dispute. A dispute between an employer and employees or their trade union usually about wages or working conditions. *Industrial disputes are often avoided by collective bargaining.*

Infancy: from Latin, *infantia*: childhood, the condition of being an infant; now used for a person who is under age, that is to say under the age of 18.

Infringe: (v) violate or interfere with the right of another person; used in particular in the context of trademarks, patents and copyright.

Injunction: an order of the court directing a person to do or refrain from doing a particular thing. *The plaintiff applied to the court for an injunction to be granted against the defendant to prevent him from continuing to breach the terms of the contract.*

Inland Revenue: the Government department administering the collection of tax.

Innominate term: the term of a contract which is of an intermediate character in that it is neither a condition nor a warranty. It literally means neither named nor classified, and consequently in such a case a party to a contract has to see the effect of the resulting breach to decide what action to take.

Inquisitorial: from Latin, *inquisitio*. A system of law in civil law jurisdictions where an investigating judge initiates all the inquiries in a criminal matter and where the trial itself is an inquiry by the court.

Insanity: unsoundness of mind. It refers to the state of mind of a person which prevents that person from knowing right from wrong, and in consequence, he cannot be held responsible for his acts. A person is presumed to be sane until the contrary is proved.

Insider dealing: dealing in shares or debentures of listed companies by persons having access to confidential information obtained from the company and which is not available to the public. This conduct is regulated by the Companies Securities (Insider Dealing) Act 1985 and is a criminal offence.

Intention: purpose or aim. The sense of a contract, which may be derived from a reading and subsequent comprehension of its contents. *As we are dealing with family relations, we will have to rebut the presumption that there was no intention to enter into a contract.*

Invitation to treat: an offer to receive an offer. *Price indications in shops, price lists and catalogues are considered invitations to treat, which are merely statements of the price, and not offers to sell.*

Irredeemable: used to describe securities for which no date is provided for the redemption or repayment of the capital sum, especially for Government loan stock and some debentures.

Issue: (v) print, publish or distribute. A writ is issued. Shares in companies are issued in exchange for cash. Sometimes there are free issues of shares known as scrip issues. The issue price is the price at which a new issue of shares in a company is sold to the public.

J

Judgment: the formal decision of a court. *The court delivered judgment in favour of the plaintiff.*

Jurisdiction: the power of a court to hear and decide on a case before it. *Juvenile matters are not within the jurisdiction of this court.*

Jurisprudence: the philosophy or science of law. *Students of law at Cambridge may choose jurisprudence as one of their optional courses.*

K

Knighthood: the lowest title of dignity in the United Kingdom. It is not hereditary. *He has been given a knighthood by the Queen for his services to the community.*

L

Landlord: the owner of land or premises which are leased to another person called the tenant.

Lapse: (v) to end, expire, run out, terminate. Legal proceedings are said to have lapsed if no step is taken within the time limits laid down by the rules of court. Lapse of time means that a particular period of time has passed or expired. *The offer lapsed because the other party failed to accept it within the stipulated period.*

Law: an obligatory rule of conduct; the body of principles recognised and applied by the state in the administration of justice; The body of rules and guidelines within which society requires its judges to administer justice. *We must by law submit our annual accounts to revision by public auditors.*

Lawful: permitted or recognised by law; legitimate.

Lawsuit: this is commonly used to refer to a legal dispute between two or more persons before a court of law. It is not a formal legal expression.

Leading case: a judicial decision which establishes the principles of that branch of the law, which is cited in text books and in court, and referred to as such on account of its importance.

Legal detriment: in the context of a contract, it means that the promisee forgoes a legal right which he might otherwise exercise, in return for a promise. It also means injury, damage or loss suffered at law. *A party to a contract incurs legal detriment if he waives his right to sue for breach of contract.*

Legislation: statute law, parliament legislates, that is to say, it makes laws. *In England, unlike Spain, legislation only comprises part of the body of law.*

Legitimacy: from Latin, *legitimatio.* Conformity to the rule of law. The condition of being born in lawful wedlock, that is, marriage.

Lessee: see tenant. A person to whom a lease is made by a lessor.

Lessor: see landlord. A person who makes a lease to another person called the tenant or lessee.

Liability: obligation or duty imposed by law. An amount of money owed to another person. *The major disadvantage of a partnership is the unlimited personal liability of its members.*

Liable: debt, indebtedness. The condition of being answerable at, or responsible by law, or subject to something. *On the expiration of the contract, neither party was liable under its terms.*

Lien: from the Latin *ligare* meaning to bind. It is a right over another person's property which may be retained until a claim against that person is satisfied. *There is a lien on those shares, and they cannot be sold.*

Limited: in the context of limited liability, it means that in the case of a company limited by shares, shareholders will not be called on to pay more than the amount remaining unpaid on their shares. *If we incorporate our business, our liability for its debts will be limited.*

Listing: from the verb to list. A company whose shares are traded on a Stock Exchange is known as a listed company. This means that the company has signed a listing agreement, *e.g.* with the London Stock Exchange for the quotation of its shares on the Stock Exchange. *Ace plc is soon to seek a listing on the LSE.*

Litigation: the procedure whereby legal action is taken by a person who is referred to as the litigant. It has been defined as a game in which the court is umpire. *Hospitals are frequently involved in litigation.*

Lock-out: a kind of industrial action by an employer where he refuses to allow employees access to their place of work in consequence of a dispute. *The managers have decided on a lock-out as the only way to stop the plant being destroyed.*

M

Majority: full age. A person who has attained the age of 18. *He will inherit the estate when he attains his majority.*

Mandamus: from Latin, we command. This was formerly a writ directed to a person or body to compel the performance of a public duty. It is now known as an order of mandamus and forms part of the procedure known as a judicial review.

Material: relevant, important, essential. *Your company's failure to have the housing finished by the start of the Olympic Games constitutes a material breach of contract and therefore discharges us from our contractual obligations.*

Member: a person who has subscribed to a company's memorandum of association or who has been allotted shares in a company or who purchases shares from a shareholder of a company are known as members. When they transfer their shares or upon death they cease to be members of the company.

Merchantable quality: Used of goods, fit for ordinary purposes taking into account their description, price and any other relevant circumstances. This condition is implied by statute.

Minor: person under the age of 18.

Minutes: a written record of meetings of the directors and shareholders of a company. *The minutes of the last board meeting must be signed by the chairman after they have been approved by the members of the next board meeting.*

Misappropriation: dishonestly appropriating or taking over another person's property. *The shareholders accused the chairman of misappropriation of the company's funds.*

Misrepresentation: a false statement which gives a wrong idea of a material fact. *"In my opinion any behaviour by words or conduct is sufficient to be a misrepresentation if it is such as to mislead the other party. If it conveys a false impression, that is enough."* Denning L.J. See *Curtis v Chemical Cleaning and Dyeing Co* (1951) 1 K.B. 805.

Mortgage: an interest in land or other property which is designed to secure the payment of a debt or the discharge of some other obligation. *If you borrow money from a bank in order to purchase a property you will take out a mortgage with the bank in order to buy the property.* The document is known as a mortgage deed.

Motion: application to a court for an order directing something to be done in the applicant's favour. The most common application is for an interlocutory injunction relating to a pre-trial matter. *X applied to the court by notice of motion for an injunction to restrain Y from removing his assets from the jurisdiction.* This is known as a Mareva injunction from the case *Mareva Compania Naviera SA v International Bulk Carriers SA* [1975] 2 Lloyd's Rep. 509.

N

Necessaries: from Latin, *necessarius*. Something necessary or essential. Refers to goods or services corresponding to the condition in life and present needs of either a minor, or a person subject to some incapacity.

Negligence: in English law it is a tort, a civil wrong. A breach of a duty of care arises resulting in damage to the person to whom the duty of care is owed. A professional person owes a duty of care to his client in the advice he gives. *A person who suffers loss or injury in consequence of a breach of a duty of care may claim damages in tort for negligence.*

Negotiable instruments: commercial paper such as a cheque, bill of exchange or promissory note representing money, which changes ownership by the act of giving it to another person.

Net worth: the value of a company when its liabilities have been deducted from the value of its assets.

Notification: a formal notice or communication. (v) notify. *The court formally notified the defendant by written notification of the hearing date for the action.*

O

Obiter dictum: from Latin, a remark in passing. Informally referred to as *obiter*. This is the name given to something which is said by a judge when delivering judgment, and which is not essential to the decision in the case before him.

Obligation: a legal or moral duty, to be contrasted with physical compulsion. *A debtor has an obligation towards his creditors.*

Offer: an undertaking by the person making the offer, and known as the offeror, that he will be bound in contract by the offer if there is a proper acceptance of it by the other party known as the offeree. A written or oral proposal to give or do something. *They have made an offer of £400,000 for that house.*

Offeree: a person to whom an offer has been made, or to whom something has been offered.

Offeror: a person who makes an offer, or who offers something.

Officer: a person who holds a position of authority in an organisation. The officer of a company acts on behalf of the company in an official capacity. Company officers include the directors and the company secretary.

Onus: burden, responsibility. *The onus of proof was on the plaintiff to justify his claim for damages against the defendant.* The plaintiff had the obligation of proving the facts to justify his claim.

Operative mistake: a mistake of fact which prevents the formation of a contract. This is an exceptional occurrence, and a good example is a mutual mistake as to the identity of the subject-matter of a contract.

Option: a right to choose something. This right may be given by contract to accept or reject an existing offer within a specified period of time. The contract is known as an option agreement. For example, a right to purchase a property.

Overheads: general expenses, also referred to as overhead expenses. *Ace's overheads are very high and it is increasingly difficult to pass them on to the customer.*

P

Partner: a person who is in partnership with others is called a partner. He or she is often referred to as a member of a partnership.

Partnership: the relationship existing between persons carrying on business in common with a view to making a profit. *I want to go into partnership with John to sell the furniture he makes.*

Party: a person who takes part in a business transaction or in legal proceedings. *He was a party to a contract with the Spanish Government.*

Perform: (v) carry out, execute: to perform a contract means to do what you are required to do in accordance with its terms and your obligations. *Failure to perform the contract according to the terms laid down may result in litigation.*

Performance: the carrying out or completion of an act. *A contract is said to be discharged by performance.*

Performance bond: a bond or guarantee normally given by a bank to guarantee the satisfactory performance of a contract by one of the parties to the contract. *The Government requires a performance bond before it will finally sign the contract with us.*

Petitioner: a person who makes or presents a petition. Used in bankruptcy and divorce cases.

Plaintiff: a person who brings an action before the courts. Also known as claimant.

Plea-bargaining: an informal procedure whereby the defendant in criminal proceedings may agree to plead guilty to a charge in exchange for the prosecution agreeing to withdraw other charges.

Plead: (v) to ask for something, to petition, or to request.

Pleadings: written statements delivered by the litigating parties alternately to one another requesting information to elucidate the questions of fact and law to be decided by the court in a claim.

Poll: a procedure whereby votes are taken, registered and counted. A form of voting at shareholders' meetings. *The members decided to vote on the resolution by means of a poll, and not a show of hands.*

Preamble: recital, preliminary or introductory part of a statute or contract. *The date, the place and the names and addresses of the parties are normally stated in the preamble to a contract.*

Precedent: a judgment or decision of a court cited in a later similar case to justify the court's decision. The High Court is bound by a previous decision of the Court of Appeal and the House of Lords. *The*

Carlill *case set a precedent for acceptance through performance.*

Presumption: an inference drawn or a conclusion reached as to the truth of some fact in question, obtained from other facts proved or which are admitted to be true. *In family matters, there is a presumption that the parties do not intend to create legal relations.*

Principal: a person who authorises another person called the agent to act on his behalf. A sum of money loaned at interest, and referred to as the principal sum. *Now I've paid most of the interest on my mortgage, I have to pay back the principal.*

Private law: that part of the law which regulates the relations directly between individuals and where the state is not involved. For example, contract law and family law.

Privity: a relationship between two parties; privity of contract is the relationship existing between parties to a contract. It has been said that in the law of England certain principles are fundamental. One is that only a person who is a party to a contract may sue on it.

Privy Council: the present-day British Cabinet was developed from the Privy Council, which is no longer the executive power in England, but it is still important. Acts of Parliament frequently give "Her Majesty in Council" power to make orders and proclamations, and in order to do so, the Queen will call a meeting of the Privy Council. Membership is for life and all Cabinet Ministers are Privy Councillors. It has two kinds of executive work, one concerning political matters referred to above, and the other concerning judicial matters. The judicial committee of the Privy Council is the final Court of Appeal on both civil and criminal matters from certain Commonwealth Countries and British overseas territories. In practice, this includes New Zealand, The Channel Islands, The Isle of Man, Gibraltar,

Mauritius and The Republic of Trinidad and Tobago, among others. It is also the Final Court of Appeal from English Ecclesiastical Courts and also hears appeals from the Disciplinary Bodies of Dentists, Doctors and Opticians.

Probation: trial period. The action of putting someone to the test. In certain circumstances a court, instead of sentencing a person to a term of imprisonment, may make a probation order, which means that the offender is placed under the care and supervision of an official called a probation officer.

Proceedings: the conducting of legal business before the courts. *You commence these proceedings by issuing a writ or summons and by doing this you are said to institute proceedings against another person.*

Product liability: the liability of persons for damage caused due to defective products. *The Distributor hereby agrees to keep the Supplier indemnified against all actions and claims except those of a product liability nature.*

Prohibition: this was formerly a writ issued out of the High Court to restrain an inferior court from exercising its powers. This is now controlled by the High Court under the remedy of judicial review, which supervises inferior courts.

Prohibitory: with the quality of prohibiting. *A prohibitory injunction is a court order preventing the continuation or ordering the cessation of a wrongful act.*

Promise: the intention to do or to forbear from some act. *A promise is made by the promisor to the person called the promisee.*

Proposal: offer, proposition. *He made a proposal to his friend to go into business together.*

Proprietary interest or right: the holding of an interest or right in something, or ownership over it. A proprietary name, for example, is the name of a commercial product which is registered by the holder or owner of the proprietary interest as a trade mark, which protects it against its use by a third party without the owner's permission.

Prosecute: (v) to pursue legal proceedings, and in particular criminal proceedings. *He was prosecuted for burglary.*

Prospectus: a document which provides details of a new issue of shares in a company inviting the public to buy shares. The prospectus has to comply with the provisions of the Companies Act 1985. *I'm going to send away for the prospectus for the new Rolls Royce share issue.*

Provision: a clause in a legal document. *That contract makes no provision for force majeure.*

Proxy: a person appointed to represent another person. A shareholder may appoint a third person his proxy to attend and vote on his behalf at a shareholders' meeting of the company. The proxy does not have to be a member of the company. It is fairly common practice at meetings for the directors to offer themselves as proxies for shareholders who cannot attend the meeting.

Public law: that part of the law which deals with the functions of central and local government and regulates the relations between the individual and the state, including administrative law, constitutional law, criminal law and tax law.

Public policy: it has been described as a principle of law which holds that no person can lawfully do anything which has a tendency to be injurious to the public, or against the public good. *Certain contracts are void as being contrary to public policy.*

Puff: trade puff; exaggerated or extravagant statement or advertisement.

Punishment: a penalty imposed by a court of law in criminal proceedings when an accused person is convicted of an offence, or pleads guilty.

Purport: (v) claim or intend; often to claim something falsely. *He purported to be a judge of the High Court.*

175

Q

Quantum Meruit: from the Latin meaning "as much as he has earned". In the case of a claim for a breach of contract, the plaintiff may be entitled to claim for work done and services performed and the court has to quantify the amount which the plaintiff should have earned, to reach a figure for damages, on a *quantum meruit* basis.

Quash: (v) annul, set aside, make void. *The House of Lords quashed the decision of the Court of Appeal.*

Quasi-contract: a situation where the law imposes on a person an obligation to repay money on the grounds of unjust benefit or enrichment, *i.e.* when he has enriched himself at the expense of another person.

Quorum: from Latin meaning "of whom" used to indicate the minimum number of persons required to be present to constitute a formal meeting. *As there was no quorum, the meeting was adjourned until the following week.*

R

Reasonable man: the ordinary citizen, envisaged as a reasonable and sensible person. This concept is important in the law of tort because the standard of care in actions for negligence is based on what a reasonable man might be expected to do taking into consideration the circumstances and the foreseeable consequences. He has been described as "the fair and reasonable man who represents after all no more than the anthropomorphic conception of justice".

Rebut: (v) (p./p.p. rebutted) oppose by contrary evidence, disprove or contradict something. *The plaintiff will have to rebut the presumption that there was no intention to create legal relations if he wishes his case to succeed.*

Rebuttal: (n) a refutation or contradiction. *The defendant's rebuttal of the allegations in the pleadings was accepted by the court.*

Receipt: an acknowledgment in writing that money or goods have been received. *Will you please sign this receipt for the delivery of 100 tons of coal?*

Recover: (v) regain something or get something back or obtain something. *George recovered damages in the libel action he brought against the newspaper.* To recover possession of property. *When proceedings are taken to evict tenants from the property and judgment is given in favour of the owner, the latter is said to have recovered possession of his property.*

Rectification: a remedy available in equity where a contract does not accurately reflect an agreement between the parties in consequence of some common mistake.

Redeemable: capable of being redeemed, that is, paid off or cleared by payment. *I asked my stockbroker to purchase New Zealand government bonds redeemable in 2002.*

Redress: remedy, relief. *He sought redress*

for all the pain and hardship he had suffered as a result of his accident at work.

Registered office: the official address of a company which every company must have at all times. It must be notified to the Registrar of Companies upon incorporation and all changes must also be notified.

Registrar of Companies: a civil servant in charge of the running of the company registry and responsible for registering companies and supervising the statutory documents required for the registration of companies.

Reject: (v) refuse, not accept. *An offer is rejected if the offeree communicates his rejection of the offer to the offeror.*

Release: the state of being set free from liability. A deed of release: document which exonerates a person from liability for any claim. The renunciation or abandonment of a legal claim.

Relief: remedy, normally in the form of damages or an injunction. The remedy sought from the court by a claimant. *He applied to the court for relief.*

Rely on: (v) depend on something, put one's trust in something. *He relied on a decision of the Court of Appeal when pleading his case before the court.*

Remedy: the means whereby the law enables a person to recover rights or to obtain reparation or compensation for a wrong. *An action brought for damages before the court is a remedy sought by the plaintiff.*

Render: (v) make, restore, give up. *The mutual mistake as to the subject matter rendered the contract void.*

Repossess: (v) take back into your possession. *When a mortgagee (lender) exercises his right to take possession of the mortgaged property, e.g. if the mortgagor*

(borrower) fails to maintain the repayment terms, then the mortgagee is said to repossess the property.

Repudiate: (v) reject or refuse to accept or recognise something. *A refusal to be bound by the terms of a contract amounts to repudiation of the contract, which generally is a breach of contract.*

Rescission: the act of rescinding, or making void. The setting aside of a contract in cases of innocent or fraudulent misrepresentation, whereby it is treated as if it had never existed.

Resolution: a binding decision made by the members of a company. From the verb *resolve. The problem of the removal of the director was resolved at the general meeting of the company when an ordinary resolution was passed to remove him.*

Respondent: a person against whom a motion or an appeal is brought or against whom a divorce petition is filed.

Restraint: limitation or restriction. A restraint of trade is a contractual term purporting to limit a person's ability to carry on business after the termination of his employment. *The contractual term was held by the court to be an unreasonable restraint and contrary to public policy.*

Reverse: (v) to set aside a judgment on appeal. *The High Court reversed the judgment of the county court.*

Revoke: (v) cancel, annul, withdraw, renounce. *An offer may be revoked at any time before its acceptance.*

Right: something to which a person has a lawful claim. *In England, there is no automatic right to personal privacy.*

Root: in the context of a contract, the root means the fundamental essential features of the contract; its basic terms and conditions.

S

Service: a duty owed by one person to another. Hence a service agreement between a company and its managing director, whereby the managing director owes a duty to the company under the agreement. The delivery of a writ or summons to a defendant.

Set aside: (v) (p. set / p.p. set) annul, cancel, make void, override. *An application was made by motion to the Court of Appeal to set aside the High Court judgment on the grounds that the trial judge committed errors of law.*

Settlement: compromise. The conclusion of a claim by an agreement between the litigating parties. Also a deed disposing of land or other property, inter vivos or by will, also known as a trust. For example, a marriage settlement. *The settlement of the claim included the payment of legal costs.*

Share Capital: the total amount which the shareholders of a company have contributed, or if the share capital is not fully paid up, the amount they are liable to contribute as payment for their shares.

Shareholder: a person who owns shares and thus becomes a member of a company. A company may also own shares in another company.

Shipment: the act of shipping freight or goods whether by sea, land or air. An amount shipped, a consignment. *The shipment of computers was slightly damaged when the aircraft hit a light plane on the runway.*

Solicitor: a person who is authorised to conduct legal proceedings or to advise on legal matters. In the United Kingdom he is the lawyer of first instance. Although solicitors may appear in court, traditionally barristers tend to do most of the advocacy, at least in the higher courts.

Specific performance: an equitable remedy which may be granted at the discretion of the court where damages would be inadequate compensation for the breach of the agreement; the effect of such an order is that the party against whom the order is made must perform his obligations under the terms of an agreement. *As there was no other way of making redress, the court ordered the plaintiff to convey the property to the defendant.*

Stake: a financial interest in a business. *John has a substantial stake in Ace plc.*

Statement of claim: a formal document known as a pleading in which the plaintiff sets out the material facts upon which he relies in support of his claim, and the relief he is seeking.

Statute: an Act of Parliament. A legislative decree of the Monarch in Parliament. When a parliamentary bill is approved by both houses of Parliament, it receives the formal Royal Assent, and becomes an Act of Parliament and is entered in the statute book, where all enacted statutes are recorded.

Statutory: established by law. Statutory instrument: a common kind of subordinated legislation. A statutory meeting: the ordinary general meeting of the members of a company.

Statutory declaration: a formal declaration made in a prescribed form before a Commissioner for Oaths.

Stipulation: an essential term or condition of an agreement; from the Latin word *stipulatio.*

Stock: capital raised by a company by the issue and subscription of shares. Also money loaned to a government, local authority or company at a fixed rate of interest.

Strike: a partial or complete withdrawal of labour by workers.

Subject to: to be bound by something, to be under the power of something or somebody, to be conditional on something. Also used in contract law when an offer which is accepted subject to contract means that no legally binding commitment has been made without further formalities. *He was subject to a court probation order.*

Subscriber: a person who subscribes for something; a person who signs the memorandum of association of a company upon its incorporation and who subscribes for shares in the company, signing the articles of association and appointing the first directors of the company.

Subsidiary: a subsidiary company is one which is controlled by a holding company. Under the Companies Act 1985 a company is defined as a subsidiary of another company if that other company either holds a majority of the voting rights, or is a member of it and has the right to remove or appoint a majority of its directors, or is a member and controls alone, as a consequence of a shareholder agreement, a majority of the voting rights in the company. *Ace plc has decided to set up a subsidiary in Kuala Lumpur in order to enter the booming Asian market.*

Succession: used in relation to the estate of a deceased person. The right by which a person succeeds to the estate or office of another person. The rules of intestate succession show who is entitled to succeed to the property of a person who dies without leaving a will.

Sue: (v) to commence or bring proceedings against a person or entity. *He successfully sued the newspaper for libel.*

Suit: any civil court proceeding; from the French word *suite* meaning the act of following.

T

Takeover bid: an offer made to the shareholders of a company by another company or by individuals to purchase their shares at a specified price in order to gain control of the company. *Ace plc has received a hostile takeover bid from Zero plc, but its shareholders are being advised not to accept.*

Tenant: a person who rents property from a landlord.

Tender: an offer; (v) to tender; to pay off his debt, a debtor should tender the exact amount of the outstanding debt to his creditor. It may also mean an offer for sale, or an invitation to make an offer. *The Ministry of Defence invites tenders for the supply of uniforms for the Army.*

Tenet: a principle, dogma or doctrine.

Term: a substantive part of a contract which creates a contractual obligation. In practice, it includes a condition, a warranty or an innominate term.

Terminate: (v) to end, bring to an end, conclude. *The contract was terminated by written notice given under its terms.*

Testator: the person executing a will. (Feminine form: testatrix.)

Testify: (v) to witness, to give evidence in court.

Third party: a person other than the principals in any court proceedings or in any contractual relationship.

Timely: opportune, suitable or well-timed.

Title: the right to ownership of land or goods, or the evidence of such right. *The title deeds are evidence of legal ownership of land.*

Tort: a civil wrong. From the Latin word *tortus* meaning twisted or distorted. It is an act which causes harm to a person, excluding any breach of contract, and the remedy is for an action for damages to be brought at common law.

Trade puff: an advertisement which contains an exaggerated statement attributed to the object in question or false praise; puff means to inflate or swell up.

Trading Account: part of a company's profit and loss account. It shows the cost of goods sold compared with the money realised by the sale of the goods, and in this way the amount of the gross profit is ascertained.

Transaction: an act or series of acts carried out in the ordinary course of business negotiations. *A business transaction could encompass a number of business acts, for example, the selling of a property, which would be referred to as a property transaction.*

Transmission: the granting of assets to another person not by way of transfer but by operation of law, for example on death or bankruptcy.

Trespass: a civil wrong, or tort. From old French, passing across. An unlawful act committed against another person or property, *e.g.* wrongful entry on a person's land.

Trustee: a person who holds property on trust for another person who is called the beneficiary.

U

Ultra vires: from Latin, beyond the power. A term used generally to refer to the excess of legal powers or authority.

Unconscionable: the state of not having a conscience. Something is said to be unconscionable if it is not in accordance with what is generally considered to be right or reasonable. In contract law, a bargain is said to be unconscionable when its terms are so one-sided and so unfair as to give rise to a presumption of fraud or injustice.

Undertake: (v) (p. undertook/p.p. undertaken) to promise, to enter into a binding obligation. *Ace plc have undertaken to supply us with software for the next twenty-four months.*

Undue influence: an equitable doctrine whereby if a person enters into an agreement in circumstances which suggest or give rise to a presumption that he has not been allowed to exercise free and deliberate judgment on the matter, the court will set aside the agreement. It may often involve improper pressure, and may arise in situations where there is a relationship of mutual confidence, such as a guardian and ward.

Unilateral contract: a contract where an offer is made in the form of a promise to pay in return for the performance of an act, which is taken to imply assent. See *Carlill v Carbolic Smoke Ball Co* [1893] 1 QB 256.

Unjust enrichment: a quasi-contractual term, which means that a person has been unduly or unfairly enriched at the expense of another person. In such a case the person enriched has to make restitution to the other person, as he is under an obligation *quasi ex contractu* to do so, as if it were a contract.

Unreasonable: The following definition has been rendered by a famous judge: "No one can properly be labelled as unreasonable unless he is not only wrong but unreasonably wrong, so wrong that no reasonable person could sensibly take that view."

Uphold: (v) (p. upheld / p.p. upheld) to confirm. *The Appeal Court upheld the decision of the lower court.*

V

Valid: legally binding or enforceable; a valid contract is legally binding on the parties.

Valuable consideration: see consideration. Consideration to be good must be valuable. It must be something which is of some value in the eyes of the law. See *Thomas v Thomas* [1842] 2 Q.B. 851. *A promises to give his Rolls Royce to B in return for B's pencil. In the eyes of the law B's pencil is of value. Contrast with the situation where A promises to give his Rolls Royce to B. There is no consideration.*

Verbal: spoken, oral. A contract may be verbal or written.

Vitiate: (v) to invalidate, to make legally defective; to make or render ineffective. *A contract may be vitiated by fraud.*

Void: having no legal force or effect: not legally binding. *The contract was void* ab initio, i.e. *empty or without legal force from the beginning.*

Voidable: capable of being set aside.

W

Waiver: the free abandonment of a claim. A waiver has to be an intentional act with knowledge. *Her decision not to sue for breach constitutes a waiver of her rights.*

Ward: a person under the legal care or protection of another person, called the guardian. *As both his parents were killed when he was a minor, he was made a ward of his uncle.*

Warrant: (v) to sanction, guarantee, vouch for, assure. *He warranted that the goods were of merchantable quality.* (n) a written authorisation issued to execute processes in both civil and criminal cases. *A warrant was issued for George's arrest.*

Warranty: a less important term of a contract. Contrast with *conditions* which are the more important terms. *A breach of a warranty does not operate to discharge a contract, but the other party can sue for damages.*

Will: a revocable declaration made by a person in the event of that person's death. It is also known as a testament. A will must be executed by the testator or testatrix (in the case of a woman) in the presence of two witnesses and they must all sign together in each other's presence.

Writ: an instrument under seal issued in the name of the Sovereign. *A judicial writ is issued by a court to commence a legal action by a plaintiff against a defendant.*

KEY

Introduction

Vocabulary – (p.2)

paragraph one –	engraved
	bold
	heeded
	parliamentarian
paragraph two –	rooted
	thoroughly
	accessible
	passage
paragraph three –	chokingly
	bewildering
	well-drafted
	paid lip service

Exercises – (p.4)

1. CIVIL   sue, plaintiff, judgment, bring an action, county court, civil wrong, injunction.
   CRIMINAL punish, conviction, guilty, imprisonment, prosecution, offence, fine, Crown Court.
   BOTH   proceedings, defendant, jurisdiction, liable, magistrates courts, appeal, trespass, release, discharge.
2. (a) give rise to
   (b) does not reside
   (c) be stated as depending
   (d) ... if he fails to leave upon request
   (e) distinct
   (f) primarily

English for Contracts

Introduction – (p.6)

1. (a) (for example) Individuals: when buying a newspaper, a house, travelling by public transport.
   Firms: when buying supplies or raw materials or selling goods.
   Governments: when signing international treaties.
   (b) Courts and legislators take care to see that the freedom to contract is not abused, and to protect the rights of each party to a contract.
   (c) Contract law underlies many areas of business – corporations, commercial paper, partnerships, landlord and tenant agreements.

2. (a) binding   (b) in writing   (c) assent to
   (d) performed   (e) commercial paper

182

3. (a) binding   enforce
    (b) arise
    (c) into   comply   compliance
    (d) in   on   expectations.

– (p.7)

4. (a) empowered   (b) enables   (c) entrusted
    (d) entitled   (e) ensure   (f) enshrined/embodied
    (g) embroiled/entangled   (h) enlighten   (i) enact

Chapter One

Read and Match – (p.8)

A   B
1 – f   1 – f
2 – d   2 – b
3 – e   3 – e
4 – a   4 – c
5 – b   5 – d
6 – c   6 – a

Sentence Writing (suggested answers) – (p.10)

1. The court enforced the contract.
2. The court ordered them to refrain from distributing the product in California.
3. Your signing the contract has committed you to performance.
4. New enactments arise from many EU directives.

Discussion – (p.13)

1. Yes.
2. No
3. Yes
4. No
5. Yes

The Court of the Queen's Bench rejected the argument. Patteson J. thought that, whether there was a benefit to the defendant or not, there was "at any rate a detriment to the plaintiff from his parting with the possession for even so short a time". Lord Denman avoided the language of benefit and detriment. "The defendant had some reason for wishing to weigh the boilers; and he could do so only by obtaining permission from the plaintiff which he did obtain by promising to return them in good condition." By one or other of these lines of argument it is, of course, possible to find a consideration, though the description of the transaction as a bargain struck by the exchange of a promise on the one side and a permission on the other wears a somewhat artificial appearance.

Discussion Cases

  (i) The court held that the agreement was contrary to public policy and illegal. No relief could be granted to the plaintiff.
 (ii) It was held by the Court of Appeal that, as the work had been carried out and paid for before the beneficiaries made their promise to repay Mrs McArdle, the consideration was past and the promise contained in the document was not binding.
(iii) The Court of the Queen's Bench held that the plaintiff could not sue the defendant and explained their decision in two different ways. Lord Denman said that the plaintiff could not "show any consideration for the promise moving from him to the defendant". Littledale J. said that "no privity is shown between the plaintiff and the defendant".

Exercise prepositions – (p.14)

a. in   b. from   c. under   d. to
e. into / by / with   f. on   g. from   h. in / on

Read and Match – (p.15)

a. Trade puffs – 3   b. Declaration of Intention – 4
c. Invitation to treat – 2   d. Response to a request for information – 1

Exercises

1. Verbs – *(p.18)*
notify; invite; terminate; manifest; regulate; communicate; oblige / obligate (NAmer); diversify; expect; certify; contemplate; consider; imply; repudiate; revoke; allege; examine; quote; determine; apply; simplify; interpret; annotate; implement; resign; qualify.

2. Like, Unlikely Alike, etc. – *(p.19)*
(a) Unlikely   (b) like/unlike   (c) Unlike   (d) likely
(e) alike   (f) unlike   (g) dislike   (h) like
(i) alike

Exercises – (p.21)

1. Finish the sentences: (for example)
    (a) On his/her 18th birthday, a minor attains his or her majority.
    (b) Regarding contractual capacity, a mentally unsound person is incapable of entering into a contract.
    (c) On signing the contract,
         (a) you have committed yourself to complying with its terms.
         (b) you have undertaken to comply with its terms.
    (d) If there is no consideration, an agreement will not be binding unless it is written under seal.
    (e) We have submitted a tender for the construction of the road.
    (f) I'm afraid our action for breach of contract has not been successful; the court has delivered judgment against us.
    (g) That advertisement is merely an invitation to treat; it does not amount to an offer.
    (h) Family arrangements do not always result in binding contracts.
    (i) The court has held that our product is infringing Kraft's patent and has issued an injunction ordering us to refrain from marketing it.
    (j) English law does not prevent minors from entering into contracts for necessaries.

2. (a) enforceable   (b) expectations   (c) negotiable
    (d) compliance   (e) inducement   (f) contracting
    (g) contractual   (h) presumption   (i) repudiation
    (j) rebuttal

Read and Answer – (p.22)

(B's answers)
 1. When a special relationship exists between the parties.
 2. The transaction can be set aside in equity.
 3. Duress is a coercion of will (one of the parties did not act under his own free will), while undue influence is found in a special relationship of inequality between the parties.
 4. No. Undue influence is an equitable doctrine, while a contract made under duress can be set aside at common law.
(A's answers)
 1. No. It depends upon the seriousness of the mistake.
 2. It is a mistake of fact which prevents the formation of a contract.
 3. Misrepresentation is a statement made by one of the parties in order to induce the other party to enter into the contract. In contrast mistakes are simply about facts, such as the identity of the parties, or subject matter.
 4. No. Innocent misrepresentations can be made.

Exercises – (p.25)

1. Mistake   render a contract void
                     arise
                     so as to
   Misrepresentation with a view to inducing
                     to be acted on
                     convey
   Undue influence   rebut
                     onus
                     trustee
   Duress   remedy
                     fail to
                     exercise

2. unenforceable   instability   mislead
   unenacted   indivisible   unaware
   illegal   illegitimate   misrepresentation
   mistake   incapacity   inadequate
   invalid   disqualify   unnatural
   inexistence   unreasonable   disagreement

Harvey and Facey. – (p.28)

1. No.
2. No.
3. No.
4. Revoked.
5. On appeal the Judicial Committee of the Privy Council held there was no contract. The second telegraph was not an offer, but was in the nature of an invitation to treat at a minimum price of £900. The third telegram would not therefore be an acceptance resulting in a binding contract.

Exercises – (p.30)

ADJECTIVE	NOUN	VERB
valid	validity	validate
acceptable	acceptance	accept
defining	definition	define
triable	trial	try
comprehensive	comprehension	comprehend
revocable	revocation	revoke
judicial	judgment	judge
existing	existence	exist
intentional	intention	intend
reliable	reliance	rely

2. (a) counsel   (b) council   (c) counsellor
   (d) councillor   (e) counsel   (f) counsel

Writing – (p.30)

(a) In the absence of a reply from the Mayor and Council, I entered into negotiations with a new buyer.
(b) The Council's delay in replying that day in Kingston led me to believe that they were no longer interested in the property.
(c) My failure to send the title deed is considered a breach of contract by the Mayor.

(d) I never committed myself to selling him the property.

Carlill v Carbolic Smoke Ball Co

Blank-filling – (p.31)

in; auction; communicated; to; implicit; as; as; return; carried; performance.

Note-taking – (pp.32–33)

1. Main points
    (a) Contract is too vague to be enforced.
    (b) Terms of the offer are too vague to be treated as definite because no time limit fixed for catching influenza.
    (c) Not clear to whom the offer is made as (i) terms wide enough to include people who used ball before the advertisement was issued (ii) an offer made to the world in general.
    (d) The offer is not definite because there are no means of checking whether the terms are carried out.

2. Introductory phrases
    (a) The defendants contend next that ...
    (b) It was argued also that ...
    (c) It was also contended that ...

Exercises – (p.33)

1. Find the expression
    (a) arises   (b) inasmuch as   (c) as to
    (d) to suppose it to be   (e) at all events
2. Sentence rewriting
    (a) Upon acceptance, does this offer form the basis of a binding contract?
    (b) Have they complied with the conditions laid down in the contract?
    (c) Let us consider the contract in question.
    (d) You led me to believe that you would give me a discount for such a large order.
    (e) We are under no obligation to fulfill the promise.

Read and take notes (suggested answers) – (p.33)

1. It was intended to be read by the public and to have the effect of making people use the smoke ball. It was intended to be understood by the public as an offer which was to be acted upon.
2. Either the protection was warranted to last during the epidemic or the smoke ball would be a protection while it was in use.
3. It was an offer made to all the world and became a contract with anybody who performed the condition on the faith of the advertisement.
4. Notification of acceptance was not necessary: performance of the condition was a sufficient acceptance without notification.
5. The inconvenience of using the smoke ball by one party and the benefit received from the use (and therefore sale) of the smoke ball by the other party both constituted consideration.

Exercises (suggested answers) – (p.37)

1. Rewrites
    (a) Immunity is guaranteed while the ball is in use.
    (b) Was the £100 reward intended to be paid?
    (c) Those are the grounds on which all cases involving advertisements have been decided.
    (d) There was no notification of acceptance by the offeree.

2. Sentence joining (suggested answers)
    (a) A reward will be paid by the Carbolic Smoke Ball Company to any person who uses the smoke ball and then contracts the increasing epidemic.
    (b) It would be an insensate thing to promise £100 to a person who used the smoke ball without having any means of checking or superintending his manner of using it.

3. Table – *(p.38)*

VERB	NOUN	ADJECTIVE
contend	contention	contentious
advertise	advertisement	advertised/ing
document	document	documentary
define	definition	defined/ing/definite
mature	maturity	mature
intend	intention	intentional
allege	allegation	alleged
promote	promotion	promotional
imply	implication	implied
endure	endurance	enduring
argue	argument	arguable
ripen	ripeness	ripe
apply	application	applicable
receive	reception	receptive

Crossword – (p.39)

Across: 1. consideration 7. fell 8. upon 9. mere 11. now 13. tort 14. against 16. revocation 18. eye 19. tender 20. binds
Down: 1. commitment 2. near 3. due 4. relevance 5. impression 6. non 10. entered 12. waiver 15. onus 17. eye

Chapter Two

Blank filling – (p.40)

(1) reached; (2) parties; (3) parties; (4) intention; (5) bound; (6) law; (7) intention; (8) leading; (9) lays down/establishes; (10) held/found; (11) parties; (12) offer; (13) intention; (14) parties.

Exercise (suggested answers) – (p.41)

1. The contract should provide for both terms and method of payment.
2. Our clients will enter into the contract provided you include a clause limiting their liability as to defective products.
3. The contract provides that all promotional material be approved by the company.
4. The distributor will provide us with all the advertising material.

Note-taking – (p.41)

CONDITIONS	WARRANTIES
nature: essential to comply with for complete performance	not an essential part of the contract
remedy: contract either discharged or aggrieved party can sue for damages as if it were a breach of warranty.	aggrieved party can sue for damages for the breach.

Exercises – (p.42)

1. Matching
   1. (d)   2. (e)   3. (b)   4. (a)   5. (f)   6. (c).

Read cases:

1. *Poussard v Spiers & Pond* [1876] 1 Q.B.D. 410
   It was held by the court that the obligation to perform as from the first night was a condition and the breach of the condition entitled the other party to repudiate the contract.

2. *Bettini v Gye* [1876] 1 Q.B.D. 183
   The court held that the undertaking to take part in the rehearsals for six days was a warranty and not a condition. The other party was entitled to damages for the breach, but could not repudiate the contract.

Exercises – (p.43)

1. Sentence completion (suggested answers)
   (a) ... you would sue them for damages for the breach.
   (b) ... she would not be bound by the promise.
   (c) ... he could avoid the contract if he so wished.
   (d) ... the contract would automatically be suspended.
   (e) ... no contract would have been formed, as the offeror would not have received the acceptance.

2. A. Use of "as" (suggested answers) – *(p.44)*
   (a) ... as the promisor.
   (b) ... as mentally disordered persons.
   (c) ... as to avoid the contract.
   (d) ... as the price paid by each of the parties for what he receives from the other.
   (e) ... as acceptance.
   (f) ... as an offer to the world at large.
   (g) ... as an invitation to treat.
   (h) ... as vitiating factors.
   (i) ... as a breach of warranty.

3. Substitution
   (a) does not constitute; merely
   (b) instance
   (c) provided that; enforce
   (d) deemed/considered as
   (e) manifested
   (f) undertake
   (g) waive
   (h) liable; arisen
   (i) is entitled to
   (j) revoked

Reading comprehension – (p.45)

1. (b)   2. (c)   3. (c)   4. (a)   5. (b).

Exercises – (p.47)

NOUN	VERB
implication	imply
presumption	presume
provision	provide
negotiation	negotiate
suit	sue
entitlement	entitle
exclusion	exclude
negligence	neglect
compensation	compensate
reliance	rely

Sentence rewrites (suggested answers) – (p.48)
(a) People say that in marriage break-ups the blame never lies wholly on one side.
(b) In a case of negligence it is the court's task to decide who is to blame.
(c) Our clients blame you for their failure to open their hotel in time for the tourist season.
(d) The police blamed the poor city lighting for the rise in traffic accidents.

Blank-filling – (p.48)

1 (b)	2. (d)	3. (a)	4. (d)	5. (c)	6. (c)	7. (b)	8. (a)
9. (c)	10. (d)	11. (b)	12. (a)	13. (a)	14. (d)	15. (b)	16. (d)
17. (b)	18. (c)	19. (d)	20. (c)				

Exercise – (p.51)

Prepositions
1. for   2. under   3. for/within   4. in/for
5. into   6. under   7. before   8. to

Sentence Writing (suggested answers) – (p.53)

1. The court's task is to ensure that the parties to a contract comply with its terms.
2. Mr Brown has made no commitment. He has merely manifested his intention to enter into a contract at a future date.
3. Where agreements are of a family nature, there is a presumption that the parties do not intend to create legal relations.
4. Unless you avoid this contract as a minor, you will be liable under it.
5. The court ruled for the plaintiff.
6. My client has suffered legal detriment, which constitutes consideration.
7. The aggrieved party can sue the breaching party for damages.
8. He complied with the terms of the contract.

Vocabulary – (p.55)

1. pursuant to
2. assign / prior written consent of
3. undertake
4. arising / expiration
5. be deemed to terminate / prior to
6. fulfil / all due
7. timely pay / the outstanding amount
8. hereto / foreseeable
9. grants / furnished
10. hold harmless and indemnify / infringement
11. set forth

Reading comprehension – (p.59)

Whereas = considering that
Whereby refers to "THIS AGREEMENT" (at the beginning of the contract)

Answers to questions – (p.59)

1. No.
2. Provided it gives the Distributor three months' notice by telex or telefax.
3. Modifications can be made to allow for currency fluctuations and freight charges.
4. Company – FOB Fairyland Port. Distributor – all costs after delivery by the Company FOB Fairyland Port.
5. Yes, and it is established in Schedule 3 of the contract.
6. For two years. It can be renewed provided the distributor has achieved a satisfactory level of sales.
7. Yes. It must try to maximise sales, and must provide the Company with sales forecasts and marketing plans.
8. The Distributor is responsible for after-sales service but the Company is liable for any product found defective within the first twelve months.
9. The Distributor, excluding product liability.
10. Yes. It must not disclose any information about the method of manufacture or design of the product, nor must it enter into an agreement with a company selling a similar product for two years after the expiry of the present contract.
11. The Distributor must return or dispose of all samples pattern books, etc., and give the Company a list of the names and addresses of all customers. It must also return all remaining products.

Boiler-plate clauses:
confidentiality/disclosure = 14
termination = 13
guarantees/indemnities = 11
exclusion of liability = not found
disputes/conflict of laws = 21

commencement = 7
standard warranties = 9 (and others)
service of notice = 19
whole agreement = 22
force majeure = 17

Vocabulary – (p.60)

1. shall
2. (a) hereinafter   (b) hereunder / hereto   (c) hereafter
    (d) hereof   (e) hereby   (f) hereunder
    (g) hereof   (h) whereby / hereto

Reading comprehension – (p.61)

A's answers to B's questions:
1. No. Yes, provided we let ABC know in writing that we are making a tender.
2. Yes. The contract says that even if one of the parties doesn't insist on correct performance at once, he can insist at a later stage.
3. We deduct the amount we've already paid.

B's answers to A's questions
1. Yes, but the other parties have to give their written consent.
2. No. It also covers any patents the Licensor may take out in the future.
3. You will have to give a three-month termination notice.

Read and Match – (p.62)

1. (d)   2. (c)   3. (a)   4. (e)   5. (b)
1 = (none)   2 = 10 (for example)   3 = (none)   4 = 17   5 = 11

Exercise – (p.63)

Sentence rewrites (suggested answers)
1. An express term always overrides an implied term.
2. The promisee submitted his tender in reliance on a certain price.
3. A contract for the sale of land, as distinct from other sale contracts, must be in writing.
4. As your client has breached a condition, my client deems himself discharged from the contract.
5. He has been served with a writ in respect of his breach of contract.

Crossword – (p.64)

Across: 1. agreement   5. LLB   6. deem   9. lease   10. all   11. ever   12. opt   15. transfers
Down: 1. at   2. release   3. e.g.   4. timely   7. example   8. client   13. as   14. us

Chapter Three

Exercises – (p.67)

1. Sentence Rewrites (suggested answers)
    (a) Both parties may agree that circumstances have changed, in which case their contract may be changed by novation.
    (b) My client, on behalf of whom I am appearing, wishes to remain anonymous.
    (c) There were four parties to this contract, all of whom will have to appear in court.
    (d) Restrictions may be placed on the export of computer technology, in which event your contract will be deemed to be frustrated.
    (e) The plaintiff will probably be awarded damages, a third of which he will have to pay to his lawyer.

2. Language of cause and result
    (a) *Result*: lead to; as a consequence; Hence; result in; give rise to.
        Cause: because; due to; result from; arises from.

    (b)   (i) Your signing this document has resulted in a waiver of your right to sue.

(ii) Our financial problems have led to Becno Inc. withdrawing their take-over bid.
(iii) Mr Smith failed to give us 30 days' notice. Hence, a breach of contract has arisen.
(iv) The faulty drafting of the contract gave rise to two important court cases.

Blank-filling – (p.68)

(1) to	(2) fails	(3) amounts	(4) discharge
(5) upon	(6) injured	(7) by	(8) rise
(9) injured	(10) against	(11) which	(12) arises
(13) performance	(14) injured	(15) sue	(16) performance

Reading for definitions – (p.69)

1. (c)   2. (d)   3. (a)   4. (b)

Exercises – (p.70)

1. Negative forms

invalid	unable	unwilling
unearned	unreasonable	unperformed
incomplete	unnecessary	illegal
unforeseen	ineffective	impractical
unavailable	inadequate	undue

2. Sentence rewrites (suggested answers)
   (a) As both parties waived their rights to make a claim, they were discharged from their contract.
   (b) The plaintiff considered that she was entitled to recover for the inconvenience she had suffered because of the airline's negligence.
   (c) A contract is discharged upon performance.
   (d) The court awarded the plaintiff damages of £50,000.

3. Opposites

(1) breach	(2) duty
(3) promisee	(4) entire
(5) partially	(6) unsigned
(7) occasional	(8) defendant
(9) beneficiary	(10) tenant

Crossword – (p.71)

Across: 1. discharge 5. earned 6. be 8 when 9. cast 11. one 12. i.e. 13. trusts 16. effective
Down: 1. due 2. sorted 3. re 4. event 7. bans 8. waive 9. court 10. set 14. sue 15. if

English for Company Law

Introduction

Read and ask – (p.72)

Answers given by B to A
 1. to purchase the business

 2. members of his family
 3. £39,000.
 4. one £1 share each
 5. the balance in cash
 6. another loan of £5,000
 7. the repayment of the loan
 8. debts owed to the company's trade

Answers given by A to B
 (a) leather merchant and wholesale boot manufacturer
 (b) Salomon and Co Ltd
 (c) memorandum of association
 (d) 20,000 £1 shares
 (e) of debentures (a secured form of loan)
 (f) went through a difficult time
 (g) liquidation proceedings

creditors

9. the company's business was in reality still Mr Salomon's

10. other creditors

(h) the company's debt on the loan

(i) company (and the unsecured creditors)

(j) indemnify the company against its debts

Exercises – (p.73)

1. Sentence completion (oral) (suggested answers)
   (a) ... carried on a business as a leather merchant and wholesale boot manufacturer.
   (b) ... to himself and members of his family.
   (c) ... of £8,994.
   (d) ... went through a difficult time.
   (e) ... the company failed to pay interest on the loan.
   (f) ... meet the company's debt on the loan.
   (g) ... of the first debentures which had been issued to him.
   (h) ... the company and the unsecured creditors were entitled to be repaid personally by Mr Salomon.

2. Verbs and prepositions – *(p.74)*

forming	*to*
retained	*of/over*
had been formed	
bought	*in*
received	*in*
to solve	*in*
to be made	
to pay	*on*
were started	
raised	
to repay	
owed	
claimed	*over*
contended	
to be repaid	
was brought	

Note-taking – (p.76)

1. He held that the company was an agent of Mr Salomon's to run his business for him.
2. He said that the Companies Acts intended that the shareholders of a company should have a real interest in the company.
3. He thought that Mr Salomon had formed the company in order to attain a result not permitted by law.
4. (a) Although a company in fact carries on business on behalf of its shareholders, this does not mean that the company is an agent of the shareholders.
   (b) The Companies Acts do not mention the number of shares that may or must be held by each shareholder, or the extent of the influence of each shareholder.
   (c) A company upon incorporation becomes a different person at law from the subscribers to the memorandum.

Summary writing (suggested answers) – (p.77)

... personally liable to the company and to its creditors; ... genuine and independent; ... a result not permitted by law; ... was reversed; ... was held; ... person; ... a mature body corporate; ... the degree of interest which may be held by each of the shareholders; ... repay the company or its creditors.

Exercise – (p.77)

Prepositions

1. in / for   2. to / in   3. in   4. on
5. in   6. upon   7. on   8. from

Chapter One

Reading – (p.78)

1. (d)   2. (a)   3. (b)   4. (c)

Exercises – (p.78)

1. Formal equivalents
   (1) establish / constitute; searched; capital;
   (2) became established; net wage; earns / his turnover is; his employees.
   (3) recovered
   (4) contributed; start the business; accumulating.

2. Sentence rewrites (suggested answers)
   (a) Each party contributed £10,000 to start the business, but it never commenced trading.
   (b) ABC's results have recovered and they have declared a dividend.
   (c) He inherited £5,000 from his father to set up his own workshop.
   (d) His net income is approximately £1,700 after paying his employees, the rent and tax.

Classifying – (p.79)

Sole trader: 2, 7, 10, 12, 19, 20.
Partnership: 2, 7, 10, 12, 14, 16, 19, 20.
Private limited company: 1, 4, 7, 8, 9, 10, 11, 13, 15, 17, 18, 21.
Public limited company: 1, 3, 4, 5, 6, 8, 11, 13, 15, 17, 18, 21.

Exercise (suggested answers) – (p.81)

1. Upon the dissolution of a partnership, the first step ...
2. He has the majority stake in that company.
3. The two companies have formed a joint venture to build ...
4. The company continued with its plan regardless of the managing director's doubts.

Blank-filling – (p.82)

1. accordance (d)   6. register (d)
2. provisions (b)   7. transferred (c)
3. share (a)   8. existing (a)
4. attain (b)   9. appointed (d)
5. fee (a)   10. notification (c)

Letter writing – (p.84)

Thank you; regarding; appreciate your trust in us; choice/option; are not; drawing up; filed; to the effect that all the requirements of the Companies Act have been complied with; former; engaged in; latter; contain; on their behalf; provided; satisfied; with the contents of the documents; issue; notice of; notice; be aware; common to; carry out other steps; obtaining; transferring; should; do not hesitate.

Exercise – (p.85)

1. (d)   2. (e)   3. (a)   4. (f)   5. (c)   6. (h)   7. (b)   8. (g).

Reading and classifying – (p.86)

1. memorandum   6. articles
2. articles   7. memorandum
3. articles   8. memorandum
4. memorandum   9. articles
5. memorandum   10. memorandum

Exercise – (p.88)

1. (a)   2. (b)   3. (d)   4. (b)   5. (c)
6. (d)   7. (c)   8. (a)   9. (c)   10. (d)

Summary writing (suggested answers) – (p.89)

carried out; sanctioned by its objects; a special resolution of the members of the company; concerned about profits; the kind of business entered into by the directors; persons supplying goods and services to a company; this doctrine ineffective; cover the relation between the shareholders and the directors of a company.

Exercises (suggested answers) – (p.89)

1. Sentence completion
   (a) His total debts amounted to £X.
   (b) If we cannot meet our mortgage payments, the building society will repossess our house.
   (c) A limited company has perpetual succession, regardless of changes in membership.
   (d) A partnership is automatically dissolved upon the death or retirement of a partner.
   (e) A quick and easy way of setting up a company is by buying one off the shelf.
   (f) All writs and official notices are served upon a company at its registered office.
   (g) In order for the proceedings of a general meeting to be valid, there must be a quorum.
   (h) The power to appoint and remove a secretary is usually vested in the directors of a company.
   (i) As the articles of association have an inherent contractual nature, they are binding upon subscribers.
   (j) Whereas the memorandum is mainly aimed at outsiders, the articles are of interest to the members of a company.

2. – *(p.90)*

VERB	NOUN	ADJECTIVE	PERSONAL NOUN
repossess	repossession	repossessed	█████████
mortgage	mortgage	mortgaged	mortgagee/or
succeed	succession	successive	successor
incorporate	in/corporation	corporate	incorporator
register	registration	registered	registrar
authorise	authorisation	authorised	█████████
subscribe	subscription	subscribed	subscriber
remunerate	remuneration	remunerative	remunerator
ratify	ratification	ratified	ratifier
dissolve	dissolution	dissolved	dissolver
confiscate	confiscation	confiscated	confiscator
convert	conversion	convertible(ed)	convert

3. Vocabulary – *(p.90)*

Hold: the Olympic Games   Celebrate: Mass
      an exam   your birthday
      a meeting   a victory in the Olympic Games
      a trial   your wedding anniversary
      the Olympic Games
      elections
      a hearing
      an opinion

Blank-filling – (p.90)

1. virtue   8. sealed   15. public
2. provides   9. member   16. private
3. subject   10. member   17. section
4. bind   11. provisions   18. by
5. members   12. draw   19. of

194

6. extent   13. sets   20. empowered
7. signed   14. regulations   21. means

Summary writing (suggested answers) – (p.92)

behalf of Phonogram Ltd; behalf of Fragile Management Ltd; paying £12,000 towards financing a pop group; Mr Rennie sent Mr Lane a cheque for £6,000; a receipt; in the account of Jelly Music Ltd; had not been formed; was brought by Phonogram Ltd to recover the money.

Reading comprehension – (p.93)

1. (b)   2. (c)   3. (a)

Exercise – (p.94)

Informal to formal expressions
1. Prior to the formation of the company
2. transaction
3. further to
4. In the unlikely event that we fail to complete/undertake ...
5. duly
6. deposited
7. It transpired
8. ruled / repay
9. purported to make / on behalf of
10. never commenced the incorporation process
11. abide by.

Exercises – (p.96)

1. Phrasal verbs
    (a) In the USA most drivers abide by the speed limit on highways.
    (b) A list of prices and minimum orders is set out on the last page of the contract.
    (c) We advise you to consult a lawyer before you draw up the company's memorandum and Articles.
    (d) Considering his entrepreneurial abilities, I wouldn't be surprised if he decided to set up his own company.
    (e) Below I have set out the steps laid down by the Companies Act 1985 for registering a company.

2. Prepositions – (p.97)
(a) to   (f) of/to   (k) in/for
(b) in   (g) to   (l) for
(c) up   (h) under   (m) to
(d) from   (i) into   (n) on/of
(e) with/under (j) on   (o) at

Blank-filling – (p.97)

1. undertake   5. conducting   8. liable
2. under   6. contracts   9. if
3. permits/empowers 7. bind   10. transaction
4. on

Crossword – (p.98)

Across: 2. partner 5. COD 6. or 7. leading 10. principals 11. name 12. issue 13. promoters
Down: 1. for 3. agency 4. registers 5. company 8. deposit 9. firmer

Chapter Two

Exercise – (p.100)

1. outnumber   2. outsell   3. outlive   4. outgrown
5. outwitted   6. outperformed   7. outbid   8. outweighs

Read and order – (p.100)

1. (f)   2. (c)   3. (b)   4. (d)   5. (e)   6. (a)   7. (a)

Read and match – (p.101)

1. (c)   2. (d)   3. (e)   4. (a)   5. (b)

Exercise (suggested answers) – (p.101)

1. In the event that the director is removed, ... OR In the event of the director's removal, ...
2. The articles provide for the disclosure of the material interests of directors.
3. The power to remove the secretary has been conferred upon the board.
4. A resolution to re-register the company as a public company was passed by the shareholders.
5. This venture has Bill Fence's backing.
6. My appointment to the board of directors comes into effect as of May 1st.
7. We were well aware that the secretary had failed to ... OR We were well aware of the secretary's failure to ...

Sentence expansion – (p.102)

1. Debentures can be distinguished from share capital in that they are loans made to the company.
2. They are secured either by a charge on specific assets or by a floating charge on all the assets.
3. Debentures can either be redeemable or irredeemable.
4. A redeemable debenture is repayable on a specified date and is usually issued when the need for finance is temporary and when interest rates are likely to fall.
5. An irredeemable debenture is not repayable until the company is wound up or fails to pay the interest due.
6. Debentures are usually issued when interest rates are low and likely to rise.
7. Although debentures carry no voting rights, interest must be paid whether or not profits are made.

Read and put into categories – (p.102)

1. ordinary shares: b, e, f, h,   2. preference shares: a, c, d, g

Discussion – (p.104)

(a) Yes.
(b) Yes.
(c) No
(d) Yes.
(e) No
(f) Yes.

Read and match – (p.104)

1. (d)   2. (b)   3. (f)   4. (a)

Blank-filling – (p.106)

A director must always act *bona fide* for the **benefit** of a company as a whole. As seen in the judgments, a director must **account** to the company for any profit he may make in the **course** of his dealings with the company's property. This accountability arises from the **mere** fact that a director makes a profit from his privileged **knowledge**; it is not a **question** of loss to the company. If a director does not **disclose** a profit made in such a way, it would **amount** to what is known as insider dealing, which can be a criminal **offence**. Insider dealing means dealing in the **shares** of a company for the purpose of private **gain** by a person who has **inside** information about those **shares** which would affect their price if it were generally known. The insider dealing **law/legislation** in England is very complex. The Company Securities (Insider Dealing) **Act** of 1985 does not employ the word "insider" but "individual connected with a company". **Thus** the legislation is clearly directed towards directors and other employees of a company.

Read and match – (p.107)

1. (e)   2. (f)   3. (d)   4. (c)   5. (b)   6. (a)

Exercises – (p.108)

1. (a) account
   (b) accountant
   (c) accountable
   (d) accounts
   (e) accounted

2. *– (p.109)*

VERB	ABSTRACT NOUN	PERSONAL NOUN
inherit	inheritance	heir
apply	application	applicant
vote	vote/voting	voter
account	accounting/accountability	accountant
issue	issue	issuer
participate	participation	participant
finance	finance	financier
offend	offence	offender
represent	representation	representative
liquidate	liquidation	liquidator

3. Sentence completion (suggested answers) – *(p.109)*
   (a) ... outnumber the women by five to one.
   (b) ... carried forward from one year to the next.
   (c) ... to forfeit his shares.
   (d) ... that they are a loan made to the company.
   (e) ... must be satisfied that the company has met all the statutory requirements.
   (f) ... holding lotteries. (For example, the gerund form of the verb is necessary.)
   (g) ... weighs the disadvantage of incorporation.
   (h) ... to raising capital through a share issue.
   (i) ... the sum of the money which the company's shareholders have been asked to pay.
   (j) ... account to the company for that profit.

Substitution – (p.110)

The directors' powers are usually **laid down** in the articles of association of the company. These powers are **granted** to the directors and only they may **exercise** them. Consequently, the shareholders of the company cannot control the actions of the directors **provided** these are within the scope of the powers **vested in** them. If the shareholders **disapprove of** the directors' actions, they may **convene** a meeting to **pass a resolution** to **alter** the articles to restrict the powers of the directors or to **remove** any particular director. A director may not **delegate** his powers to somebody else. The directors may **appoint** a managing director if the articles **provide for** such an appointment. It is usual for the managing director to have a contract of employment stating his powers and duties and terms of employment, and **in this respect** he **acts in a dual capacity** as a director and as an employee.

Blank-filling – (p.111)

1. (c)	2. (a)	3. (c)	4. (d)	5. (a)	6. (c)
7. (c)	8. (b)	9. (c)	10. (d)	11. (a)	12. (c)
13. (b)	14. (d)	15. (b)			

Fill in the blanks – (p.112)

1. Turnover   2. operating profit   3. profit on ordinary activities before taxation   4. profit for the year 5. dividends   6. fixed assets   7. cash at bank and in hand   8. current assets   9. net current

assets 10. total assets less current liabilities   11. provisions for liabilities and charges   12. net assets   13. called up share capital   14. profit and loss account   15. shareholders' funds

Read and Decide – (p.115)

A pressure group ... **True**
The A.G.M. was called ... **True**
The reduced turnout ... **False**
The chairman of Prettywoman ... **False**
A proposal was made ... **True**
Shortly after the A.G.M. .... **False**
An extraordinary general meeting ... **True**
The preference shareholders ... **False**

Exercises – (p.116)

1. Negative forms

destabilise	unpaid	unwise
disapprove	impartial	disregard
unusual	incorrectly	unable
irrespective	unlimited	invalid

2. Vocabulary

(a) unlawful   (b) accountability   (c) unlisted
(d) negligent   (e) outnumber   (f) misappropriation
(g) Insider   (h) discharge   (i) consultancy
(j) downsize

3. Sentence rewrites (suggested answers) – *(p.117)*
   (a) Upon subscription of the memorandum, Mr Wallis became ...
   (b) Prettywoman's shares will soon be listed on the London Stock Exchange.
   (c) The directors ... at the request of members holding not less than one-tenth of the paid-up capital.
   (d) All the members entitled to attend an AGM must be served at least 21 days' written notice.
   (e) He will have to account for the profit he made on that transaction.
   (f) We plan to continue with the business regardless of the dissolution of the partnership.

Reading – (p.118)

It corresponds to "The AGM was called exclusively to ..."

Exercise – (p.120)

1. out   2. in   3. up   4. down   5. up
6. off   7. on   8. even   9. for   10. with

Put in order – (p.121)

The Annual Return

When **the annual accounts** have been approved by **the shareholders** at the A.G.M., they must be annexed, along with the directors' and auditors' report, to **the annual return**, which must be made to **the Registrar of Companies**. The return must also include details about the directors and members of the company and particulars about the **share capital**. Failure to comply with **the requirements** is a **criminal offence**, and the company in default and each of **its officers** becomes liable to **a fine**. The law requires the public to have access to information on **the members**, officers and finances of each company granted the privilege of **incorporation**.

Crossword – (p.122)

Across: 1. accountant 6. entitled 8. too 9. assets 11. undue 13. gilt-edged
Down: 1. agenda 2. cut 3. null 4. audited 5. turnover 7. inherit 10. sued 12. e.g.

Chapter Three

Read and discuss – (p.125)

Vulture became the purchaser and Prettywoman the vendor.
Vulture's lawyers: (a)   (b)   (g)   (h)

Prettywoman's lawyers: (c)   (d)   (e)   (f)
Both: (i)   (j)

Exercises – (p.126)

1.   Vocabulary
closure = closing down (of factory); disclosure = making public (of information); doubtful = adjective; doubtless = adverb (He will doubtless come soon); appear = a film star appears in a film, a lawyer appears for his client; disappear = vanish; security = safety, also invested money (government securities); insecurity = lack of safety, confidence; appoint = put somebody in a position; disappoint = to let somebody down.
relevant and irrelevant are real opposites.
respect and disrespect are real opposites, but respect can be used in expressions: in respect of, with respect to.
action and inaction can be opposites (inaction = lack of action), but an action is also used in law (to bring an action against somebody).

2.   Sentence rewrites (suggested answers) – *(p.126)*
   (a) In default of instructions, the proxy will vote or not as he thinks best.
   (b) In the event of adjournment, the proxy vote will still be valid.
   (c) Because of the court case, the director has tendered his resignation.
   (d) You are recommended to seek advice.
   (e) You must contact the solicitor through whom the sale was effected.

3.   Oral comments. – *(p.127)*
The students should use
   (a) deny/denial
   (b) reject/rejection
   (c) refuse/refusal

Text completion – (p.128)

failing / creditor / safeguard / ensuring / over / suitably / provides / body / authorised / rules / body / obtained.

Read and match – (p.128)

1. liquidator   2. administrator   3. administrative receiver

Writing – (p.129)

   I regret to inform you that on 10th October an administrative receiver was appointed to the Home Ranch Café.
   This was due to the company's inability to pay the debenture called for by the bank. The People's Bank was empowered under the terms of the debenture to appoint a receiver in the event of non-compliance with a demand for payment.
   Unfortunately, the company's financial position shows that it is impossible to continue trading. It is probable that a liquidator will be called in to wind up the company. It is doubtful whether any surplus assets will remain to distribute to the members of the company.
   I would be very pleased to answer any questions you may have regarding the matter. Please feel free to contact me at any time.

Reading – (p.129)

   1. False. The company was unable to pay its interest payments.
   2. False. He handed in a letter of resignation four weeks after the administrative receiver was appointed.
   3. False. It held that Mr Griffiths had been employed until the company had accepted his resignation.
   4. True.
   5. True.

Discuss and put in order – (p.131)

(d)   (a)   (e)   (f)   (c)   (b).

Exercises – (p.132)

1. Over- and under-

(a)

(i) overnight	(ii) overall	(iii) undergo	(iv) over/undersubscribed
(v) overdraft	(vi) overdue	(vii) over/undertake	(viii) overhear
(xi) over/undercharge	(x) overseas	(xi) undergraduate	(xii) override
(xiii) over/undervalued	(xiv) overthrow	(xv) underwrite	(xvi) underage
(xvii) overrule	(xviii) overpower	(ixx) underlying	(xx) over/understate

(b)

(i) oversubscribed	(ii) underage	(iii) overvalued
(iv) overdue	(v) underlying	(vi) undertaken

2. Sentence completion (suggested answers)
   (i) ... in a dual capacity.
   (ii) ... be delegated.
   (iii) ... contains the profit and loss account and the balance sheet.
   (iv) ... out in the profit and loss account.
   (v) ... for its business to be validly transacted.
   (vi) ... convene an extraordinary general meeting.
   (vii) ... them to reject it.
   (viii) ... at general meeting or by a postal vote.

3. Word building – *(p.133)*

receivership	appointment	insolvency	security
membership	allotment	arbitration	acceptance
approval	accounting	transfer	chairmanship

Read and choose – (p.133)

(c)   (e)   (g)   (i).

Blank filling – (p.133)

The Home Ranch Café Ltd has decided to **wind up** its English **operation**, as it is **unable** to satisfy its **creditors**, and has serious **cash-flow** problems. The company has presented a petition to the **court** for an order for the **appointment** of a **liquidator** to realise the **assets** and pay off the **creditors**, any **surplus** funds being **divided** among the **shareholders**. When the company's affairs are **wound up**, the **court** will make an order **dissolving** the company. The **liquidator** will register the order with the Registrar of Companies and the company will be **removed** from the **register**.

Crossword – (p.134)

Across: 1. debenture 6. use 7. companies 9. overstate 13. uneven 15. be 16. re 17. testify
Down: 1. disclosure 2. boom 3. turn 4. US 5. reject 8. answers 10. elect 11. AD 12. every 14. net

INDEX